I HAVE A DREAM . . .

THE LIFE AND TIMES OF

MARTIN LUTHER KING, JR.

LENWOOD G. DAVIS

NEGRO UNIVERSITIES PRESS
WESTPORT, CONNECTICUT

Library of Congress Cataloging in Publication Data

Davis, Lenwood G
    I have a dream; the life and times of Martin
Luther King, Jr.

    Reprint of the ed. published by L. G. Davis,
Salisbury? N.C.
    Bibliography: p.
    1. King, Martin Luther, 1929-1968. I. Title.
E185.97.K5D34 .1973   323.4'092'4 [B]   70-154202
ISBN 0-8371-5977-6

Originally published in 1969 by Lenwood G. Davis

Reprinted with the permission of Lenwood G. Davis

Reprinted by Greenwood Press, Inc.

First Greenwood reprinting 1973
Second Greenwood reprinting 1974
Third Greenwood reprinting 1977

Library of Congress catalog card number 70-154202
ISBN 0-8371-5977-6

Printed in the United States of America

2

Dedicated to my Mother, Mrs. Lucy M. Davis

and Grandmother

Mrs. Beaulah A. Pickett

Preface

In this book I aim to give a detailed unbiased account of the life and times of Martin Luther King, Jr. from birth to his untimely death. I hope that this book will provide a greater understanding of this man who has accomplished so much in such a short period of time.

Dr. King's philosophies were drawn from the teachings of Jesus Christ, Mahatma Ghandi, Henry David Thoreau, Immanuel Kant, and Georg Friedrich Hegel. As these men influenced his philosophies, the examples set by his father influenced his character.

Reverend Martin Luther King, Jr. was what I call an "idealist-realist" and although he may have been a dreamer, his dreams were practical. He was a realist because he tried to make his dreams into reality. During his trial, at which time he was charged with violating Alabama's anti-boycott law, King was optimistic enough to hope for the best, but realistic enough to prepare for the worst.

During the Montgomery boycott, Martin Luther King, Jr.'s presence alone was a tonic for the weary commuters. In many instances more than a tonic was needed. "We have been exploited economically, excluded socially and dominated politically. But we are funny. The Negro is funny, he can endure. He can smile. He can keep hoping and striving," King told a mass audience.

There is no doubt that the Republican Party realizes, now, the fatal mistake it made during the 1960 campaign in not speaking on King's behalf as Kennedy did. Quite naturally, out of loyalty and respect for King, many Negroes voted for the Democratic nominee for the presidency. One of the most important campaign moves was undoubtedly the late President

Kennedy's telephone call of sympathy to Mrs. Martin Luther King, Jr., when Dr. King was in jail in Montgomery, Alabama.

I have spent many restless and sleepless nights before I undertook this momentous assignment, in trying to select an appropriate title for this book. I did not simply want to call it a biography of Martin Luther King, Jr. When I first started writing this book, I thought *A Man From Atlanta* would be a good title. Later as he became more and more known, I decided to call it *Martin Luther King, Jr. : Man or Myth*. After Victor Lasky, however, wrote *J.F.K. The Man and The Myth,* I abandoned that title. When King delivered his brilliant "I Have A Dream" speech, I was convinced that this was the one and only title for the book.

Contents

Chapter One

THE EARLY YEARS

"King felled over a second-floor railing to the concrete. Blood gushed from the right jaw and neck area. His necktie had been ripped off by the blast," said Rev. Jesse Jackson, one of his aides. Jackson also surmised: "He had just bent over. If he had been standing up, he wouldn't have been hit in the face. When I turned around, I saw policemen coming from everywhere. We didn't need to call the police." Rev. King was immediately taken to St. Joseph's Hospital where despite emergency surgery for the gunshot wound, he died at 8:30 p.m.

Dr. King's death had a profound effect upon every segment of American life. Television programs were cancelled; banks, schools, colleges, stores, and other institutions were closed; sporting events were re-scheduled—all in honor of Martin Luther King, Jr.

Most citizens of America and the world were shocked and saddened over the assassination of Dr. King. People everywhere began to wonder why a man who preached nonviolence had met such a violent death.

Perhaps, if I told something of the world in which Martin Luther King, Jr. grew up, one could better understand him and his mission. When his first son was delivered, Martin Luther King, Sr. told Dr. Charles Johnson to put "junior" on the birth certificate. Dr. Johnson, however, knowing the father informally as "Mike," put the name "Michael" Luther King, Jr. instead. When the father discovered this error a few days later, he went to the hospital and requested that "Martin" be substituted for "Michael" on the infant's record. He was assured that this mistake would be corrected. Years later, however, it was discovered that the mistake had not been corrected.[1] It was not until 1943, at which time Martin Luther King, Sr., needed to clear his own name in order to get a passport for a trip abroad, that he had both his first name and that of his son legalized to Martin.

Willie Christine, first child of the Kings was born in 1928, just a year before Martin. Alfred Daniel, the third and last child, was born a year after Martin. At home Willie Christine was known as "Christine," and sometimes as just "Chris." Martin as "M. L." and "Mike." Alfred Daniel as "A. D." The children called their mother "Mother Dear" and father "Daddy." "Mama" was reserved for their grandmother and "Granddaddy" for their grandfather.

All the King children were born and reared in Atlanta, Georgia, at 501 Auburn Avenue Northeast. Atlanta was more than a birthplace to Martin Luther King, Jr., since he grew up, went to school and finished college there. Even when he went away from Atlanta, like the prodigal son, he always returned.

I

Atlanta, Georgia, has often been called the "New York of the South." It was the South in King's youth, but even then not the rural south as we know it. It was more modern than some northern cities. It was the largest southern city and the state capitol. Consequently, the people were more educated, more prosperous and more sophisticated. Atlanta was different from most southern cities, since it was industrialized and commercialized.

Atlanta has not and perhaps will not forgive General William T. Sherman for the destruction that his forces did in 1864. As we students of history know now, he went through Atlanta like a "bat out of hell," seizing, burning and destroying everything that he could not use. The day General Sherman marched on Atlanta is one of the "darkest" days in its history.

For a while Atlanta had a branch of the Communist Party of the U.S.A. and was the headquarters for the Ku Klux Klan. These organizations, however, were counterbalanced by the Commission on Interracial Cooperation, B'Nai B'rith and the National Association for the Advancement of Colored People.

Atlanta's colleges then, unlike now, were segregated; however, from them a small group of "liberals" emerged. Generally, the city's "elite," both Negroes and whites, got together at concerts, book reviews, teas and forums—generally at Morehouse College or Atlanta University.

Newspapers almost everywhere mold public opinion and are very influential in community activities. The morning *Atlanta Constitution,* representing traditional local interests, was reasonable and stood for quiet "process" in race relations. The afternoon *Atlanta Journal* policy remained conservative.

Ralph McGill editor of the *Constitution* for nearly two decades was a Southern "liberal" with a national reputation. A month rarely passed that he did not write some article for some national magazine. He tried to keep evenly balanced the three forces pulling against him—North, South, and Negro. They demanded more and faster concessions to equality than the Southerner would or could afford to yield. Yet Mr. McGill still remained a "liberal," until his death.

Then, unlike now, all of Atlanta's facilities were segregated; her movies, airports, busses, restaurants, hotels, motels, courthouse, jails, and stores. Even though the King family never did use these segregated facilities, they left a stigma of Martin's childhood that he could not forget.

Generally speaking, this was Martin Luther King, Jr.'s Atlanta. Even though it was southern, it was different from most southern cities. It was more dynamic and exciting. There was some interracial goodwill and real friendship. A number of Negroes were loved and respected by whites and a number of whites were loved and respected by Negroes. Subsequently, the whites could not conclude that "All" Negroes were "bad" and vice versa.

II

Every large city has its famous "Negro" streets. In Harlem there is 125th Street and 7th Avenue; in Durham, North Carolina, Pettigrew; in Washington, D.C., U Street; and in Chicago, 47th and South Parkway—to name a few. Atlanta was no different, for there was Auburn Avenue, King's neighborhood.

To be born on Auburn Avenue was different from being born on almost any other well-known street where Negroes lived and played—for it was here that the Negro spirit came alive. Auburn Avenue was like most "famous" avenues and streets—it had many faces. In the daylight, its Negro-owned Citizens Trust Company; the Mutual Federal Savings and Loan Association; *The Atlanta Daily World;* Radio Station WERD; Yates and Milton Pharmacy, and the Odd Fellows and Elks usually stayed busy. And at night the Clubs removed their masks. There were numerous smaller establishments also, such as service stations, jewelry shops, grocery stores, liquor stores, beer taverns, a job printing plant, restaurants and barber shops. There was a branch of the Public Library, since Negroes could not use the main one downtown.

Ebenezer Baptist Church, Big Bethel A.M.E. Church, and Wheat Street Baptist Church, were three of the Street's most widely known sanctuaries. They frequently served as rallying points during election time.

After 1944, when Negroes won the right to vote in the Democratic primary, which was the decisive election in Georgia and most of the South, they built themselves into a balance of power and voted in blocks, locally. Since Atlanta had over a quarter of a million people, and every one out of three was Negro, some twenty thousand votes could swing almost any municipal election.

Auburn Avenue had a variety of personalities and each possessed a certain individual "air" about him. Since this book is not about Negroes in Atlanta in general, I will only mention a few men who lived on or were connected with Auburn Avenue. There was N. B. Heron, President and Treasurer of the Atlanta Life Insurance Company; E. M. Martin, Vice President and Secretary of Atlanta Life Insurance Company; John P. Whittaker of Mutual Federal Savings and Loan Association; C. A. Scott, Editor-in-Chief of the *Atlanta Daily World;* William Holmes Borders of Wheat Baptist Church; Rev. D. T. Babcock, and the Rev. H. I. Bearden of Big Bethel AME Church; the Rev. Martin Luther King, Sr., of Ebenezer Baptist Church; Attorney A. T. Walden; Dr. R. A. Billings; A. F. Hendon, the barber; and numerous other personalities.

III

The King family was closely knit. Because of the closeness of the children's ages, they were more of a group. They shared a common interest in each other's problems. Christine was never a big sister—only a sister. A. D. was never a little brother—only a brother.

Martin Luther King, Sr., remembering his early childhood, meant to be kind to his family and give them love and affection. He was glad to provide for his wife and children, but in his home, his word, considerate and benevolent as he tried to make it, was final.

The children were taught to love and respect their parents and their elders. Honesty, thrift, order and courtesy were adhered to faithfully. Education was looked upon as the path to competence and culture. The church was the path to morality and immortality.

The King family lived like most minister's families during that time. There was plenty, but nothing fancy, and nothing went to waste. Each child was given a weekly allowance for the Sunday School and Church collection plates, for his individual coin bank and extra ice cream cones.

The family was basic to the environment in which the King's children developed. Most of Reverend King's children gained their precepts from two institutions—the church and the school. Most of their friends were selected from the girls and boys in the neighborhood with whom they attended church or school.

The King Children spent a great deal of time at Ebenezer, since their pastor was also their father. When Reverend King was not at home, he could usually be found at the church.

Both Mrs. King and Mrs. Williams participated in church activities. Mrs. King played the piano or organ and directed one of the choirs. During Martin's childhood, she taught him to play the piano. At four years of age, he could sing well enough to appear before churches and church conventions. His mother accompanied him at the piano and he sang with rollicking gospel beat. His favorite song was "I Want To Be More Like Jesus."

The church members, like most congregations, usually did nice things for the pastor and his family. Some of the "sisters" would bake pies and cakes for the Reverend and sometimes invite him to Sunday dinner for "Southern fried chicken" and other delicious foods. Almost everyone on the East Side knew of or had heard of the Reverend King and his children.

During King's childhood, he loved to play games. There were sand-lot and street baseball, basketball, and times of flying kites, model airplanes and riding his own bicycle.

King played with anyone who came along. The neighborhood was lower middle class, and upper lower class, with the Negroes of "wealth" living on the West Side. Neither the children nor the father or mother drew class lines, but there was parental concern about the behavior pattern of playmates.

For a while two of Martin's playmates were white boys, sons of the neighborhood grocer. Although the children got along extremely well, one day the white mother informed Martin that her son could not play with him anymore. Afterward, Martin went home and asked Mother-Dear why the boy's mother said they could not play together anymore. Mrs. King had the unpleasant task of explaining why.

IV

When Chris started attending the Young Street Elementary School, King was only five, but somewhat talkative as a youngster, he insisted on going also. So he slipped in and enrolled by pushing his age up to six. Later, he was "put out" when he forgot to keep his secret by describing the details of his last birthday party. He had to wait a year.

King enjoyed going to school. He was such a good student that he skipped about three grades during his elementary and secondary education. He was a B+ student and enjoyed studying. He was interested in extra-curricular activities and participated in a few.

He remained at Young Street for a couple of years, then transferred to David T. Howard, completing the sixth grade there. From Howard he went to the Laboratory High School of Atlanta University, where he and his sister studied together. He helped her with mathematics and she helped him with his spelling. By national standards, public school education in Atlanta was "fair," but at Laboratory School it was "superior." This private institution was discontinued after Martin had been there for two years. He completed his high school education at the Booker T. Washington Public High School, where he skipped both the ninth and twelfth grades.

King and Chris were drawing closer together, while he and A. D. were drifting apart. By the time Martin had completed elementary school, his younger brother ceased to be a regular companion. Martin was making new friends of his own. A. D. was not upset by this shift, however, for he was a forceful personality in his own right and had many pals. As King grew up, he developed a taste for fine clothes. He liked tweeds so much that his boyhood pals called him "Tweed." [2]

At eight, King began selling the weekly Negro newspaper, and at thirteen, had a paper route for the *Atlanta Journal*, the city's afternoon daily. He worked himself up to assistant manager of one of the paper's deposit stations. This was a responsible position because it meant that he would help the manager to see that each of the thirty or more newsboys got the correct number of papers for his route; that complaints from customers were given proper attention; and that if any emergencies arose, necessary arrangements would be made. King, the youngest assistant manager the *Journal* had at the time, never became station manager. Even in Negro neighborhoods assistant manager posts were reserved for whites because it involved handling money and coming into the downtown office where the cashiers and clerks were generally, if not always, young white women. And the newspaper company did not want Negro "employees" coming in contact with white employees.

King did not recall his first encounter with the race question, but the experience of losing the white playmates from the grocery store was no doubt the first time the race question became a visible problem.

But King never forgot an incident that occurred when he was only six years old. His father had taken him to a downtown shoe store in Atlanta. They took seats in the "front" of the store while waiting to be served. After being there for a while, a young white man finally came forward and said,

15

"I'll be happy to wait on you if you'll just move back there to those seats in the rear." The elder King said forcefully, "There's nothing wrong with these seats, we are quite comfortable here." "Sorry," said the young white clerk, "but you'll have to move." Reverend King said, "We'll buy shoes sitting right here or we won't buy any of yours at all."

There was a brief pause. It was almost unheard of for a Negro to talk back to a white man like that. Then Reverend King and his son, Martin, left the store. Martin remembered walking down the street beside him as he muttered, "I don't care how long I have to live with this system, I will never accept it."

Reverend King was always alert to discourtesy coming from anyone, and especially coming from a white person. The elder King did not permit white agents to use some of the traditional names given to Negroes, such as "Uncle," and "Auntie."

One day while out riding Reverend King accidentally passed a stop sign. A policeman pulled up to the car and said, "All right, boy, pull over and let me see your license." The Reverend King replied indignantly, "I'm no boy." Then pointing to Martin, "This is a boy. I'm a man and until you call me one, I will not listen to you." The policeman was so shocked that he wrote the ticket up nervously and left the scene as quickly as possible.

Even before King was born, his father had refused to ride the city busses—after witnessing brutal attacks on Negro passengers. He had led the fight in Atlanta to equalize teachers' salaries, and also helped to eliminate the segregated elevators in the courthouse. Being Pastor of Ebenezer Baptist Church, with a congregation of four thousand, he had become very influential in the Negro community and was quietly respected by the whites.

The father's warrant respect undergirded the life of the son. King never forgot another incident that happened to him when he was a senior at Booker T. Washington High School. Miss Sarah Brace Bradley, the speech teacher, took some of the students to Valdosta, Georgia, for an oratorical contest, by bus. And on the return trip the students had to give their seats to some white passengers. The students, including King, stood up for 90 miles.

King, on the other hand, abhorred segregated movies and attended one only once. He could not enjoy the picture while sitting in the "Crow's Nest." Nor could he adjust to the separated rest rooms, waiting rooms and eating facilities— partly because the very idea of separation did something to his sense of dignity and self-respect.

King did, however, have some pleasant contacts with friendly whites, especially his two young white friends and also his biology teacher at the Laboratory High School.

A. D., unlike Martin, would retaliate if he were struck. Martin would not since he was against striking others and would do so only as a final resort. A. D. enjoyed teasing his sister and often made her cry. Martin beseeched A. D. to stop, however, he did not. Unable to tolerate this harassment any longer, Martin struck A. D. against his head with the telephone and knocked him senseless. A. D. from that day on never harassed his sister or brother again.

King was knocked, kicked, and beaten numerous times during his childhood, but he never fought back. One such instance was while he was at David T. Howard School where he was beaten up by his school's bully; as usual he did not fight back. Another time at a supermarket, a boy jumped on him and beat him up; yet, King never said or did anything in his defense, when three boys ganged him.

Even though King was a person of energy and probably could handle himself physically, he usually could talk himself out of most situations. Martin has always been considerate of others, however, he would always deal with himself violently.

Before he was 13 years old, Martin had attempted suicide twice and each time it was because of the love he had for his grandmother. A. D. once accidentally knocked his grandmother unconscious while sliding down the banister. Martin was so preoccupied with the belief that she was dead, rather than merely unconscious, that he went to a second story window and jumped out, falling some twelve feet to the ground, but emerging uninjured. Another time he tried to commit suicide was on May 18, 1941, when he was twelve. As he was watching a parade he had slipped away from home to see, his grandmother suffered a heart attack while speaking at Mount Olive Baptist Church and on arrival at the hospital was pronounced dead.

When he heard about his grandmother's death, he ran all the way home as fast as he could. When he got there, he found the whole family crying. Feeling remorseful for slipping off to watch the parade, he went up to the second floor of the house and again jumped out of the window. Again he was shaken up a bit, but not hurt. This was the first time that he was aware of anyone dying so close to him, for his grandfather had died when he was only two. Because King was almost raised by his grandmother and she was like a second mother to him, he was deeply disturbed over her death. The family moved to 193 Boulevard soon after his grandmother's death.

Most of Martin's first fifteen years had been fortunate. One of his grandfathers had been a sharecropper, the other a college graduate minister. One grandmother he loved dearly and the other he never knew personally. His mother was gentle; his father protective. He and his brother and sister were bound together by hundreds of common experiences. He had many pals of his own and was recognized and accepted by his friends and family.

Martin Luther King, Jr., was healthy, "wealthy," and "wise." He wore good clothes and had a little money in the bank. He was happy with his family, his neighborhood, his school and most of the time his city. The church was nearly part of the home. Rarely did unpleasantness come upon him, but when it did, he would stand up and be counted for what he believed was fair and right. At the same time, by nature and by choice, he was opposed to physical forces as an instrument of dealing with human beings. By now, only a lad of fifteen, he was ready for Morehouse College in Atlanta, Georgia.

Chapter Two

THE MOREHOUSE YEARS

King like thousands of other young men was inspired to attend Morehouse College, by its president, Dr. Benjamin Mays who was a colorful and dynamic personality. Dr. Mays, unlike the traditional poorly trained ministers, that Martin had seen at conventions, was a "notorious modernist," a compliment in religious circles. He was then, as now, popular with both the common people and the collegiate group.

Since King lived near the college, he had always heard his father talk about it and often visited it as a boy. When he matriculated in the fall of 1944, he had a different feeling, for he was now a part of it and a "Morehouse Man." The institution, like most colleges, had freshmen to come a few days earlier, to give them a chance to become oriented to the college and college life. There were 205 freshmen in Martin's class, some of whom he knew. Martin took the college entrance examination and passed it while he was in the eleventh grade, thereby, skipping the twelfth grade. Because most of the students lived on the campus, it did not take the men long to know each other. Martin lived off-campus at home with his family.

Morehouse College is composed of the College of Arts and Science and the School of Religion. Being a liberal arts college, the students received a broad outlook on life nurtured in an atmosphere of academic freedom. Morehouse College is an institution for the education of young men for constructive leadership and service.

I

The students ran their own affairs. At Morehouse, they had their own newspaper—the *Maroon-Tiger*, ran rallies and contests among the Spellman girls for their Homecoming Queens and staged elections on campaigns for class officers.

Morehouse College has probably produced more college presidents than any other Negro institution of higher learning and more than its share of prominent doctors, lawyers and ministers. Ability and self-confidence were characteristic qualities of the men of Morehouse. The students had every right to believe in its slogan, "A Morehouse man cannot fail." One look at its president, who was on the national board of the N.A.A.C.P., and a half dozen other civil rights organizations and who was not afraid to think and speak out, would surely be incentive enough for any Morehouse man.

At Morehouse contact between professors and students was close. The professors were at their best when engaging in the art of civilized conversation, and their impact on young minds was powerful. They taught not so much by instructions and skill as by living examples. Proud citizens of the academic world, they cast their students into the classical mold by making the great thoughts and deeds of the past come alive.

King found the place congenial. He liked the leisurely academic life as much as he liked the intellectually earnest men that prevailed. The environment was small-town, and the campus was composed of a few buildings—mostly ante-bellum. Since the student body usually numbered about five hundred, everyone got to know everybody else. All the student body assembled together each morning for a half hour, Monday through Friday. A brief devotional service was followed by the remarks of some local or national speaker on the vital issue of the day. Sometimes the students would sponsor their own programs. On Tuesday, the President usually gave an informal talk.

Morehouse, being a private college, was free of the pressures that were felt by state-supported institutions and the special pressures felt by Negro state colleges in the South. Since it was a private institution, it could select students from the upper third of the graduating high school senior classes.

Some of the professors who most impressed Martin Luther King, Jr., while at Morehouse College, were Samuel W. William, professor of philosophy; Claude B. Dansbury, professor of mathematics; Gladstone L. Chandle, professor of English; Walter R. Chivers, professor of sociology.

King majored in sociology and minored in English. These two subjects combined proved later to be of immense value to him in communication with his followers. He did not participate in many activities as he might have had he lived on campus. King was, however, a member of the Glee Club, the Atlanta University-Morehouse-Spellman Chorus, the Y.M.C.A., the N.A.A.C.P., and the Faculty-Student Discipline Committee.

Some of King's closest friends, Walter McCall and Robert Williams, were clear about their "calling" into the ministry, whereas, he was slow in making up his mind. Most of King's closest friends, were like himself, non-fraternity men. King, being the intellectual type, did not have time for the horseplay of the Greek letter organizations.

Like most first and second year students, King took the courses in core curriculum. In his sophomore year he also spoke well enough to win second place honor in the Webb Oratorical Contest. Even by his sophomore year, he was still not sure whether he wanted to be a doctor, lawyer or minister. By his junior year, he was turning more to the ministry and away from law and medicine. By his senior year, he had decided upon the ministry. Many of King's friends took a personal interest in his well-being and set many fine examples for him to follow. Some were persuasive in helping him make up his mind. Thus with the image of his father, who wanted him to become a minister but did not push the point, the encouragement of Dr. Mays, and the influence of Professor Kelsey, Martin Luther King, Jr., turned to the cloth.

II

King, like thousands of other college students, spent his summer vacation earning spending money. He worked with a railway express company during the rush season, but quit when the foreman called him a "nigger." He also worked in an Atlanta mattress factory. One summer he traveled with other Morehouse men to Connecticut to work in the tobacco fields. While there, the young men were exposed to a new experience. Unlike in Georgia, they were "free" to go into many theaters, restaurants and other public places. Even though the association with white persons was at a minimum, the men still felt that they had a new birth of freedom.

As the King family grew older, the three children were developing wills of their own. They wanted to be confronted with problems and then try to solve them. So the problem of children versus parents developed, as expected. The three children had their individual reactions to their father's well-meant assumption that he knew what was best for them. A. D. was somewhat disappointed with himself at times, especially since he was not doing too well in college. In fact, he withdrew from college and married his childhood sweetheart, Naomi Barber, and started a home of his own. King developed the technique of listening to what his family had to say and then doing what he thought best.

Things were going splendidly for everyone in the King family except A. D. Mrs. King had gone back to Morris Brown College to complete the work for her baccalaureate degree. The Rev. King was on the Board of Directors of the Citizens Trust Company, Atlanta University, Morehouse College, the National Baptist Convention, and the N.A.A.C.P.

Martin Luther King, Jr., finished Morehouse College in June 1948. At nineteen years old, he was healthy, interested in furthering his vocation, articulate, optimistic, and as a student, draft-exempted.

As Plato said, "The direction in which education starts a man will determine his future life." So Martin Luther King, Jr.'s experience at Morehouse College would determine his future life. He thought that by being a Morehouse man, he was ready for the world and could take on anything that it could give.

Chapter Three

THE CROZER YEARS

Crozer Theological Seminary is a graduate school for the education of men and women for the Christian ministry at Chester, Pennsylvania. It originated a century ago out of the desire of Baptists for a seminary within the Middle Atlantic region. The University of Lewisbury, now Bucknell University, was founded in 1864. John Price Crozer established the theological department in 1865.

Although the Seminary was founded by Baptists and the majority of its Board of Trustees were Baptist ministers and laymen, from the beginning it sought to render wider than denominational services. It has been ecumenical in its interests and in the composition of its faculty and student body. In particular, it has been a valuable meeting place for northern and southern Negroes, Canadians, and overseas Baptists.

Crozer is proud of its heritage. Scholarships have been the key to its reputation, yet it has not abandoned the churches at home and abroad for abstract research. It has been deeply rooted in the free church tradition of American Baptists, yet expressing in its daily work a prayer for the ultimate unity of the Church of Christ.

I

It was by no accident that Martin Luther King, Jr., chose Crozer Theological Seminary for his professional training. Even though he received scholarships from other institutions, he selected Crozer because it was among the top theological schools in the country, and he was also offered a full tuition scholarship for three years.

King was an A student during his three years. As one compares King's academic record at Morehouse and at Crozer, he will find that he made a much better record at Crozer. Perhaps, one of the reasons was the interracial environment.

He was always conscious of the fact that everyone expected him to do better than anyone else. He always tried to be punctual for his classes. He thought that when he entered the classroom everyone's eyes were on him. Wherever he appeared in public, he strove to act like a gentleman.

During King's first year, he studied criticism of the Bible, church history, and special phases of the lives and works of the major prophets. For his third and final year, he took the psychology of religion, ethics and social philosophy. At the same time, there were the courses on the techniques involved in performing the tasks of the ministry, including church administration.

Martin's favorite and most impressive professor was Dr. George W. Davis, who taught Systematic Theology, and taught it most systematically. Martin contended that Professor Davis was a "marvelous teacher, conversant with the trends of modern culture and yet sincerely religious. He was warm and Christian. It was easy to get close to him." [3]

Another one of Martin's professors that left a favorable impression on him was Professor Kenneth Lee Smith, who "had a tremendously large capacity to grapple with big ideas." [4] Professor Smith enjoyed an intellectual "debate" with his students. He encouraged them to hold independent views. For hours and hours after class he and King would tangle over the social philosophy of the Reverend Walter Pauschonbuisch and the neo-orthodox views of Dr. Reinhold Niebuhr.

King also recalled Dr. Morton Scott Enslin, who "was one of those precise scholars and superb linguists, who had a rather iconoclastic manner of criticism." [5] Professor Enslin's course in the New Testament was so shocking that the fundamentalist beliefs of some of his students were completely up-rooted. Dr. Enslin also "knocked King out of his dogmatic slumber." [6]

King received further enlightenment from visiting lecturers such as A. J. Muste and Dr. Mordecai W. Johnson. Dr. Johnson was a profound and colorful public speaker in the great tradition of Southern Baptist preachers. He was a Morehouse man of the Class of 1911. He taught at Morehouse for two years and later went into the ministry.

While Dr. Johnson was president of Howard University in Washington, D.C., he began to read about Gandhi's own works in young India. He also talked with Charles Andrews and others he met who had been to Asia. The Indian way seemed to offer an answer to Dr. Johnson's question of social justice. He went to India. After he returned, he was so indoctrinated with Gandhi's philosophy that he spread it throughout the country. Among the places he spoke was the Fellowship House in Philadelphia, about twelve miles from Chester, and among those who heard him was King.

King became so inspired by Dr. Johnson's talk that he began to read all of the books on Gandhi that he could find. The more he read, the more he wanted to know and the deeper he became involved with Mahatma's philosophy. At last he had found a philosophy that was worthwhile and offered an answer to his sense of social obligations.

While at Crozer, King was elected president of the student body. He took several special classes in philosophy at the University of Pennsylvania to supplement his courses at Crozer. He also attended the Penn Relays during each of his three years there.

The students at Crozer came from all parts of the country and from abroad. They generally were a friendly and a congenial group. Normal contacts usually make relationships free and easy, but no matter how select the students are, there is usually going to be one that will not or cannot conform. One North Carolinian found it difficult to accept Negroes as associates. Occasionally, he used the word "darkie."

In their playful moments the students sometimes indulged in horseplay. One prank was to slip into a hallmate's room during his absence and overturn his bed, chairs and other pieces of furniture. Everybody would participate in these pranks, including the North Carolinian and King. One day, someone upset the North Carolinian's room. When he returned to his room and found it upset, he went directly to King, in anger, and accused him of upsetting his room and to the shock of several students, he pulled a pistol, threatening to shoot him. King calmly told him that he had not been a member of the gang that had done the upsetting. Later, the incident was brought before the student government, but Martin would not press charges against him, preferring to let the matter drop. But both the student body and faculty felt that such a serious act could not easily be brushed aside. After much meditation and contemplation, the North Carolinian finally got enough courage to publicly confess his wrong and apologized.

For refusing to press charges and acting calmly in the face of an apparently dangerous situation, King was easily the man on the campus—in the eyes of the student body and faculty.

Apparently the North Carolinian and King became friends before they graduated, because some years afterward when the North Carolinian was passing through Atlanta, he felt he knew King well enough to look him up and ask for a small "loan." King was glad to help him out.

King usually encountered no difficulty in the use of public facilities in Pennsylvania. He did realize, however, that there was some discrimination in the north as well as the south.

There was an unpleasant incident that he vividly recalled. One evening he and his friend, Walter McCall, were taking their dates out riding and decided to stop and have something to eat at a restaurant on a New Jersey highway, a few miles from Camden. The foursome got out of the automobile and went into the restaurant and took a table. After being there for a while, they realized that the waitresses were purposely passing them up. Consequently, they asked for the proprietor, who said that he was not going to serve them.

Being well informed and up to date on the laws of the state, they knew that New Jersey, like most northern states, had a civil rights law that prohibited discrimination because of race, color or creed. Therefore, they decided to go back and sit at the table. The proprietor became so angry just seeing them sitting there and refusing to leave that he went outside and got his pistol and fired into the air and declared vehemently, "I kill for less."

The foursome quietly and calmly left, but later returned with a policeman and had the frightened restaurateur arrested.

King and his friends asked some of the other people in the restaurant if they would testify as witnesses and three University of Pennsylvania students agreed to do so.

The case was turned over to the Camden Branch of the N.A.A.C.P. and a suit was filed against the restaurateur. The N.A.A.C.P. had a clear cut case had the witnesses testified as they had agreed, but upon second thought, they decided against doing so. Therefore, the suit was thrown out of court for lack of "objective evidence."

II

Being the son of a minister, King had a great advantage over most of his classmates. From the time he was born, he had heard inside discussions on church affairs. In 1947, he had been ordained and elected assistant to the pastor at Ebenezer, while only a junior in college. And during the summer vacation, while attending Morehouse, his father let him take charge of operating the church.

Ebenezer was evidently well-administered for it was financially independent. It was free of debt and had reserved funds in the bank. It was somewhat different from some of its neighboring churches that engaged in raffles or lotteries or some other money-producing ventures. Perhaps some credit for Ebenezer being financially sound was due to Martin's father, for under his pastorate, the enrollment of the church increased from four thousand to six thousand. Most of the congregation consisted of skilled, semi-skilled and few domestics.

In recent years, however, Ebenezer has attracted some doctors, public school teachers, postal employees, businessmen, and college professors. The elder King usually sent all persons on the church roll a reminder or "church bill." A mimeographed statement was issued each month which listed the contribution of church members.

King also attended some of the state and national Baptist conventions and become familiar with the inside church functions. These first-hand experiences were very helpful since they were not included in the Crozer curriculum.

The years at Crozer were some of King's happiest and in a sense, they were his golden ones. He was graduated in 1951 with a B.D. degree. Besides being class valedictorian, he was also the recipient of the Peral Plafkner Award for scholarship, and the Lewis Crozer Fellowship of $1,200 for two additional years of graduate study. There was no doubt that he had done much better at Crozer than at Morehouse.

King had suffered no major defeats. He was graduated with honors and was loved and respected by his fellow students and faculty as well. He was healthy, successful and happy, for he was living the "good life."

Chapter Four

THE BOSTON YEARS

When King announced his intentions of continuing his schooling there were mixed reactions among his friends and neighbors. Some thought that he had sufficient training for the Baptist ministry, since there were not many Negro Baptist ministers with two earned degrees. Some felt that he would be too educated for his congregation.

When Martin pointed out that he had a $1,200 Fellowship, many of his friends had to agree that this did make a difference. In September 1951, King arrived on the Boston University campus in his green Chevrolet, his graduation present from his parents, and enrolled as a candidate for the PhD degree. At that time Boston University and the University of Southern California were the two leading universities in the nation for the study of personalism. King was especially interested in this rather new turn in modern philosophy which placed great emphasis upon the value of human personality.

For the first semester, he had a room at 170 St. Botolph Street, about an eight minute drive from the University, where several other Boston University students also rented rooms. During the second semester, King and another Morehouse man, Philip Lenud, who was studying for his B.D. at Tufts University, rented a suite at 397 Massachusetts Avenue.

Martin Luther King, Jr.'s life in Boston was far different from his life at Morehouse or Crozer. Working toward a doctorate is largely an individual and independent project that requires a great deal of intensive research and leaves little, if any, time for social life. King and Lenud did find time, however, to organize as an extra-curricular activity, the Philosophical Club. At first, it was composed of a weekly meeting for fifteen or twenty Negro graduate students who were studying at various institutions of higher learning in and around Boston. One evening they would meet, drink coffee and talk. At each meeting, someone would read a paper on a subject of his choice and the others would give constructive criticisms. Sometimes, the students became so involved in these "philosophical" discussions that they would "debate" until dawn. As time passed the reputation of the Club spread, and subsequently it became both interracial and co-educational.

I

King's favorite teacher at Boston was the famous Dr. Edgar S. Brightman with whom he studied for only a semester and a half. Dr. Brightman was taken seriously ill, and died soon afterward. King considered him not only a distinguished teacher, but also a brilliant scholar as well. Dr. Brightman rated King highly. King was also impressed with L. Harold De Wolf, who was a disciple of Brightman.

De Wolf was also impressed with King, as he later remarked that of "all the doctorate students I have had at Boston University—some fifty in all—I would rate Martin Luther King among the top five." [7]

Despite the extensive doctoral requirements, King arranged to enroll as a special student at Harvard University.

II

While at Boston, King found the young ladies exceptionally withdrawn and reserved. Since there were not that many young ladies "available," King talked to Mrs. Mary Powell, an old friend from Atlanta who was studying in Boston and who agreed to help. A few days later, Mrs. Powell suggested two names to him. He had met one of the girls, but the description of the other one enchanted him so that he asked Mrs. Powell to get her telephone number. He also asked her to tell the girl about him. Later he called Miss Coretta Scott. When King first telephoned Coretta, she did not receive him warmly. However, after listening to him, she found something very appealing about his voice and personality. So she agreed to have lunch with him the next day.

At lunch the conversation went smoothly and he asked her for another date. She suggested that he escort her to a party to which she had been invited the next night. Before King took her home from the restaurant, he had made up his mind about Coretta and he told her what he thought. "You have all the qualities that I expect to find in the girl I'd like to have for a wife," he remarked suddenly.[8]

In the following months they became serious about each other and later began to talk about marriage. This was a very difficult question for Coretta because there was her career to think about. She had come a long way from Marion, Alabama, as a baby born April 27, 1927, then through Lincoln High School in Marion, and then to Antioch College in Yellow Spring, Ohio, and now at the New England Conservatory of Music in Boston.

Coretta also thought about her parents when the question of marriage arose, even though she was at the Conservatory on a scholarship. Her father, Obrie, had always been a hard working man and had also managed his own general store, his home, three trucks for hauling wood, a chicken farm and a considerable amount of land. Though her mother, Bernice McMurry, had little formal schooling, she wanted her children to get a good education. Coretta was the second of the three children; her sister Edyth was two years older; her brother, Obrie Leonard, was three years younger.

III

From an early age, Coretta had been interested in getting an education. After finishing Lincoln High School, she did not expect to go to college, since her sister Edyth, was in college at Antioch. To have two children in college at the same time, would present a hardship on her family. She was hopeful and confident, however, that a door would open for her. That door opened two months before graduation when she received word that she had been granted a scholarship to Antioch College.

All these things ran through Coretta's mind. She had hoped that the right man would come along a year or so after she had completed her education and got started as an artist. King had appeared at the right place, but at the wrong time.

31

Moreover, she had never intended to marry a minister. Another question arose. Would the wife of a minister have to give up thoughts of a separate career for herself? The groom-to-be assured her that he thought their marriage and her singing career could be happily combined. Not long afterwards Coretta realized that she wanted him and needed him so much that if need be, she would gladly give up her career.

The wedding was held on June 18, 1953, on the lawn at Coretta's home. No doubt it was the largest social event in Perry County that year. King's father performed the ceremony and his brother was the best man.

They returned to Boston and rented a four room apartment for $35 a month. The marriage did not interfere with their education. For awhile, Coretta decided she would have a better chance for a part-time career as a music teacher than as a concert artist; therefore, she changed from the four year course in voice to the three course in public music. After graduation, Mrs. King returned to Atlanta and spent the summer with her in-laws.

Chapter Five

GO SOUTH YOUNG MAN, GO SOUTH

King had to return to Boston to complete his residence requirements and by the end of the summer of 1954 he had completed his research. Even though he had finished his research he did not have to stay in Boston to write up his findings for the dissertation, since the final copy could be submitted by mail.

In the meantime, King thought that it would be wise to start thinking about a job, so that he could start working in September of 1954. There were two churches in the North interested in him—one in New York and one in Massachusetts. Three colleges had also offered him attractive and challenging positions. An administrative position, including a deanship and teaching position.[9] Meanwhile, he had received a letter from the officers of the Dexter Avenue Baptist Church in Montgomery, Alabama, saying that they were without a pastor and would like for him to deliver a sermon when he was in that section of the country. The officers who sent him the invitation had heard of him through the elder King, in Atlanta, and other ministerial friends. Since King would be home in Atlanta for the Christmas holidays, he wrote immediately saying that he would be happy to come to Montgomery to deliver a sermon one Sunday in January.

Even though the congregation of the church was relatively small—with only about three hundred members, it nevertheless had many influential and respected citizens among its membership.

The Saturday before the Sunday that he was to preach, he was aware of a certain anxiety. Although he had preached many times as associate pastor of his father's church, he was conscious that he was on trial. While he was reviewing his sermon, several questions arose. Should he attempt to interest the educational segment of the congregation with a display of scholarship? Or should he preach as he had always done, depending on the inspiration of the spirit of God? He subscribed to the latter course. He said to himself, "Keep Martin Luther King, Jr., in the background and God in the foreground and everything will be alright. Remember you are a channel of the gospel, and not the source." [10]

The next day, at eleven o'clock, he was in the pulpit delivering his sermon before a large congregation. His topic was: "The Three Dimensions of a Complete Life." The congregation was very much impressed with him, and he left with the feeling that God was ever present. Later, the officers of the church asked him if he would accept the pastorship, if they decided to endorse him. He told them that he would give it some consideration.

About a month later the officers of the Dexter Avenue Baptist Church sent him an air-mail special delivery letter stating that he had been unanimously selected as their choice for the pastorship and if he would reply at once, he could start immediately. Even though he was happy to have the offer, he did not reply at once, because he was to fly to Detroit the next morning for a preaching engagement the following Sunday.

As he was traveling on the airplane, several questions ran through his mind. He was torn in two directions. Should he accept a pastorship, and if so, should it be the one in the North or the one in the South? Or should he go into the educational field? After much meditation and after discussing it with his wife, he decided to go SOUTH and accept the offer from the Dexter Avenue Baptist Church in Montgomery, Alabama.

His father, as expected, did not agree with his son. He wanted to groom him as his successor. He also had a bad impression of Montgomery as a place to live. As usual Martin listened to his father, and then made up his own mind. The South was his home, despite all of its shortcomings. He loved it and had an intense desire to do something about the problems that he had felt so keenly as a youngster.

After exploring arrangements with the officers of the church, he accepted the pastorate. Because of his desire to spend at least four more months of intensive work on his doctoral thesis, he asked for and was granted leave from full-time pastorate until September 1, 1954. During this interim he did agree, to come to Dexter Avenue Church once a month, to keep things running smoothly.

On a Sunday in May 1954, he preached his first sermon as minister of the Dexter Avenue Baptist Church and for the next four months, he commuted by planes between Boston and Montgomery.

I

On September 1, 1954, the Martin Luther King, Jr.'s were able to move into the parsonage at 309 South Jackson Street, and he was now a full-time pastor. The first few months were busy with getting to know the congregation and becoming adjusted to a new job, a new house, and a new city. Even though he preached well and was friendly with everyone, his youth was somewhat against him.

During the five months that King was pastor, he saw an increase in attendance and an increase in financial support. The Dexter Avenue Baptist Church was often referred to as the "big folks' Church." Revolting against this idea, King was convinced that worship at its best is a social experience, with people of all levels of life coming together to realize their oneness and unity under God. He thought that whenever the church consciously or unconsciously caters to one class, it loses the spiritual value and force of the "whosoever will, let them come" doctrine and is in danger of becoming little more than a social club with a thin veneer of religiosity.

While King was pastor of the Dexter Church, the auxiliary program was broadened through the establishment of a committee to revitalize religious education, a social service committee for the sick and needy, a social and political action committee, a committee to raise and administer scholarships for high school graduates, and a cultural committee to give encouragement to promising artists.

For several months Reverend King had divided his time between completing his thesis and carrying out his duties with the church. He rose every morning at five-thirty and spent

35

three hours writing the thesis, returning to it later at night for another three hours. The remainder of the day included weekly services of personal conferences, visiting the sick, marriages, and funerals. A minimum of fifteen hours a week was spent in preparing his Sunday sermon. He usually began an outline on Tuesday. On Wednesday, he did the necessary research and thought of illustrative material and life situations that would give the sermon practical content. On Friday, he began writing and usually finished the writing on Saturday night.

He also found time to take an interest in the larger community of Montgomery. The city's economic life was greatly boosted by the Gunter and Maxwell Air Force bases. One in every fourteen employed civilians in Montgomery worked at these bases and almost one in every seven families was an Air Force family—either civilian or military.

Since there are not many industries in or near Montgomery, about 59 percent of the Negro women are domestic workers and about 45 percent of the Negro men are laborers or domestic workers.

Reverend King found Montgomery far different from Atlanta; there were no integrated professional organizations of teachers, physicians or lawyers; no interracial ministerial organizations; no local Urban League or NAACP. The Baptist minister, therefore, began working with the Alabama Council on Human Relations and also the NAACP.

As time went on, he discovered several things had to be remedied, in the Negro community before any real social progress could be made. First, there were too many spiral groups in the community that divided the Negro leadership. There was the Progressive Democrats, under the leadership of E. D. Nixon; the Citizens Committee, headed by Mrs. Mary Fairbanks and Jo Ann Robinson. There were also several smaller groups. Since the vast majority of the people were indifferent and complacent, some efforts had to be made to unite all of these groups.

Many Negro ministers were not concerned with the struggle for racial justice. Most of them thought that they should not get involved with such earthly, temporal matter as

36

social and economic improvements; they were to preach the gospel, and keep the people's minds on the Bible and Heaven!

While Rev. King was participating in civic affairs, Mrs. King was also keeping busy by continuing her career. In November, 1954 she appeared in a concert at the Shiloh Baptist Church in Brunswick, Georgia. She made her first debut in Montgomery at the First Baptist Church on March 6, 1955. Later, Mrs. King appeared at Carmen, Ala. Because she was expecting her first child, her career had to be temporarily discontinued. The Martin Luther King, Jr.'s first child, Yolanda Denise King, was born on November 17, 1955.

Just five months before their first child on June 5, 1955, Martin Luther King, Jr., was awarded the Ph.D in Systematic Theology. The dissertation investigated the philosophies of Paul Tillich and Henry Wieman. By the fall of 1955, Martin Luther King, Jr. had a wife, a daughter, a Ph.D., a Church and was well liked by his congregation. Except for his unusual educational background, he and his family were a "typical" American one.

Chapter Six

THE NEGRO AND THE MONTGOMERY MOVEMENT

The Montgomery protest has been treated adequately in *Stride Toward Freedom;* Therefore it will be referred to briefly in this book. As we all know by now, Martin Luther King, Jr., did not become internationally known until the boycott.

Montgomery could not or would not be the same after December 1, 1956. It was the day that Mrs. Rosa Parks, a Negro seamstress was arrested for refusing to obey the bus driver's order to move from the seat in which she was sitting to let a white passenger sit down. Mrs. Parks was returning home from work and after being tired from standing all day, she sat in the first available seat, which happened to be reserved for white riders. Since Mrs. Parks refused to move, she was arrested.

The reactions of the Negro community in Montgomery were mixed. At first there was some speculation about why Mrs. Parks did not move. Some people in the white community said she had been "planted" by the NAACP as a test case. As a matter of record, the NAACP did not plant her there. In fact, it did not aid or abet the boycotters at the early stages of the movement.

No one can understand why Mrs. Parks reacted the way she did, unless she had been pierced by the Zeitgeist—the spirit of the time. And her crying soul screamed out, "I can't take no more."

There were only one or two people, including E. D. Nixon, who knew of Mrs. Parks' arrest and signed her bond. After word got around, the reaction in the Negro community to boycott the buses was set off, like a gigantic missile. Since the Women's Political Council suggested the boycott first, they wanted a man to master-mind their idea; therefore, they asked E. D. Nixon and he readily agreed.

Early Friday morning Nixon called Martin Luther King, Jr. and told him of the incident and concluded by saying, "We have taken this type of thing for long enough already and I feel that the time has come to boycott the buses. Only through a boycott can we make it clear to the white folks that we will not accept this type of treatment any longer." Reverend King agreed, at once, that some protest was necessary and that a boycott would be an effective method of protesting.

On Friday night a mass meeting was called and virtually every group and organization of the Negro community was represented, including businessmen, doctors, union leaders, lawyers, postal employees and ministers. Since E. D. Nixon had to leave town earlier in the afternoon for his regular run on the railroad, he could not be present. In his absence, Reverend L. Roy Bennett, president of the Interdenominational Ministers Alliance, agreed to preside.

The meeting began about seven-thirty with H. H. Hubbard leading a brief devotional period. Afterward Reverend Bennett explained the purpose for the meeting. He proposed that the Negroes should boycott the buses on Monday. "Now is the time to move. This is no time to talk! It is time to act," he concluded.

For almost forty-five minutes after his statement, confusion reigned. Several people wanted further clarifications of Mrs. Parks' actions and arrest. Some wanted to know how long the protest would last. Others wanted to know how commuters would be transported to and from their jobs. Even though many questions went unanswered, it seemed to have been the consensus of the group that the boycott should take place.

The ministers overwhelmingly endorsed the plan and promised to go to their congregations on Sunday morning and encourage them to stay off the buses Monday.

While the meeting was still being held, a committee was formed to prepare a mimeograph statement. It read:

Don't ride the bus to work, to town, to school or anywhere Monday, December 5.

Another Negro woman has been arrested and put in jail because she refused to give up her bus seat.

Don't ride the buses to work, to town, to school, or anywhere Monday. If you work, take a cab, or share a ride, or walk.

Come to a mass meeting Monday at 7:00 P.M., at the Holt Street Baptist Church for further instructions.

The *Montgomery Advertiser* got hold of leaflets and made the boycott a front page story. This story later turned out to be the Negroes' advantage since it informed other Negroes who had not received leaflets.

When the bus drivers went on their routes Monday, December 5, 1956, the buses were empty except for six or seven passengers. Instead of the 60 percent cooperation the leaders had hoped for, it appeared as if the boycott was almost 100 percent effective. A miracle seemed to have taken place, for the complacent Negroes had been awakened. During this period many forms of transportation were used — private taxis, private cars, horse-drawn buggies, mules, and horses. Some people even walked, sometimes as much as ten miles.

The same day, December 5, Mrs. Parks was tried and found guilty of disobeying the city segregation ordinance. She was fined ten dollars and the cost of court, which totaled fourteen dollars. She had her attorney, Fred D. Gray, to appeal in the case. Mrs. Parks' arrest and conviction did two things; it helped to steer the Negroes into some positive thinking and action. Secondly, it was a test of the validity of the segregation law itself.

Later during the day, Rev. Ralph D. Abernathy, Rev. E. N. French and E. D. Nixon met and discussed the need for some organization to guide and direct the protest. At a mass meeting the Montgomery Improvement Association was organized with Martin Luther King, Jr. as president.

The Montgomery Improvement Association was the name suggested by Abernathy at the same meeting. Although King was the spokesman for M.I.A., most of the decisions were the collective results of the whole association.[19]

As president, King related what had happened to Mrs. Parks to another mass rally the same night at the Holt Street

40

Baptist Church. After reviewing the history of abuses and insults that people of color had experienced on the city buses, he concluded "but there comes a time that people get tired. We are here this evening to say to those who have mistreated us so long that we are tired of being segregated and humiliated; tired of being kicked about by the brutal feet of oppression. We had no alternative but to protest. For many years, we have shown amazing patience. We have sometimes given our white brothers the feeling that we liked the way we were being treated. But we come here tonight to be saved from that patience that makes us patient with anything less than freedom and justice."

He also urged the people not to force anybody to refrain from riding the buses. Their methods must be that of persuasion and not coercion; the Christian doctrine and their consciences should be their guide. They must heed the words of Jesus echoing across the centuries; "Love your enemies, bless them that curse you and pray for them that despitefully use you." So the main theme of the entire movement was that of Christian love.

The meeting concluded with the following resolution which called upon the Negroes not to resume riding the buses until:

(1) Courteous treatment by the bus operators was guaranteed.

(2) Passengers were seated on a first-come, first-served basis— Negroes seated from the back of the bus toward the front while whites seated from the front toward the back.

(3) That Negro bus operators be employed on predominantly Negro routes.

Everyone at the meeting expressed his determination not to ride the buses until conditions were changed.

From the beginning of the protest, the major problem was that of transportation. For the first few days, the Negro taxi companies agreed to transport the people for the same ten cent fare that they paid on the buses. During the negotiating, however, it was implied by Police Commissioner Clyde Seller that there was a law that required taxis to charge a minimum; therefore, the taxis had to be abandoned because of a later city order making it illegal to charge less than the minimum fare.

Where will we go from here? What method of transportation will be used? How much will it cost? Can the Association afford it? Where will the money come from—were questions pondered by the leaders.

Remembering that Reverend Theodore Jemison had led a bus boycott in Baton Rouge, Louisiana, and that he and his associates had set up an effective car pool, King suggested that the same method be used in Montgomery. The M.I.A. agreed that this was a good idea.

After a call went out for volunteer workers who would drive or loan their cars, over a hundred and fifty people responded and later a total of 300 were used. At first, the M.I.A. had been able to support the 300 car pool, but as time went on, the car pool expenses rose to $500 a month.

Although the M.I.A. never made a public appeal for funds, contributions later began to come in all sizes and from all places over the world. This no doubt was due to the fine coverage that the newspapers had given the movement. Gifts ranged from $5 to $5,000, with the total contribution nearly a quarter of a million dollars.[12]

The second problem of the M.I.A. was keeping the people together. From the beginning, the basic philosophy of the movement was that of Christian love. Now reference was made concerning the principles of non-violence and passive resistance.[13]

About a week after the protest had begun, Miss Juliette Morgan, a white lady, wrote a letter to the editor of the *Montgomery Advertiser* with the thought in mind to compare the Montgomery movement to the Gandhian movement in India. From this day on the philosophy of non-violent resistance emerged as the technique of the movement.

Every mass meeting followed a simple outline; songs, prayer, Scriptures, opening remarks by the president, collection, reports from various committees and the main address of the evening. Every speaker was asked to make non-violence the hub of his theme.

King once told a mass rally, "We have known humiliation, we have known abstinence, abusive language, we have plunged into the abyss of oppression, and we decided to rise up only with the means of protest. It is one of the greatest glories of America that we have the right to protest."

"There are those who would try to make this a hate campaign. This is not a war between the white and the Negro, but a conflict between justice and injustice. This is bigger than the Negro race revolting against the white. We are seeking to improve not the Negro of Montgomery, but the whole of Montgomery," Reverend King continued.

He concluded by inserting that, "If we are arrested every day, if we are exploited every day, if we are trampled over every day, don't ever let anyone pull you so low as to hate them. We must use the weapon of love. We must have compassion and understanding for those who hate us. We must realize so many people are taught to hate us, that they are not totally responsible for their hate."

Even though not all Montgomery's Negroes believed or understood this new philosophy, most of them followed it to perfection and did so only because they had confidence in their leaders.

I

The Montgomery story is one with 50,000 actors and each playing a different role. It is impossible to name and to give equal space to all of the personalities. Since the Montgomery Improvement Association's Executive Board, however, played such an important role it is appropriate to direct our attention to some of the thirty-odd members.

King relied heavily on Rev. Ralph Abernathy who was second in command throughout the entire movement. He was also the Chief Negotiator of the Movement. Fred D. Gray was the brilliant young attorney who represented the M.I.A. after being out of Western Reserve University Law School only one year. Mrs. Jo Ann Robinson was another stalwart worker. Jo Ann, as she was popularly called, was unstoppable. She was active at every stage of the movement, including editing the M.I.A. Newsletter. The Rev. Robert Graetz, pastor of the Negro Trinity Lutheran Church, was the lone white member of the Executive Board of the M.I.A. He not only supported the movement, but also participated as an active member.

Rev. Graetz was also a constant reminder to the Negroes that many white people were applying the "love-thy-neighbor-as-thy-self" doctrine. E. D. Nixon, a pullman porter, had often been referred to as "the Man behind the Man," during the movement. Nixon withdrew his name from the presidency of the MIA because as a pullman porter, he would be out of town a great deal, and because he felt that someone with more education should represent the organization. He did, however, agree to be treasurer and he worked hard at it.

Mrs. Rosa Parks will probably go down in history as the lady who precipitated the Montgomery boycott. Her courage and patience made her one of the most respected people in the community, the state, and the world. What role, then, did Martin Luther King, Jr., play in the movement? He was the spokesman, philosopher and the symbol of the bus boycott. He was the one who preached nonviolence and christian love.

Many people did not expect the boycott to last as long as it did. The white community thought that it would die out in a few days. Since the Negroes had never joined together for a common cause before; the white community had no idea that this time would be any different. Therefore, when the city officials saw that the Negroes meant business and that they were not going to give up as easily as expected, the city and bus officials agreed to negotiate, and a meeting was called. The meeting was largely due to the influence of the Rev. Robert Hughes, executive director of the Alabama Council on Human Relations; the Rev. Thomas P. Thracher, and Dr. H. Trenholm, president of Alabama State Teacher College, both members of the Council also. The meeting took place December 8, 1956 at eleven o'clock at the City Hall.

The MIA Executive Board appointed a Negotiating Committee of twelve with Martin Luther King, Jr. as the spokesman. Present also at the meeting were Thrasher, Hughes, Trenholm, the three commissioners—Mayor W. A. Seller, Commissioner Clyde Seller, Commissioner Frank A. Parks, J. E. Bagley and Jack Crenshaw, representatives of the bus company.

At the meeting three proposals were presented: (1) a guarantee of courteous treatment; (2) passengers seated on a first-come-first served basis, the Negroes seating from the back; and (3) employment of Negro bus operators on predominately Negro routes.

Mr. Crenshaw, the attorney for the bus company, argued that, "If we grant the Negroes these demands, they would go about boasting of a victory that they had won over the white people; and this we will not stand for." The meeting lasted for four hours without any settlement.

On Monday, December 9, 1956, another meeting was called. At the meeting Luther Ingalls, secretary of the Montgomery White Citizens Council, was present, and once again little was accomplished as Mr. Ingalls was about to make a statement when King jumped to the floor and challenged his right to speak since he was not a member of the committee. "Furthermore, we will never solve this problem so long as there are persons on the committee whose public pronouncement are anti-Negro," said King. The white committee members tried to divide the Negroes by saying King was the cause of the stalemate. Reverend Abernathy soon took the floor and said vehemently that King was the spokesman for the group and the Negro community was behind him all the way.

Another attempt was made to reopen negotiations by the Men of Montgomery—an organization made up of the most influential businessmen of the city. They realized that their businesses were being hurt financially and any postponement of the negotiations could very well be disastrous. The bus company lost more than $750,000. Several members of the Men of Montgomery met with the MIA in an effort to settle the protest; and if it had not been for closed-minded men, a solution may have been reached.

After compromise failed, opponents of the movement tried to block it by causing dissension among the Negro community by spreading false rumors about their leaders. One throwaway was circulated December 18, 1956. It read:

ARE YOU TIRED OF WALKING

Sure You Are . . . But Why Walk While Our
Leaders Ride . . . In Big Cars Too.

45

Why?

Because They're Playing For Suckers
While They Get Rich On Our Money.

No Wonder They Want To Keep The Boycott Going. . .
No Wonder They Don't Tell Us There Isn't a Chance
In The World Of Breaking Segregation In Montgomery.

WAKE UP AND GET SMART

We'll Be Walking To Work Till Judgment Day If They
Have Their Way . . . We'll Be Losing What Friendship
We Have Left And Making Our Situation Worse Instead
Of Better If They Have Their Way. . .

We'll Be The Joke Of The Whole Country. . .
Walking While Our Leaders Ride In A Big Car
Walking While Our Leaders Get Rich On Our Money.

DON'T SWALLOW THEIR MESS ANYMORE

DON'T BE A FOOL, IT'S OUR MONEY AND OUR FEET

Of course, all of these rumors were unfounded. King told
a mass rally in his appeal for funds to support the movement:
"We have to be very careful that no one exploits this movement. We all know that the Till case was exploited too much.
We need money, but we are not going to do anything and
everything to get it. No one is going to get any handouts."

Some members of the white community implied to several
leaders of the protest that the problem could be solved if King
were removed. And if someone else were their leader, things
would change overnight.

King became so disturbed over these incidents that he
called a meeting of the Executive Board and offered to resign.
He told them that he would be the last person to stand in the
way of a solution to the problem. And that he still would be
an active member in the movement. The Executive Board
gave him a vote of confidence and made it clear that they were
pleased with the way he was handling things and that they
would support him to the end.

Another attempt was made to divide the Negroes again on January 22, 1957. The commissioners announced in the local newspaper that they had met with a group of prominent Negro ministers and worked out a settlement. Later this settlement proved to be nothing more than a hoax. The commissioners thought that once the Negroes began riding the buses in large numbers the boycott would collapse. King and some of his associates were able to identify the "three prominent Negro ministers." They were not members of the MIA, and they publicly repudiated the commissioners' announcement.

V

After the hoax failed, these distraught men were now becoming desperate. They now injected a "get tough" policy— a series of arrests for minor and often unfounded traffic violations. Some drivers in the car pool were stopped and questioned about their license, insurance, and even their employers.

Gradually, the volunteer car pool began to weaken, and it became more and more difficult to get a ride because some drivers were afraid that their licenses would be revoked, or their insurance cancelled. King was even arrested and put in jail for allegedly speeding thirty miles an hour in a twenty-five mile zone.

After the "get tough" policy failed, the officials became more desperate. By the end of January, King and his family were receiving as many as forty or fifty threatening telephone calls a day telling him to get out of town or else; "you niggers are getting yourselves in a bad place;" " 'nigger' we've taken all we want from you;" "before next week you'll be sorry you ever came to Montgomery."

Once again King was near the breaking point, and had only one person to turn to that he knew would understand— God. One night, he prayed to God aloud. "I am here taking a stand for what I believe is right. But now I am afraid. The people are looking to me for leadership, and if I stand before them without strength and courage, they will falter. I am at the end of my power. I have nothing left. I've come to the point where I can't face it alone."

At that moment, King later remarked that he experienced the presence of the Divine as he had never experienced him before. It seemed as though he could hear the quiet assurance of an inner voice saying: "Stand up for righteousness, stand up and God will be at your side forever."

After their negotiations, intimidations and "get tough" policy had failed, the concerned officials resorted to their last desperate hope-violence. On January 30, 1956 King was speaking at the First Baptist Church when he received word that his home had been bombed. He immediately went home to see if his wife and daughter were safe. As he walked calmly to the front door, he noticed a large crowd of Negroes and policemen on his lawn. When he went into the house and investigated, he learned that when his wife and Mrs. Mary Lucy Williams, a member of his congregation, who came to keep his wife company in his absence, had heard the sound of something falling on the front porch, they jumped up and ran to the back porch.

Also in the dining room was Mayor Gayle, Commissioner Seller and several white reporters. Both Gayle and Seller expressed their regrets that "this unfortunate incident had taken place in our city." That statement later proved to be more true and significant than they had ever dreamed possible. The bombing of Martin Luther King, Jr.'s home made headlines the world over and from that night on Montgomery, Alabama would know no peace.

By this time the crowd outside was in an angry mood. The policemen had failed to disperse them. The crowd would not leave, until they were assured that King's family was all right. Reverend King walked out to the porch and asked the crowd to come to order. He assured them that his family was all right. "Now let's not become panicky; if you have weapons, take them home, if you do not have them, please do not seek to get them. We cannot solve this problem through retaliatory violence. We must meet violence with non-violence. We must remember the words of Jesus: "He who lives by the sword will die by the sword. We must love our white brothers."

When King had finished, the Police Commissioner began to speak to the crowd, but to no avail. After Reverend King made a plea to them to hear what the Commissioner had to say, the crowd stopped booing.

It should be noted at this point that soon after the bombing, the threatening telephone calls stopped—almost overnight. Two days after the bombing the bus boycotters filed suit in Federal court, calling for the end of bus segregation and asked that the Mayor and the City Fathers be restrained from violating the civil rights of Negroes. This suit also had another far-reaching effect that the boycotters had not expected—the aid of the NAACP. Do not think that the opposition sat idle without some counter-attack.

On February 13, the Montgomery County Grand Jury was called to determine whether Negroes boycotting the buses were violating the law. After about a week of deliberation, the Grand Jury found the boycott illegal and indicted more than 115 men and women. The city supported its case on an old State law against boycott-conspiracy to destroy a legitimate business.

At the time of the indictments, King was at Fisk University, Nashville, Tennessee, giving a series of lectures. After receiving word of the indictments from Ralph Abernathy, he cancelled his remaining lectures and returned to Montgomery. He went directly to the jail since his name was on the indictment also. After he had received a number and been photographed and fingerprinted, one of his church members paid his bond and he left for home. Before King arrived in town, many Negroes went down to get arrested purposely. Another miracle must have taken place because the Negroes were no longer frightened. In fact, some of them were somewhat disappointed when they found their names were not listed. Once again the Negroes proved that they could endure any hardship thrust upon them and they could even laugh. And that was what the white community could not understand about them.

The following Sunday Reverend King told his congregation in his sermon on "Faith in Man" that integration is the great issue of our age, the great issue of our nation and the great issue of our community."

"We are in the midst of a great struggle, the consequence of which will be world-shaking; but our victory will not be for Montgomery's Negroes alone; it will be a victory for justice, a victory for fair play and a victory for democracy. Were we to stop now; we would have won a victory because the Negro has achieved from this a new dignity. But we are not going to stop. We are going in the same spirit of love and protest—the same dignity we have shown in the past," he concluded.

Since the protest had started, there had been a few out-of-state reporters, and after the bombing even more came for the trial that was set for March 19. The trial was covered by more than twenty newsmen from France, India and England, as well as from various parts of the United States. Montgomery was now becoming world known and almost anything that happened there would be reported.

The reporters followed King everywhere, from the time he got up in the morning until he went to bed at night. King was in the news almost every day and making headlines everywhere. He was not only becoming a national hero, but an international one as well.

On March 19, Judge Eugene W. Carter convened court. The defense attorneys waived their rights to a jury trial. Few spectators were admitted to the courtroom because of the large number of defendants and witnesses—thirty for the prosecution and forty-six for the defense.

The State called Reverend King as the first defendant. William F. Thetfort, solicitor for the State, was attempting to prove that King and the boycotters disobeyed a 1921 statute that outlawed boycotts of legal business, "without legal excuse or just cause." The statute was originally designed to be used in labor strife and had never been applied otherwise. The penalty was a one thousand dollars fine or six months in jail.

The conference attorneys Arthur Shores, Fred Gray, Peter Hall, Charles Langford, Ozekk Billingley and Robert Carter, presented arguments to show that the prosecutor's evidence was not sufficient enough to prove that King or the other defendants had violated Alabama's anti-boycott law.

50

When the defense witnesses were brought to the stand, they looked the solicitor and the judge in their eyes with a dignity that they had never experienced before. Attorney Shores contended that the indictment was so vague that the defendants could not tell the nature of it; it violated the rights of free speech, freedom to worship, peaceful assembly, and equal protection under the law.

It was generally agreed that the reason for raising the constitutional question at this point was to lay the ground work for appealing the decision, should it be a conviction, to the United States Supreme Court.

The Solicitor ran into difficulty with three of the witnesses that he called—James H. Bagley, transportation superintendent of the Montgomery City Lines; the Reverend A. W. Wilson, member of the MIA, and Mrs. Eva A. Dunges, financial secretary of the MIA. The attorneys for the defendants raised objections to almost every document offered as evidence. Judge Carter upheld many of the objections by refusing to admit testimony not directly relating to King.

On March 20, Judge Carter ruled that the State had established a prima facie case in the trial of Martin Luther King, Jr. On March 22, Carter found Martin Luther King, Jr. guilty of leading an illegal boycott against the Montgomery Bus Lines and fined him $500 and $500 for costs of court or 386 days at hard labor in the county jail. The fine was converted into the jail sentence. The sentence, however, was suspended after the defense attorney served notice of appeal. The case of the eighty-nine Negroes arrested in connection with the protest against the bus line was continued pending appeal.

Judge Carter announced that he would find King guilty, but would fine him only half of the possible penalty, because he had continually urged his followers to observe a policy of nonviolence. Ironically, Judge Carter, who had been on the bench twenty years, taught men's monthly Bible Class at the Dexter Avenue Methodist Church, almost, across the street from Reverend King's Church.

Several friends had come to sign King's bond. Later, he left the court house with his wife and a host of friends at his side. In front of the court house hundreds of Negroes and whites were waiting. On the steps of the court house, he told the gathering "I was optimistic enough to hope for the best, but realistic enough to prepare for the worst." This will not mar or diminish in any way my interest in the protest. We will continue to protest in the same spirit of nonviolence and passive resistance and using the weapon of love."

The following night King spoke at a prayer meeting at the Holt Street Baptist Church. It was decided to extend a spontaneous one-day boycott until the bus company improved conditions. Again King told the gathering, "This conviction and all the convictions they can heap on me will not diminish my determination one iota. God is using Montgomery as his proving ground and maybe here in the 'Cradle of the Confederacy,' the idea of freedom in the Southland will be born." Once again King had restored to his followers their faith in God and justice.

By now all the world knew of Martin Luther King, Jr. He was the Man from Atlanta. He was a Man who had almost become a legend in his own time. He was part martyr and part hero.

Chapter Seven
MANDATE FOR A CHANGE

After Reverend King and several other leaders of the boycott were denied permission to establish an all-Negro bus company, they filed suit in the Federal District Court asking for an end of bus segregation on the ground that it was contrary to the Fourteenth Amendment.

The hearing was set for May 11, 1956, before a three-judge Federal Court. The trial was held on that date and the judges deliberated for about three weeks. On June 14, 1956, Judge Richard T. Rives of the Fifth Circuit Court of Appeals, and Judge Frank M. Johnson, Jr., of the Middle District of Alabama, signed the majority opinion. It held bus segregation violated the due process and equal protection clause of the Fourteenth Amendment of the Federal constitution. The city attorneys immediately announced that they would appeal the case to the United States Supreme Court.

Although the battle was not over, the Negroes could walk with new hope. Bus segregation was dead and the only thing uncertain now was the burial date. King called the ruling a "great victory for democracy and justice." He thought that all people of goodwill would accept the Court's ruling as a great victory, not only for Montgomery's 50,000 Negroes, but for people everywhere. The opposition however, was not ready or willing to admit defeat.

The United States Supreme Court decision on the boycotters' appeal was still pending. The city officials and other desperate men were still refusing to accept or face reality. Insurance companies cancelled the insurance on most of the cars in the pool—almost overnight. By September all the policies would be cancelled. Consequently, the leaders were able to solve this crisis by taking out insurance with Lloyds of London.

As one last desperate effort to block the car pool, the city decided to take legal action against the car pool itself. The leaders of the boycott, therefore, filed a request in the Federal Court for an order restraining the city from interfering with the car pool. United States District Judge Frank M. Johnson, Jr., however, refused to grant the request. The hearing was set for November 13.

During the hearing the United States Supreme Court acted without listening to any argument; it simply said the motion affirmed is granted and the judgment is affirmed. At the hearing the city was granted a temporary injunction to halt the motor pool.

The next night another mass meeting was held and the Executive Board of the MIA called off the protest and asked the people to refrain from riding the buses until the mandate reached Alabama. The leaders of the movement thought that it was going to take four or five days for the mandate to reach Montgomery. Later it was discovered that it would take several weeks or maybe a month. While the Negroes were waiting for the mandate to come, the leaders went to work to prepare the people for the integrated buses. As always at the mass meetings, nonviolence was stressed. "Suggestions for Integrating Buses" were mimeographed and distributed all over the city. The leaflet read:

INTEGRATED BUS SUGGESTIONS

This is a historic week because segregation on buses has now been declared unconstitutional. Within a few days the Supreme Court Mandate will reach Montgomery and you will be re-boarding **integrated** buses—if there is violence in word or deed it must not be our people who commit it.

For your help and convenience the following suggestions are made. Will you read, study and memorize them so that nonviolence determination may not be endangered. . .

1. Not all white people are opposed to integrated buses. Accept goodwill on the part of many.
2. The WHOLE bus is now for the use of ALL people. Take a vacant seat.
3. Pray for guidance and commit yourself to complete nonviolence in word and action as you enter the bus.
4. Demonstrate the calm dignity of our Montgomery people in your actions.
5. In all things observe ordinary rules of courtesy and good behavior.

6. Remember that this is not a victory of Negroes alone, but for all Montgomery and the South. Do not boast! Do not brag!
7. Be quiet but friendly; proud, but not arrogant; joyous, but not boisterous.
8. Be loving enough to absorb evil and understanding enough to turn an enemy into a friend.

Even though the Negroes made an effort to prepare themselves for bus integration, not a single white group would take the responsibility of preparing the white community. Instead of taking positive steps for law and order the WCC and other groups issued statements and provoked violence. Anonymous appeals also went out to the Negroes to rebel against the leaders who had guided them in the Movement. Once again the distraught men tried to conquer by dividing the Negroes.

The United States Supreme Court's order banning bus segregation in Montgomery went into effect December 20, 1956. A mass meeting was called for that evening at the St. John AME Church, to give the people final instructions before riding the buses the next day.

At the meeting, Reverend King delivered a message to the jubilant crowd which said in essence to patronize the buses, but warned against violence; to be calm, use restraint, and not to let emotions run wild. He warned that if they become victimized with violent intents, they would have walked in vain. And twelve months of glorious dignity would be transformed into an eve of gloomy catastrophe. "God is working in Montgomery. Let all men of goodwill, both Negro and white, continue to work with Him. With this dedication they would be able to emerge from the bleak and desolate midnight of man's inhumanity to man to the bright and glittering daybreak of freedom and justice," he concluded.

The next day King, Abernathy and Nixon were among the first to ride and integrate the buses in Montgomery, Alabama. There were no major incidents on the first day. The first day of peace and quiet, however, was by no means a precedent. If the desperate men were to save face and fulfill their prediction, a new "reign of terror" had to emerge. Between December and January a number of bombings to houses and churches occured. A shotgun blast was fired into King's home on December 22, while he and his family were sleeping. Panes of glass were shattered, but the damages were slight and no one was hurt.

Reverend King told his congregation about the blast at the regular Sunday morning services. He included the shooting announcements among others—the need for Christmas baskets for the poor—both white and Negro, and a plea to make sure that the sick were visited. He told the congregation that he would like to meet those who had done the shooting to tell them that surely they must know they could not solve the problem that way. Still without raising his voice, he said that he would like to point out that even if he were killed his attackers would have 50,000 other Negroes to "get."

King went on to say that as the walls of segregation continued to crumble in the South, "it may be that some of us may have to die." But he called on his congregation never to falter, never to forget that in the midst of changes in life, of changes in man, even "if the stars no longer bedeck the Heaven, God's love for all things and for all men would continue. After the announcement of the attacks, the congregation calmly picked up the hymnals and sang "Silent Night, Holy Night."

During this "reign of terror" Reverend Ralph Abernathy's home was also bombed. The Bell Street Baptist and Mt. Olive Baptist Churches had been almost completely destroyed. Two other churches were damaged also. Even Reverend Graetz's home had been bombed the previous summer. After the bombings, most of the Negroes in the community were in low spirits.

During this "reign of terror" the city officials cancelled the bus company's franchise. At this point, King had become discouraged and felt a sense of personal guilt for everything that was happening. At a mass meeting, he broke down in public for the first time and two of the ministers had to help him to his seat. This was the scene that caused the press to report, mistakenly, that he had collapsed.

On January 28, another wave of terror broke out. The People's Service and Cab Stand was bombed. Allen Rebertson, sixty-year old Negro hospital worker's home was bombed. It was never discovered why these two victims had been singled out. The same day twelve sticks of dynamite were found still smoldering under King's porch.

On January 31, seven white men had been arrested in connection with the bombings. All of the men, however, were released on bonds ranging from $250 to $13,000 and the City Court passed the charges on to the County Grand Jury without testimony. The Grand Jury indicted five of the seven men and dropped the charges against the other two. . . Even though the men had signed confessions, the Grand Jury still returned a verdict of not guilty! Once again justice had been miscarried.

II

The most significant result of the Montgomery Protest was the United States Supreme Court's Mandate banning bus segregation in Montgomery. It has been over ten years since the order was issued, and the buses are still not completely integrated. Most of the elderly Negroes still sit in the rear. Bombings still occur. Yet, things are better now than they were then. The Negroes know that they have the right to sit anywhere on the buses they desire, even if they do not exercise that right.

An important aspect of the Movement was the "togetherness" the Negroes possessed during the entire ordeal. They proved to the world that Negroes could and would "unite" for the common cause. There was no longer the Negro doctor, lawyer, teacher, preacher, laborer, domestic—only the Negro striding toward freedom. The Negro "elite" came from out of his ivory tower and shared the same common interest with the plain, simple, everyday Negro. The Ph.D and the no-D's were bound together in a common venture.

Today the Negro citizen in Montgomery is respected in a way that he has never experienced. In the stores the Negroes are treated courteously and a few Negroes are employed as clerks and salesmen.

The Negro emerged from the Movement with a new sense of dignity and obligation. He is no longer afraid of the white man. He will, now, speak up and take a stand for what he believes to be right, even if it means death. Perhaps, the

57

dignity for freedom during the boycott is best summed up by an elderly Negro woman, who said, "I'm not walking for myself, I'm walking for my children and my grandchildren." Another woman put it more symbolically when she replied, "my feet are tired, but, my mind is rested." The white community learned that there is amazing power in unity and that they were no longer dealing with the "old" Negro, but with a "new one."

Another important by-product of the Montgomery Movement was the new philosophies of nonviolence and passive resistance, with Martin Luther King, Jr. as chief architect. He received world-wide recognition for the way he had translated Ghandi's philosophy of passive resistance. Dr. King more than anyone else was the "backbone" of the Movement, even though he was captivated into its leadership.

Between 1956 and 1958, Martin Luther King, Jr. was the recipient of numerous awards, degrees and citations. In fact, honors were coming in faster than Mrs. King could find space for them. The awards, came from a wide variety of donors— churches, Greek letter and fraternal orders, beauty culturists, and institutions of higher learning. And whenever possible Dr. King would receive the award in person. Of all the awards that King received, between that period, he was deeply honored by the Spingarn Medal that was awarded by the NAACP.

III

During the same time King was receiving brilliant coverage by the press and news channels. Most of the major newspapers and magazines covered his speeches, wherever he appeared. Martin Luther King, Jr. had perhaps, become more widely known in such a shorter space of time than any Negro since Marcus Garvey. He has been called the "American Ghandi," "the Moses of his People," "A 20th Century Moses," "Saint Martin." And a few less complimentary names—"Uncle Tom," "a trouble-maker," "an outsider," "coon," "agitator," "Nigger," and "A Communist." *The New York Times, Nation, Hue, Chicago Defender, Los Angeles Tribune, New York Post, Liberation, New Leader, Journal and Guide, Redbook, Baltimore Afro-American, and the New*

York Amsterdam News carried the most detailed descriptions on him.

He was receiving requests for speaking engagements from all over the country. He was the main speaker at the NAACP National Convention in San Francisco. At the Convention, he told the "Montgomery Story," and related it to the history of the Negro in America and the current world struggle of subjective peoples.

Martin Luther King, Jr. also received some unfavorable criticism. Usually, it came from the active opposition. Such as the *Alabama Journal, The States' Rights Advocate,* and the *Alabama Labor.*

The *Adult Student* ran an editorial in its February 10, 1957 edition. It began, "A Baptist, the Reverend Dr. Martin Luther King, Jr. has attained sainthood in a Methodist publication."

The Birmingham Advertiser's editor, Grover Cleveland Hall, Jr. attacked King personally by referring to Claude Thompson's Sunday School lesson guide, where Professor Thompson wrote: " . . . The Kingdom was set into history with a cross. It will not be extended without pain. This is not reserved for exceptional saints . . . like . . . Martin Luther King . . . He must come home every Sunday and teach . . ."

Many letters and statements came in attacking Mr. Thompson, church literature, the boycott, King and integration in general. Professor Thompson, however, withheld any comments he had for more than a month. On March 26, Thompson wrote a letter to the editor of the *Advertiser.* It read:

> A recent editorial had taken me to task for my reference to Dr. Martin Luther King as "an exceptional saint." The editor supports his criticisms by reference to Webster's definition of sainthood.
>
> But the Church looks at sainthood a little differently than does the famous lexicographer. The Roman Catholic Church for example, requires two things in a saint: One—that he has performed some attestable miracle. And that he must be dead.
>
> As for Dr. King, he is not dead, though doubtless some of his enemies wish he were. So on this score he cannot qualify.

But as for the other test, he has performed one of the most notable miracles in America. In the midst of a dangerously explosive situation, at grave danger to himself and his family, he guided the Negroes of Montgomery in the achievement of their legal rights as citizens of a democracy. And he did it without violence on the part of the Negroes. Furthermore, and even more remarkable, he has refused to hate or fight back at people who have threatened him, ridiculed him, sought to bribe him, and even have set off bombs at his house.

I submit: this is a miracle of the first order.

Any other candidates care to compete with the Reverend Martin Luther King for the saintly crown in Montgomery? In my way of thinking this is amazingly similar to the way Jesus of Nazareth faced the enemies of his day. This is Sainthood in man's church.

Claude H. Thompson

Even though King was away from his family most of the time on speaking engagements, he did not forget that he was a human being, an individual, a person, a son, a husband, with certain obligations to his family and himself, apart from the views of observers and headlines. The Montgomery Movement also had its effects on King and his wife's families in Atlanta and Marion. Martin Luther King, Sr. had showed concern for his son's safety from the very beginning of the movement. He was in Montgomery frequently and once to bail his son out of jail.

The King family had reunited. Chris was teaching at Spellman College and A. D. had reconciled his differences with his father. A. D. had also gone back to Morehouse College. The whole family was with King all the way in every way. Coretta stood up well also. At first she was frightened and upset when the telephone calls and threatening letters came. Later she became adjusted to them. She wanted to participate more, but she realized that she was a mother and had a baby to take care of. She once told a reporter, "Frankly, I worry about him, he never has a minute to himself. When he isn't in court, he is attending meetings of the MIA. When he is home, he is on the telephone. . . I try to protect him as much as possible, so he can rest, but there is little that I can do."

Mrs. King never gave up completely her dream for a part-time singing career, despite the boycott and her child. Her day came in New York on December 1, at the Manhattan Center. This was the anniversary of the beginning of the boycott. The receipts from the program went to the MIA. Coretta was billed as "Mrs. Martin Luther King, Jr." She shared the spotlight with Harry Belafonte and Duke Ellington.

The concert was a success, in all respects—musically, educational, and financially. Mrs. King sang and afterward she made a little speech. She spoke on "Why we walked in Montgomery." After her appearance, she received invitations from all over the country. She was able to make a few, although she was expecting her second child. She appeared in Washington, D.C.; Philadelphia; Gary, Indiana; and Augusta, Georgia.

Chapter Eight

PRAYER PILGRIMAGE TO WASHINGTON

After the boycott was over many of King's associates thought that he was taking too many bows. Many of his colleagues began to look at him more objectively. They would question his judgment, and criticize matters that would have previously gone through without being questioned.[14]

It should be pointed out here that from his hundreds of invitations to speak, King never charged social betterment organizations in the South anything beyond his expenses. During 1957 *Jet* portrayed him as "Man On The Go," listing 78,000 miles by plane and 208 speeches. King received less than his expenses for those appearances.

After the boycott and after traveling thousands of miles and making hundreds of personal appearances, the hero was fatigued and frustrated. There was nothing else for him to do but take a long deserved rest and pull himself together. King and his wife, therefore, accepted the invitation of the In Friendship Organization and prepared to go to Africa. He also received invitations both from Jawaharial Nehru and Kwane Nkrumah. Dexter Avenue Baptist Church voted him $2,000 for the trip and the MIA gave another $1,000.

When the Kings left by plane from New York City, they shared the same plane with the Honorable Richard Jones, Minister to Liberia, the Honorable Norman Manley, Dr. Ralph Bunche, Adam Clayton Powell, A. Philip Randolph, and Mrs. Louis Armstrong.

In Africa the big event was the coming of a new nation. What had been a colony and protectorate of the British Empire would emerge a self-governing member of the British Commonwealth of Nations. Both the United States and the Soviet Union were there, with the hope of winning friends among the

African Nations. In fact nearly seventy countries were represented for this historical occasion. The United States was officially represented by the then Vice President Richard M. Nixon.

At 11 p.m., March 5, 1957, the old assembly of the Gold Coast Colony was no longer in existence. The ceremonies were held in the Polo Grounds in the capital city, Accra. More than 50,000 people attended the ceremonies. Nkrumah and his associates of State were on the speaker's stand. One minute after the stroke of midnight, Nkrumah spoke in a joyous voice and with deep emotion: "The battle is ended! Ghana, our beloved country, is free forever." Then a tremendous shout came from the crowd, "Freedom, Free-dom! Ghana is Free!" The Union Jack came down and the flag of Ghana— green, gold and red stripes with a single star in the center of it was raised.

The celebration continued for several days. Mr. Nixon recognized King from the *Time* magazine cover picture and invited him to come to see him in Washington. The Kings were enjoying themselves. They also had a private lunch with Nkrumah.

Before the Kings departed from Ghana, however, both became ill. Mrs. King was only slightly ill and Dr. King more seriously with a fever. In fact he was so seriously ill that three doctors had to be called before his condition improved.

While recuperating, King received a visit from Dr. Homer A. Jack, who reported the visit in the *Christian Century* for April 10, 1957, under the title "Conversation In Ghana." It read:

> Of all the clergymen in Africa, one has symbolized in the past decade the best of the church working for justice and against colonialism: Micheal Scott. Of all the clergymen in America, one has symbolized in the past segregation: Martin Luther King, Jr. Ironically, Scott of Africa, is a white man, while King of America is a black man. Appropriately, both were guests of Prime Minister Kwame Nkrumah to witness the independence celebration of Ghana.[15]

In a few days, the Kings were better and able to travel. They visited Nigeria, briefly, before flying on to Rome, Geneva, Paris and London. They were back in Montgomery by March 28, having been absent for nearly a month.

Long before King's trip, the leaders of the Montgomery boycott had been conferring with other leaders throughout the South. Since the Montgomery Movement had been successful, other leaders in the South were looking to Montgomery for advice. Dr. King, therefore, issued a joint call for a Southwide Conference at Atlanta, Georgia, for January 10-11, 1957. Sixty persons from 29 communities and 10 southern states attended.

During the meeting Reverend Abernathy's church and home were bombed, along with several others in the Montgomery Negro community. Both King and Abernathy rushed back to Montgomery and left the following day.

From the two day meeting emerged a preliminary organization called the Southern Leadership Conference on Transportation and non-violent integration. The 60 conferees represented a cross-section of the Negro world. There were state and local NAACP officials, businessmen, labor leaders, college professors and farmers. The theme of the conference was nonviolence, and the essence of the conference was "our democratic vitality is sapped by the Civil Rights issue . . . that nonviolence is not a symbol of weakness or cowardice, but transforms weakness into strength and breeds courage in the face of danger."

President Eisenhower was requested to come South, immediately, to make a major speech in a major southern city to urge all southerners to accept and to abide by the United States Supreme Court's decisions as the law of the land. . .

Vice President Nixon was urged to "make a tour of the South similar to the one made in behalf of Hungarian refugees, 'report on' economic boycotts, reprisals, bombings directed against persons . . . who assert their rights under the Constitution."

Attorney General Herbert Brownell was asked to set up a meeting of the Southern Negro leaders with the United States Department of Justice to discuss the question of federal responsibilities in maintaining order in "areas where Negroes and whites who stood up for justice feared for their lives." The conference then adjourned and a meeting was scheduled for a later date.

King made public a telegram from Mrs. Eleanor Roosevelt. It said that she was "deeply distressed by violence which occurred," and would suggest and appeal to the President, since this is the Supreme order. Reverend King said the telegram had arrived after the conference.

Within a few days, King received replies from the White House and the Department of Justice. Sherman Adams, aide to President Eisenhower, said "It is not now possible for the President to schedule such a speaking engagement. . ." The Department of Justice said, "A conference at this time would not be helpful or appropriate, since the department was daily receiving information upon this matter of civil rights." As expected, the white southern newspapers played up these rejections from Washington.

On February 14, another meeting was held in New Orleans. At this meeting, ninety-seven persons and thirty-four cities representatives from 10 Southern states attended. Martin Luther King, Jr. was elected president. Once again, as King later remarked, he was captivated into the leadership. It was a matter of choosing him to direct a defiance that had already erupted. Reverend Ralph Abernathy, King's "right arm," was elected treasurer. The name of the organization was changed to Southern Negro Leaders Conference and then changed to Southern Negro Leadership Conference.

At this conference another telegram was sent President Eisenhower and Vice President Nixon. It said:

> While we are sensitive to the burdens of your responsible office, we believe that human life and the orderly, decent conduct of our communities are at stake. Their imperative considerations leave us quite reluctant to accept as final that a speech by you in the South cannot be scheduled. It is our sincere belief that action on your part now can avert tragic situations by cooling passion and encouraging reasonableness. In saying this we are not unmindful of the immense responsibility of your office on the conduct of our national and international affairs. However morality, like charity, begins at home. Here at home, as we write, we are confronted with a breakdown of law, order and morality. This sinister challenge and threat to our government of laws, drastically calling for attention and remedial action.

The President was also asked to "call a White House conference" on Civil Rights that would be similar to the meeting that had been held on Education and Juvenile Delinquency.

It was pointed out to him that, "If some effective remedial steps are not taken, we will be compelled to initiate a mighty Prayer Pilgrimage to Washington. . . We will ask our friends, Negroes and white, in the North, East, and West to join us in the moral crusade for human dignity and freedom."

On March 25, King met in New York City with Asa Philip Randolph and Roy Wilkins. The purpose of the meeting was to outline the general theme of the March and set a date for all the colleagues and advisors to get together to map out final plans.

On April 5, the "Big Three" met with more than seventy associates and aides at the Metropolitan Baptist Church in Washington, D.C. Here for the first time the fairly distinct lines of Negro leadership were joined.

Asa Philip Randolph was the oldest of the "Big Three" at 68. He was a southerner and his real education came by way of the labor movement. He organized the Brotherhood of Sleeping Car Porters. Mr. Randolph no doubt knew about nonviolence and civil disobedience before King was born. Roy Wilkins was a Northerner, even though born in St. Louis, he was taken to Minnesota at the age of four by his mother upon his father's death. Mr. Wilkins was backed by the most powerful Civil Rights organization in the country—NAACP. It had over 250,000 dues-paying members. When King, Randolph and Wilkins met together, the religious, labor and intellectual organizations were together like a giant web.

The three men were named co-chairmen by common consent of what was agreed should be called "Prayer Pilgrimage For Freedom."

The five objectives of the meeting were:

(1) A demonstration of Negro unity.
(2) Provision for Northern aid to Southern "freedom fighters."
(3) Defense against "crippling of the NAACP in some Southern states."
(4) Mobilizing support for pending Civil Rights legislation.
(5) Protest against violence.

The meeting was to have a religious theme and the emphasis was to be placed upon nonviolence. It was to take place on May 17, 1957, in front of the Lincoln Memorial. It was also the anniversary of the date of the United States Supreme Court's momentous decision. Most of the details were left in the hands of Mr. Wilkins, even though both Mr. Randolph and Dr. King made a few suggestions.

The NAACP would underwrite most of the expenses, which were estimated between $10,000 and $15,000. King and Randolph's organizations would also contribute part of the money. The Reverend Thomas Kilgore, Jr. was named National Director of the project, with Reverend Ralph Abernathy as his associate. There were six honorary chairmen chosen along with a national sponsoring committee of 50 prominent persons. "Special Organizers," such as Bayard Rustin and Miss Ella Baker were borrowed from the In Friendship Organization.

The W.C.C., as expected, opposed the pilgrimage. An Alabama paper ran full-page advertisements calling the Pilgrimage a "conspiracy" of King and the NAACP to destroy the Southern way of life.

To counterbalance this opposition, the mayors of both New York City and Los Angeles and the Governors of California, Maryland, Iowa, and Missouri proclaimed May 17 as a Pilgrimage Day. District 65, the Retail Wholesale Department Store Union, 1,200 members sacrificed a day's wages and then paid their own expenses to Washington. Support also came from the garment, transportation, automobile, steel, hat and bartender's local unions.

II

As early as May 16, the day before the Prayer Pilgrimage to Washington, many travelers were arriving. Most of them had come by buses, trains, cars, and few airplanes. The largest delegation, about 11,000, came from New York City.

About 11:45, the crowd gathered in the area between the Lincoln Memorial and the lake. The crowd was somewhat impressive, but smaller than what the leaders had hoped would attend. The leaders estimated the crowd at 37,000, the *Washington Post* at 25,000, and the District Police at a mere 15,000.

People came from some 33 states, and from all walks of life. Actress Ruby Dee, Actor Sidney Poitier, Harry Belafonte, Jackie Robinson, John O. Killen and Sammy Davis, Jr. were also there. Most of the marchers were composed of American Negroes. Only about 10 percent were white and they were mostly ministers.

At noon the official program began, with the traditional national anthem. Bishop Sherman L. Greene delivered the invocation, which was followed by the singing of the "Battle Hymn of the Republic." A. Philip Randolph presided and delivered the opening remarks:

> We have come to demonstrate the unity of the Negroes and their allies—labor, liberals, and the Church—behind the Civil Rights bill now before Congress, in order that they might not be strangled to death by committee maneuverings and filibuster. . .
>
> We have gathered together to proclaim our uncompromising support of the fight of the NAACP for Civil Rights and democracy under the able, resourceful and constructive leadership of Roy Wilkins.
>
> We have come to call upon President Eisenhower, our great national and world leader, who is undoubtedly possessed of a high sense of humanity, to speak out against the lawlessness, terror, and fear that hang like a pall over the hearts of citizens of color of the South. . .

Next came Roy Wilkins, who took his message from a verse in Paul's letter to the Ephesians:

Put on the whole armor of God that you may be able to stand against the wiles of the devil.

For we wrestle not against flesh and blood, but against principalities, against spiritual wickedness in high places.

He also spoke out against the Federal Legislators and the way they handled the Civil Rights Legislation. He concluded by saying:

> We are troubled . . . yet not distressed;
> We are perplexed, but not in despair;
> We are persecuted, but not forsaken;
> We are cast down, but not down, but not destroyed. . .

Mahalia Jackson sang "I've Been Buked, I've Been Scorned," and the crowd gave her a wild ovation. The tempo was beginning to pick up.

Congressman Charles Diggs spoke next and pointed out that the Negroes must demand political action of both parties. Congressman Adam Clayton Powell made a jest and loosened up the audience. Mr. Powell said, "We are here in front of the Lincoln Memorial, because we are getting more from a dead Republican than we are getting from live Democrats." The crowd roared. He also pointed out the urgent need for a third nonpartisan political force based on passive resistance, mass demonstration, picket lines and political unity.

The crowd was getting restless and only one person in the Civil Rights world could calm them. Mr. Randolph presented to the marchers what they had been waiting for, when he said, "I give you Martin Luther King, Jr."

Before King came to the platform he received thunderous applause. This time King spoke from a manuscript; there was too much excitement to depend upon his memory. He started slowly until he reached the climax:

"Give us the ballot . . ." and we will no longer plead to the Federal Government for passage for an anti-lynching law. . .

Give us the ballot . . . and we will transform the salient misdeeds of blood-thirsty mobs into the abiding good deed of orderly citizens.

Give us the ballot . . . and we will fill our legislative halls with men of good. . .

"Give us the ballot . . . "and at this point the audience picked up the words and repeated. "Give us the ballot" and they waited for King to add, "and we will place judges on the benches of the South who will do justly and love mercy."

When King finished, the crowd gave him a standing ovation. It was indeed King's message that highlighted the Prayer Pilgrimage and he emerged from it with increased national prestige.

The audience stood and sang "America" and remained standing for the benediction. The Pilgrimage was a success in many respects. It received brilliant coverage by the newspapers, networks and wire services. The Police Department reported that it was one of the most orderly crowds of its size that Washington, D.C. had seen. No violence occurred. King, perhaps more than any other person at the meeting, received the best reviews.

Miss Ethel Payne wrote in the *Chicago Defender* for May 22, "Those who a few months ago thought of young King as a brilliant comet shooting across the sky never to be seen again, came away from the rally with a firmer conviction than ever of his mature, wise leadership. . ." [16] James L. Hicks wrote in the *Amsterdam News* for June 1, that "Martin Luther King, Jr. had emerged from the Prayer Pilgrimage to Washington as the number one leader of 16 million Negroes in the United States. . . At this point in his career, the people will follow him anywhere." [17]

Chapter Nine

KING'S MEETING WITH DESTINY

After the Prayer Pilgrimage to Washington King accepted the invitation that Vice President Nixon extended in Ghana. Sherman Adams had written King that the President was pleased to know that he would meet with Mr. Nixon.

On June 13, King, along with Abernathy, met with Nixon, and James P. Mitchell, Secretary of Labor, at the White House.

King and his aide, Reverend Abernathy, had prepared definite points that they intended to make. King began the meeting by describing the situation in the South, the corruption of the legal system, the bombings, disfranchisements, intimidations, and various pressures put on the outspoken white "liberals."

After King had finished opening the talk Abernathy inserted his views and described the conflict more vehemently. He said in essence that the Negroes wanted their rights now and would not be frightened from their desires. He explained that most of the opposition was represented by the Ku Klux Klan and White Citizens Council. Abernathy also said he was convinced that the President did not fully realize the complexity of what the situation was or else he would have spoken out, adding with a smile that the Vice President had spoken out "more" clearly than had the President.

Mr. Nixon smiled, also, but came to the President's defense, quietly and pleasantly. He pointed out that the President was not making as many speeches as was the Vice President. Therefore, he did not get around to all of the subjects. The President, moreover, had called together the Republican members of Congress and told them that he did not believe in platform hypocrisy and that Civil Rights was in the Republican platform.

The discussion once again centered on the Civil Rights bill, but more directly this time. At the present time a debate was going on in Congress. Nixon voiced his opinion that a Civil Rights bill would be passed by the House of Representatives and had a fifty-fifty chance of getting through the Senate.

Vice President Nixon declared that there were some insincere legislators who played politics by introducing Civil Rights bills that they knew had no possible chance of passing, just so they could say back home: "You see, I'm for Civil Rights." King inserted that neither party had done much to push the bill.

Nixon asked once again about the cooperation that came from Southern white ministers. Both King and Abernathy agreed that privately many reluctantly endorsed the Supreme Court's decision but would not take a stand publicly. And, perhaps, more would take a stand if the President and the Vice President would speak up strongly for United States Supreme Court's decisions.

Then King asked the Vice President to come South and make a speech for law and order. Mr. Nixon agreed that the general idea was good but had some misgivings about the best way for it to be executed. "If he came South at the request of Negroes, then he would be speaking to Negroes," he said. Nixon thought that he could come South naturally in connection with the work of the Committee on Government Contracts, with which he had worked ever since he had been in office.

Now it was the Secretary's turn. He gave a description of the Committee's operations and the way it sought to persuade concerns that held Government contracts to abide by the clauses that prohibited discrimination in employment on the basis of color, creed, or national origin.

The Vice President asked where in the South would it be most appropriate for him to appear, if he could make just one stop. King suggested Atlanta or New Orleans. Atlanta seemed a good choice to both Nixon and Mitchell, since the Committee on Government Contracts would be there soon.

As the meeting came to a close, one question still had not been answered. What would the President do? Nixon suggested that perhaps Mr. Eisenhower would like to hear first hand about the conditions in the South. He also thought that perhaps it would be better to wait until the Civil Rights question in Congress was concluded and then if King would send him a memorandum on it, he would help arrange a meeting for him and his associates with the President.

Later at the press conference, King spoke less about the meeting with Nixon than about his own plans. He said he had pleaded with the Vice President to do three things: (1) come South and speak; (2) urge all Southerners to support the law as interpreted by the Supreme Court; (3) call together Republicans in Congress and urge them to fight for the enactment of the Civil Rights Bill.

More than seventy-odd newspaper men were present, and King got a good press, except for Louis Lautier's article that appeared in the *Afro* for June 22 with the heading "Was King Ready?" The article stated:

> The Reverend Martin Luther King, Jr., leader of the Montgomery bus boycott, is an estimable young man and excellent pulpit orator, but he is not yet ready for the political big-times . . . he showed that he has more homework to do. . .

For Congress, the big domestic issue of the summer was the Civil Rights Bill. The Bill passed the House, but it was weakened by the opposition in the Senate. The single issue, the right to vote was the only thing that passed. And the Negro leaders, including King and Wilkins, accepted the "weak bill."

The *Chicago Defender,* that wanted an "all or nothing" Bill ran a front page editorial for August 31, declaring:

> In accepting the Senate version . . . Roy Wilkins . . . Reverend Martin Luther King . . . have committed the gravest tactical blunder that has ever been made by Negro leadership throughout . . . our turbulent history in America.

King did not reply. Roy Wilkins did. He said, "If you are digging a ditch with a teaspoon and a man comes along and offers you a spade, there is something wrong with your head if you don't take it because he didn't offer you a bulldozer!"

The Bill was finally passed and signed by the President. It provided for a jury trial only in cases where the fine of judge exceeded $300. Even though it was very weak, it was the first Civil Rights legislation that Congress had passed since 1875, a span of eighty-two years.

King called together his fellow Southern leaders to meet August 7 and 8 in Montgomery. And once again, the name of the organization was changed to the Southern Christian Leadership Conference. At the meeting, perhaps the most significant event was the $11,000 that the Packinghouse Workers of America gave to the voter registration campaign the Conference was sponsoring.

During this time there were numerous rumors to the effect that the SCLC and NAACP were at odds, both competing for funds and supporters. Actually, King had just taken out a $500 life membership in the NAACP for himself and the MIA. The rumors soon stopped.

Meanwhile as the summer was ending and school was opening, Little Rock, Arkansas, was dominating the headlines around the world. And the MIA and King sent a telegram to Mrs. Daisy Bates, who directed the Movement saying: "Urge the people of Little Rock to adhere rigorously to a way of non-violence at this time. . . ."

I

During October King was visited by Jeffrey Hayden and John O. Killens, who wanted to do a movie on the Montgomery boycott. As expected the whole city was intrigued by the thought that it would become a movie. The city officials agreed to the project. Later, Hayden and Killens left town and said they would return, probably in the spring, to begin shooting.

The project failed, however, when the city fathers learned that King would be characterized as the "good guy" and the hero of the movie and they would be the "bad guys" or villians. Therefore, they wrote to Hayden denouncing the project and threatening to do anything and everything in their power to stop the movie from being made in Montgomery. Word came back from Hollywood that there really was not sufficient detailed data on King for the story.[18] The project therefore was dropped.

About the same time NBC announced that King would appear on "Look Here," Sunday, October 27. This was a half-hour interview program with Martin Agronsky asking questions. Suddenly the WCC, WSFA, the local television station, finding no valid ground for declining to carry the program, offered to satisfy the opposition by giving equal time for a reply to whatever King might say. This apparently was not enough for the WCC. The news went out to the whole nation that NBC and King were having trouble with free speech in Montgomery.

About five minutes before the program was to come on, the station itself blacked out and went off the air completely. What had happened? No one knew! Later, it was learned that a large chain had been thrown around one of the TV transmitters causing a short circuit and power failure.

WSFA, finding is difficult to keep on good terms with NBC, the Federal Communications Commission, and WCC, announced after some hesitation that it would show a film of the telecast the next Sunday.

Once again King had to return to court. As pointed out previously, his lawyers appealed his case when he was convicted in March 1956. The lawyers were confident that the conviction of the lower court would be reversed. But the court reporter was late in completing the transcript of the trial and King's attorneys forgot to see to it that the transcript was forwarded. Thus they were not ready when that trial date came. They expected the prosecution attorneys not to press the issue of the delayed transcript. These men were playing for high staked-political survival. The prosecution took advantage of this technicality by charging improper procedure. The State Court of Appeals denied King's motion on procedural grounds.

After missing their chance for a review based on the constitutional issue involved, the best King's side could hope for was a simple "settlement" or a "package" agreement: (1) King paid his fine of $500; (2) all other cases against Negro boycott leaders dropped; and (3) *all* cases against the white bombers dropped.

When King was asked why he agreed to such a settlement, he replied that "it would have been a needless waste of time and money to continue the case. We decided . . . to pay . . . move on to another phase of the battle. . ."

King still had many hurdles to overcome. He was out for a week in November with the Asian flu. In December, he encountered another major setback when the MIA attempted another institute on social change through nonviolence and it failed. King became quite upset. In fact he was beginning to wonder if he had lost his usefulness in Montgomery. The truth was that the MIA could no longer continue the same program that it had fostered during the boycott.

In addition King was moving like a whirlwind—in a thousand different directions. He was trying to maintain the Herculean pace that he had maintained all along. He was still flying all over the country on speaking engagements. He still had his pastoral duties to perform, besides being President of the MIA and SCLC. As 1957 came to a close, King did get away for a short vacation between December and January. In fact, he was inaccessible to everyone but his family and secretary.

II

As King became less tied down with the MIA, he devoted more of his time to the SCLC. In January, 1958, he called a board meeting of the SCLC to discuss last minute details for the Citizenship Crusade on Lincoln's Birthday. When February 12 came the crowd was in high spirits. The crusade, however, obtained only a few new voters on the books during the coming months.

On April 30, the SCLC board met again. The Reverend John L. Tilley who had done a splendid job on voter registration in Baltimore, became the Executive Director and moved in the Atlanta office with Miss Ella Baker as Associate Director.

The board also made plans to hold a conference in Mississippi for May 29. When May 29 came the conference was held peacefully, to some people's dismay for violence had been forecast.

At this conference, the SCLC composed a letter and sent it to President Eisenhower saying in essence:

> Amid continued violence in the South and the dreadful prospect that some areas may close rather than obey Federal Court orders to desegregate in September, we urgently renew our request that you grant an immediate conference to Negro leaders in an effort to resolve these problems. . . Since quite some time ago you

promised to meet with Negro leaders and because the present climate of lawless defiance threatens to produce incidents that will shame America at home and abroad when school opens in September, we respectfully request an immediate audience.

About a week later, King received word by telephone that the President would see him and a few others on June 9. While in Washington, King met with White House aides Rocco Siciliano and E. Frederick Morrow and a member of the United States Attorney General's staff. At this preliminary meeting the date was set for June 23.

The next question was, who should attend the session? King's first thought had been to suggest the names of the top officials of the SCLC, since the White House bid had come in response to the SCLC' requests. But, he also felt that a conference of this kind might be so significant that a national representation rather than a strictly sectional one should be made. Therefore, he suggested his fellow Co-chairmen of the Washington Pilgrimage.

Asa Philip Randolph was acceptable, but there was some objection to Roy Wilkins from the White House representatives on the grounds that perhaps the President would not want to talk to anyone who had spoken of him the way Mr. Wilkins had at the previous conference. This conference was made up of about four hundred heads of organizations, scholars, and others attending the National Negro Publishers Association held in Washington on May 12-13. Most of the Negro leaders attended, except King, because he had a long-standing commitment to the American Jewish Congress which was meeting the same time in Miami, Florida.

President Eisenhower was the speaker at the conference. He urged his mutual security, defense and foreign aid program. Next he spoke on Civil Rights, saying:

> . . . that every American, if we are to be true to our Constitutional heritage, must have respect for the law. He must know that he is equal before the law. He must have respect for the Courts.
> He must have respect for others. He must make perfectly certain that he can, in every single Kind of circumstances, respect for himself. . . .

In such problems as this, there are no revolutionary curves. They are evolutionary. I started in the Army in 1911. I have lived to see the time come when in nine of the Armed Services is practiced any kind of discrimination because of race, religion or color.

In the Federal Government this same truth holds steady. . . But I do believe that as long as there are human problems . . . we must have patience and forebearance.

I do not decry laws, for they are necessary, but I say that laws themselves will never solve problems that have roots in the human heart and in the human emotions. . .

Most of the Negro newspapers rejected "patience and forebearance," in the editorial on the conference

Roy Wilkins remarked:

I understand the President of the United States gave you some startling advice this afternoon. I guess from where he sits, this makes sense. If you were president, you would want everything to go smoothly. You wouldn't want anyone to kick up a fuss-labor, Democrats, the Negro. If you could convince the Negro that he was being impatient, I guess you would do so. From where Mr. Eisenhower sits, I suppose this makes sense. I don't sit there.

King also called Eisenhower's words "potentially dangerous," and adding that they would "encourage those who have defied the Supreme Court's decisions and who have created the climate of tension and crisis culminating across the South."

Later at the meeting with the White House aides, King indicated that if Wilkins did not come he would not come. Therefore, Wilkins was acceptable. The aides then mentioned Lester B. Granger, who was a conservative liberal and a Republican who was Executive Secretary of the National Urban League. After the preliminaries were concluded, King notified each man and told him that he would be receiving an invitation from the White House.

Later it was agreed that the four men would meet Sunday, June 22, the day before the White House meeting, and draw up an official statement to give to the President.

The four men met at the Washington headquarters of the NAACP and each man brought along with him the six page memorandum sent to him by King and his advisors, with some corrections.

The other men had arrived about 9 a.m. King, however, did not get there until later. This group put a lot of work into the meeting. They worked far into the morning. They talked, wrote and rewrote until they came up with a seven-page statement.

The four men also decided on the procedure they would use. Randolph would start by making the opening remarks; then King, Wilkins, and Granger each would discuss three of the nine points of the joint memorandum.

The next day at 10:30, the group met in the outer office reception room of the White House. They were told that they would not quote him directly to the press.

At 11:15, the President met with the conferees. After the preliminaries were over, Randolph began. He read aloud the nine points:

(1) The President of the United States should declare in a nation-wide pronouncement, prior to September, that the law will be vigorously upheld with the total resources at his command.

(2) Much emphasis has laid on the need for restoring communication between white and colored Southerners who are troubled by a common fear of reaction. The President can well set the example in this matter by convoking a White House Conference of constructive leadership to discuss ways and means of complying peacefully with the Court's rulings.

(3) Information, resources, and advice of the appropriate government agencies addressed to the problems of integration should be made available to all officials and community groups seeking to work out a program of education and action.

(4) The President should request both parties to lay aside partisanship so that the Congress can enact a Civil Rights bill which will include Part III originally in the 1957 bill, in order that constitutional rights other than voting rights may be enforced by the United States Attorney. Lack of adequate and clear statutory authority had made the federal government a mere spectator in the disgraceful maneuverings at Little Rock.

(5) We urge the President to direct the Department of Justice to give all legal assistance possible under the law, including filing of a brief as a friend of the court and appearance of counsel, in the appeal from the Lemley decision in the Little Rock case.

(6) The President of the United States should direct the Department of Justice to act now to protect the right of citizens to register and vote. In the nine months since the enactment of the 1957 Civil Rights Act, overt acts have been committed against prospective Negro registrants in some areas and numerous complaints have been submitted to the Department, but to date, not a single case has reached the courts.

(7) The President should direct the Department of Justice to act under existing statutes in the wave of bombings of churches, synagogues, homes and community centers, also in the murderous brutality directed against Negro citizens in Dawson, Georgia, and other communities.

(8) In order to counteract the deliberate hamstringing of the new Civil Right Commission, the President should recommend to the Congress the extension of its life for at least a full year beyond its present expiration date.

(9) The President should make it clear both in statement and in act that he believes in the principle that federal money should not be used to underwrite segregation in violation of the federal constitution rights of millions of Negro citizens, and that this principle should be applied whether in matter of federal aid to education, hospitals, housing, or any other grants-in-aid to state and local government. In support of national policy, the Federal Government should finance continuation of public schools where states' fund are withdrawn because of integration.

The President listened intently, then, on cue from Randolph, each man discussed each section of the statement. Wilkins was perhaps the most moderate of the group, while Granger was the most outspoken.

King was also surprised to find that the President did not know that Negroes were displeased with his administration for not taking a strong position and supporting the Supreme Court's integration decrees. The President spoke in broad terms, saying that he believed in law and order and that all Americans should have their rights.

Next Attorney General William Roger extended the President's remarks with special emphasis on what the present administration had done for the so-called benefit of Negroes.

The Presidential Aides asked the group not to release their nine points statements to the press, but they did. Wilkins served as spokesman for the group and expressed encouragement from the meeting. Randolph said, "The conference has put a new hope into the hearts of the colored people."

A week after the conference King gave his evaluation of the meeting. He declared that two positive results took place. First, the excellent press coverage of the nine points. The American people, therefore, got a chance to learn what was on the minds of American Negroes and what they expected of their government. Secondly, the President also learned this. All had agreed that the document presented to the president and the world represented masterful thinking on the part of leaders!

III

On the morning of September 3, King accompanied his associate, the Rev. Ralph Abernathy to the municipal court where he was to testify in the case of a man being tried for assault on him. As the Rev. and Mrs. Abernathy and the Dr. and Mrs. Martin Luther King, Jr. arrived at the door of the municipal court, the guard told them that the courtroom was full and no one could go inside. Rev. Abernathy informed him that he was a party to one of the cases being heard and added, this is my wife here with me." The guard informed him that his wife could not go in unless she had been subpoenaed.

By this time Dr. King and his wife emerged and asked what the trouble was, and Mrs. Abernathy told them what the guard had said. King, feeling that maybe an attorney in the court could get them admitted, asked the guard if he could speak to Attorney Fred Gray, who was representing Abernathy. The guard replied, "Boy, if you don't get the hell away from here, you will need a lawyer yourself." At that very same moment and before anyone could say anything two policemen came up from behind the group and one of them remarked. "Boy, you done it, let's go." Then grabbing King and twisting his arm, hustled him to the police headquarters around the corner in the same building.

Mrs. King hurriedly followed the policemen. One of them looked over his shoulder and said, "Gal you want to go too? Just nod your head." King pleaded, "Don't say anything darling."

In a minute they had him inside the police station, still twisting his arms while asking for the key to the cells. "Put him in the hole," the desk officer yelled, tossing out the keys. No one was aware that a photographer was on hand taking pictures all the time.

When they got King to the cell they told him to raise his hands above his head, frisked him and kneed him. They then

81

seized him by the throat, spun him around and kicked him as he was thrust into the cell and the door was locked.

In about ten minutes the officers returned for King and he was permitted to sign a $100 bond for appearance in the City Court September 5th to answer the charge. Altogether King was jailed for about 15 minutes. During this time something must have happened from a high level and this major blunder had been discovered.

The news was soon on the wires in the late afternoon and the next morning's papers all over the nation carried the story. King accused the police of "brutality" and the accompanying pictures graphically showed proof of it. Police Commissioner of Public Safety, Clyde Sellers, was quoted as saying that Dr. King had been treated as anyone else would be and arrested as anyone else. This was probably true, at least for Negroes. The Commissioner, a member of pro-segregation White Citizens Council, described Rev. King's charge as "just the kind of statement he would expect from King, that's all he ever says."

As Dr. King left the building he was surrounded by a crowd of Negroes protesting his arrest. He told the group that the incident had illustrated how deeply racial feeling was ingrained in the minds of many people. He promised to stand up for what he thought was right, even if it meant further arrest or even death.

Between the arrest and his trial date, messages and advice had poured into his office and home from many parts of the country. Roy Wilkins of the NAACP sent a telegram to the White House asking the President to condemn what had happened.

At the trial on September 5th Dr. Martin Luther King, Jr. was found guilty of refusing to obey a policeman and fined $10 and cost of court, totaling $14 or fourteen days in jail. The original charge was loitering, but was changed. Loitering is a misdemeanor under the city code, punishable by a maximum $100 fine and 60 days in jail.

In pronouncing the sentence, Judge Loe said:

> It is regretable the case arose. There was a crowd out on the street which extended from the police station to the fire station next door and there was serious danger of an accident.

I don't find evidence excessive force or brutality was used and I believed that high position King holds make it his duty to obey an officer quicker than others.

Attorney Grey told the court that his client would serve out his time. At this point King stood and told the court: "Your Honor . . . I could not in all good conscience pay a fine for an act that I did not commit and above all for the brutal treatments that I did not deserve." The court had not expected that statement from King and it was therefore caught off guard. King was taken to a detention room later to be tried or taken to the city jail. Meanwhile, a large crowd was gathering on the outside of the courtroom and was disappointed when their hero did not come out until someone announced that he had voluntarily decided to go to jail instead of paying the fine.

During this time King's fine had been paid by someone and he was free to leave jail. He wanted to know who had paid it, but the clerk who accepted the fine said he did not know.

King then went back to see the judge who had tried the case, but the judge declared that there was nothing that he could do.

Dr. King then left the jail and went to the Dexter Avenue Baptist Church where a mass meeting was being held with prayers and testimonials in his behalf. At the church he spoke to the crowd. That same night he spoke again at the rally, where he declared:

> Today, in many parts of the South, the brutality inflicted upon Negroes has become America's shame. . . Something must happen to awaken the dozing conscience of America before it is too late. . . Somewhere the Negro must come to the point of refusing to co-operate with evil. . . But you, must go out of here with love and nonviolence. I have no malice toward anyone, not even the white policemen who almost broke my arm, who choked me and kicked me. Let there be no malice among you. . .

Commissioner Sellers later identified himself as the person who paid the fine that resulted in King's release. The Commissioner said he could not permit Dr. King to "use the facilities of the city of Montgomery for his own selfish purpose." Mr. Seller also said that King's tactics was just another "publicity stunt" intended to further his self-assured role as a martyr and also to boost the sale of his forthcoming book, *Stride Toward Freedom: The Montgomery Story.* The Commissioner continued to assert that he "elected to spare the taxpayers of Montgomery the expenses of feeding and housing King during the next fourteen days."

IV

Since the bus boycott had ceased, Martin Luther King, Jr. had wanted to write a book based on it. On September 17, 1958, his book, *Stride Toward Freedom: The Montgomery Story* was published. As part of the sales promotion for the book, the author made many personal appearances including one in New York, where he almost met instant death.

On Saturday afternoon, September 20, King sat at a desk in L. M. Blumstein's department store at 230 West 125th Street in Harlem, autographing copies of his book. Several persons were seated near, including Arthur B. Spingarn, President of the NAACP, and Mrs. Anne Hedgman, a member of Mayor Wagner's staff. An honor guard of girls from Walleigh Jr. High School were standing at both sides of the desk. Twenty persons were in line waiting to get books autographed.

Suddenly, a Negro woman who was not in line stepped through a narrow opening leading to the desk, leaned over and asked, "Are you Mr. King?" Dr. King nodded at this time. The woman pulled an eight inch Japanese letter opener from her bag and stabbed him. She was quoted as saying, "I've been after you for six years. I'm glad I've done it."

Walter Pettiford, an advertising representative of the *New York Amsterdam News,* who happened to be present, grabbed the woman and pinned her arms to her side as she attempted to escape. Soon the ambulance from Harlem Hospital arrived. Dr. King, still seated in the chair, was carried into the ambulance.

News of the stabbing spread quickly through the neighborhood and attracted over 1,500 persons to 125th Street. About 40 persons went to the hospital to donate blood. Others at the hospital were former Governor Averell Harriman, Roy Wilkins, A. Philip Randolph, Hulan Jack, Manhattan Borough President, and Robert Magum, Deputy Hospitals Commissioner.

Dr. Aubrey Maynard and an interracial surgical team went to work at once. Dr. Maynard said the blade of the letter opener had "impinged on the aorta, a blood vessel near the heart." He said a *puncture* of the aorta would have caused instant death.

The woman who stabbed Reverend King was identified as Mrs. Izola Ware Curry, 42 years old, of 127 West 122th Street. Detectives found a fully loaded 25 calibre Italian automatic inside her dress. She said she had purchased the automatic last year in Daytona Beach, Florida, while she was working there as a domestic. She was booked on charges of felonious assault and violation of the Sullivan Law.

Inspector John Saxton, quoted Mrs. Curry as saying she did not know Dr. King was in the store when she went there. He said she suffered from a "persecution complex." Mrs. Curry was quoted as saying she stabbed Reverend King because "then he would listen to my problems because I've followed him in buses and people have been making me lose my job." Police Commissioner Stephan P. Kennedy said that Mrs. Curry appeared to be "deranged" and that she was making many "incoherent" statements.

News of the stabbing was covered by all of the news channels. Telephone lines in New York, Montgomery and Atlanta were busy. Mrs. Coretta King flew from their home in Montgomery to be near her husband. Christine King and her father, the Reverend Martin Luther King, Sr., also came to New York. After a visit with her husband, she told reporters that she felt no bitterness toward Mrs. Curry. "She was obviously disturbed and no doubt is not completely responsible for her actions," Mrs. King said.

Mrs. Curry was arraigned in Felony Court before Magistrate Vincent P. Rao on charges of felonious assault and possession of firearms. "I understand this is the woman who is accused of stabbing the Rev. Dr. King with a knife," the Magistrate said. "No, it was a letter opener." Mrs. Curry shouted. She later interrupted the arraigned proceeding to shout, "I'm charging him as well as he's charging me."

The Magistrate asked her what did she have against King. Mrs. Curry replied that she was charging him with being mixed up with the Communists and that she had reported the case to the F.B.I. and it's being looked into.

The Magistrate stated that she was ill and ordered her removed to Bellevue Hospital. Later at Bellevue, psychiatrists indicated that Mrs. Izola Ware Curry was insane and she was therefore ordered to the State Hospital for the Criminally Insane.

While King was in the hospital, his condition took a sudden turn for the worse when he developed pneumonia. The change prompted the hospital staff to summon Dr. Robert H. Wylie, a thoracic surgery specialist who was director of Chest service at the Columbia University medical section in Bellevue Hospital. Dr. Maynard said, "Everything was being done for King."

News of the change in Rev. King's condition brought Governor Averell Harriman to the hospital where he spent four hours and he was assured that Rev. King was progressing satisfactorily.

Later during the week the minister showed improvement. While in the hospital, Rev. King received hundreds of telegrams and letters of sympathy from people in all walks of life.

Among the letters he received was one from Vice President Nixon, that said:

> I was terribly distressed to learn of the attack that was made on you in New York Saturday. To have this incident added to all of the unfortunate indignities which have been heaped upon you is indeed difficult to understand.
>
> I can only say that the Christian spirit of tolerance which you invariably displayed in the face of your opponents and detractors will in the end the great majority of Americans for the cause of equality and human dignity to which we are dedicated.

Perhaps King himself best expressed the unhappiness that prevailed by saying, "Our Society needs to be more concerned about mental health and social problems which contribute to this matter. We should go out with determination to solve many of the social problems which contribute to conditions that lead up to incidents like this and that one of the causes of the assault might be 'racial tension' and lack of brotherhood, which cause people to lose their sense of belonging."

Once again Martin Luther King, Jr., proved that with faith, perseverance, and with the help of God, anyone can endure all difficulties. King's doctors had said that he was within mere inches of "instant death" and a twist of the body would have been fatal. Yet, King survived even after one of his ribs and part of his breastbone were removed. No doubt Governor Averell Harriman best described King when he said, "Dr. King is a man of tremendous courage."

Another message from the White House came from Rocco C. Sicilano, one of President Eisenhower's aides, saying:

> Your courage in the face of adversity is well known, and I am certain that this time will be no exception. My best wishes for a complete and quick recovery.

Rabbi Israel Goldstein, President of the American Jewish Congress, visited the hospital and delivered a letter in which he said that Jews would pray for Rev. King's recovery at their Yom Kippur services that were being held that week.

The International Rescue Committee, the Brooklyn Catholic Interracial Council, the American Friend Service Committee, and the Union of American Hebrew Congregation also sent letters.

After being in the hospital over two weeks, and feeling much better, King held a press conference. He told the reporters that the messages were great sources of strength and support all cherish-freedom and equality for all men.

He expressed his heartfelt appreciation to the thousands of people of all faiths and races in all walks of life who had indicated by telegrams, letter, calls, cards, flowers and other gifts their warm concern for his well-being.

The stabbing of Martin Luther King, Jr. left many unanswered questions for the American people. Perhaps the most obvious one was why should anyone want to kill a man who is an exponent of love and nonviolence? Why would anyone and especially a Negro, want to kill a champion of his own cause?

There are no simple answers to the above questions. One may argue that, apparently, King was not a hero to all Negroes. The answer is plausible, since some Negroes do not like changes and prefer living the same traditional simple life— being a part of this desegregation "mess."

Chapter Ten

RETURN OF THE PRODIGAL SON

The year 1959 was perhaps the most peaceful one that Martin Luther King, Jr. had since coming to Montgomery. There were no bombings and few major incidents. This was the year that he made his very significant pilgrimage to India and strengthened his belief in using non-violence to achieve racial justice. This was the year that his book, *Stride Toward Freedom*, won an award for the best book of the year on race relations. And above all, this was the year that he had to make the most soul searching decision in his life— whether to return to Atlanta.

I

Before the stabbing in September, 1958, King had always wanted to travel to India and study more closely Ghandi's techniques of non-violence. During his recovery in November and December, King thought that after he recovered he would do some traveling. Therefore, after talking the situation over with his wife and making arrangements with the American Friends Service Committee and also studying Ghandi's teaching, King decided to go to India. This would be a very important journey for Martin Luther King, Jr. since he had used the Ghandian teachings of non-violence. King and Mrs. King departed for India February 8, 1959.

After arriving in New Delhi, Dr. King remarked, "To other countries I may go as a tourist, but, to India I come as a pilgrim." While in India, Dr. King lectured at the universities and public meetings whenever asked. And at every meeting he was besieged with questions on segregation in the United States. He would always tell the gathering that all of the United States is not segregated, only a few states, and that one day the people in those states would come to realize that all men are brothers in the eyes of God.

In New Delhi King was given international recognition as the architect of the Montgomery Movement. He was the guest of Prime Minister Jawaharial Nehru and other high officials. This was an honor for a nondiplomatic visitor and King was very pleased with what he heard from them. He concluded that India was integrating her untouchables faster than the United States was integrating her Negro minority. He said that the Indians liked Americans individually but were disturbed by America's foreign policy.

The Kings saw the good and clean places in India as well as the filthy and poverty stricken areas. They also saw hundreds of people lying on the roadside while cattle roamed the countryside.

After traveling in India for a month, the Kings returned to the United States on March 17. For them it was an unforgettable experience to learn and understand some of the ways of the Indians. And for Martin Luther King Jr. especially, it was no doubt most significant since the pilgrimage had strengthened his belief in using non-violence to acheive racial justice.

Since King was booked for speaking engagements for two years in advance he did not accept any new ones. He did, however, relate the experience that he had received while traveling in India whenever possible. One who heard him speak before he went to India and after he returned concluded that this was a "new" Martin Luther King, Jr. speaking.

He told his church congregation that:

> The Negro must have Christian strength to meet hate with love. You must say to your tormentor that you have his evil deed yet love him in the process. You must say: you will match his capacity to inflict suffering with your capacity to suffer. You will not abide by his unjust laws, but you will not hate him for making them. Non-violence is the most potent weapon available to people in the struggle for human dignity. The old eye-for-eye philosophy ends leaving everybody blind.

On April 8th, after being back little over a month, King received a joyous surprise—the Amis Field-Wolf Award for his book, *Stride Toward Freedom* and a stipend of $1,000.

After being back over two months King devoted most of his time between the Southern Christian Leadership Conference and his church. The SCLC had as its first goal voter registration among Negroes. Therefore, some representative of the SCLC was usually present at most major registration drives whenever possible.

King proposed that the best way of urging Negroes to vote was through ministers. First, because of their unique training. Secondly, because of the church itself, for Christians must be concerned with "social conditions" that corrupt the soul.

Through the church, the SCLC hoped to implement the court's desegregation decision at the local level. The civil rights act would, however, not mean anything if Negroes were afraid to follow it through.

King was traveling back and forth from Montgomery, where his church and the MIA were to Atlanta, Georgia, a venture which proved to be unwise and uneconomical. On December 1, King announced, after much soul searching, that he would move to Atlanta by February 1, 1960. This was indeed a very difficult, if not almost impossible decision to make. For here lived the people that he grew to love and respect so much. Here in Montgomery, Alabama, "The Cradle of the Confederacy," was where he held his first full-time job as pastor of a church. Here is where his home was bombed and here is where he led the boycott and became internationally famous. It was indeed an almost heartbreaking decision to make. But since the SCLC's headquarters were in Atlanta, and he was devoting more and more of his time to the SCLC, he decided to move to Atlanta.

II

Even before Martin Luther King, Jr. actually returned to Georgia, the Governor was quoted as saying that King would be placed under constant surveillance if he moved there. "Anyone who comes across the line with the avowed intention of breaking the laws will be kept under surveillance all the time," said the Governor.

Once again King was accused of being a lawbreaker before committing any so-called unjust deeds. When he announced his intentions of moving, there is no doubt that the WCC of Montgomery was glad to get rid of the outside "Agitator." Violence still prevailed however, in Montgomery, even after King left the city. Some citizens thought that things would return to normal when he left, but as we know, this did not happen.

As the year 1960 unveiled, King viewed it no differently from previous years. He was still traveling all around the country making speeches. As early as January 2, 1960, Martin Luther King, Jr. spoke to about 2,700 Negroes at a protest rally in Richmond, Virginia. He told the Negroes: "Never underestimate what they were doing and he could assure them that it would have far reaching effects." He ended by stating that they must not sell their birthright of freedom for a mess of "segregated pottage." Once again Martin Luther King, Jr. gave fresh hope to these school-less Negro children. The children had had no public schooling since the summer of 1959, when the public schools were closed by the State of Virginia rather than integrate.

Even before Martin Luther King finished Boston University, his father had a dream that his son would return to Atlanta and share his pastorship with him. Martin Luther King, Sr. thought that one day he would gradually retire and thus, let his son be his successor.

Thus, on February 6, 1960, Martin Luther King, Sr.'s dream was fulfilled, when his son, Martin Luther King, Jr. became his co-pastor. Now the elder King was truly happy to have his world renown son at his side; despite the fact that Martin, Jr. was frequently out of town on speaking engagements.

Martin Luther King, Jr.'s return to Atlanta was welcomed by some, and opposed by others. After being in Atlanta less than two months, he was arrested at his office in the Ebenezer Baptist Church, February 16, on charges of perjury.

After appearing before Judge Jeptha C. Tanpsley, Reverend King was released on a $2,000 bond. It was later learned that the perjury charges grew out of income tax statements filed by King in 1956 and 1958. The indictment accused him of not having reported $31,000 income for the two years. This charge was another attempt on the part of the

Alabama officials to harass him, presumably for his civil rights activities. King later remarked that he had no idea why he had been indicted.

Alabama law, unlike the Federal law, does not claim income tax evasion as a felony. Swearing to a fraudulent return constitutes perjury; fraud is a felony. The penalty for perjury is one to five years imprisonment.

Martin Luther King, Jr. first announced that he would fight the attempt to extradite him to Montgomery for the trial. After thinking the situation over and consulting his attorneys, however, he decided that it would be best if he returned to Montgomery to face trial for the perjury charge. If he contest the extradition, perhaps some would think that he was hiding something. The implication from the indictment was that he had embezzled money belonging to the MIA, and this was one thing that he wanted cleared up immediately.

One of the persons who had previously accused King of mishandling funds donated to the MIA was the Reverend Uriah J. Fields, who had set up a rival Negro organization in Montgomery. Rev. Fields had said that King had deposited over $100,000 in two Atlanta banks. Another statement was made that he was going to build a $35,000 home in Atlanta. Since the bus boycott, rumors to this effect had been spreading, but King denied them.

King went to Montgomery to post $4,000 bond on the perjury charges. While he was there he spoke at a mass meeting of the MIA. He told the gathering not to resort to violence, and to keep calm. Most Negroes in Montgomery did not approve of King's arrest and thought that something had to be done.

While King was in the city, a "reign of terror" broke out. The opposition had become so obsessed with destroying the protest movement of the students of Alabama State College that it gripped the whole city. In fact, Dr. King asked the President to intervene, by instructing the Attorney General of the United States to take immediate action in his name to restore law and order in the capitol of Alabama. As expected, the Governor declared that he had his state under control, and he did not need any help from the Federal Government.

Therefore, when the protest was staged by the students, the governor closed the college. To actuate the protest the students had marched to the steps of the capitol and had sung "My Country Tis of Thee," in protest of segregated lunch counters, and the arrest of Martin Luther King, Jr. Later, the leaders of the protest were arrested and expelled. The same day, policemen arrived on the campus armed with shotguns and tear gas. When the entire student body protested to the Governor, the Board of Trustees, and the President of the college, by refusing to re-register until their leaders were reinstated in college; the state officials closed the dining hall in an attempt to force them to re-register and "behave" themselves. The policemen stopped the students from convening in an orderly protest on their campus and also from holding religious services. These two incidents, probably more than any other, stirred up the whole community.

While King was preparing for his trial, a group of his associates placed a full page ad in the *New York Times* soliciting funds for his defense.[19] The *Montgomery Advertiser* said in an editorial on April 6; that the advertisement in the *Times* was replete with "lies and crude slander." In its lead editorial it declared:

> There are voluntary liars, there are involuntary liars. Both kinds of liars contributed to the crude slanders against Montgomery broadcast in a full page advertisement in the **New York Times,** March 19.
> And it is up to the **New York Times,** and the involuntary liars to purge themselves of their false witness.
> The **Times** boasts that it screens advertisement to eliminate what is . . . or in bad taste. Perhaps demonstrable lies will at some future time be screened and found unfit to print.

Montgomery's three city Commissioners, also, demanded a retraction by the *New York Times* as well as the Attorney General of Alabama. After two weeks the city of Montgomery filed a $500,000 libel suit against the *New York Times* in state court on behalf of Mayor Earl D. James, and city Commissioners Frank W. Parks and L. B. Sullivan.

Governor John Patterson of Alabama, acting as Governor and ex-office Chairman of the Alabama State Education Board, also, protested the *New York Times'* advertisement.

After receiving the letter from Governor Patterson, the *New York Times* retracted the statement in the advertisement by saying:

> The **Times** never intended to suggest by the publication of the ad, that the Honorable John Patterson . . . was guilty of "grave misconduct or improper, and omission" . . . The New York Times hereby apologizes to the Honorable John Patterson. . .

III

While Martin Luther, Jr. was waiting his trial on the perjury charges, he became more involved with the sit-ins and their leaders. More than two months passed before any effort was made to coordinate the movement. Encouraged by the Southern Christian Leadership Conference, leaders of the movement from all over the United States met in a conference at Shaw University in Raleigh, N.C., April 15-17, 1960. From this conference emerged the Student Nonviolent Coordinating Committee whose designated functions were in the areas of coordination and communication, and it acted under the guidance of Dr. Martin Luther King, Jr. and SCLC.

The first act of the Committee was to draft the following philosophy of the movement:

> We affirm the philosophical or religious ideal of nonviolence as the foundation of our purpose, the presupposition of our belief and the manner of our.
>
> Nonviolence, as it grows from Judaic-Christian tradition seeks a social order of justice permeated by love. Integration of human endeavor represents the first crucial step toward such a society.
>
> Through non-violence, courage displaces fear. Love transforms hate. Acceptance dissipates prejudice; hope ends despair. Faith reconciles doubt. Peace dominates war. Mutual regard cancel enmity. Justice for all overthrows justice. The redemptive community supercedes immoral social systems.
>
> By appealing to conscience and standing on the moral nature of human existence, nonviolence nurtures the atmosphere in which reconciliation and justice become actual possibilities.
>
> Although each local group in this movement must diligently work out the clear meaning of this statement of purpose, each act or phrase of our corporate effort must reflect a genuine spirit of love and good-will.

The sit-ins began somewhat inconspicuously in February of 1960, in Greensboro, N. C. The setting was a Woolworth lunch counter. The four participants were freshmen at the then Agriculture and Technical College of North Carolina. They took seats at the counter with a casualness that belied their uneasiness. After their request for service was denied, they sat silently until the store was closed. Then they went to the local branch of the NAACP for advice and legal aid.

Dr. King called for a national "selective-buying" campaign against businesses that practice segregation. This was the opening of the first South-wide conference of Negro student leaders of the sit-in movement. The conference was under the auspices of the SCLC, CORE, American Friends Service Committee, and the National Student Association and fellowship of Reconciliation.

More than 100 students from forty Southern communities and ten states attended the session on the campus of Shaw University. About ten white students, some of them from the North, also attended.

In his speech to the conference of over 2,000 people, King said that since the demonstration, "more" Negro freedom fighters had revealed to the nation and the world their determination and courage than had occurred in many years. They have embraced a philosophy of mass, direct, non-violent action. They are moving away from tactics which are suitable for gradual and long term change. Consideration of a nationwide campaign of selective buying is a "must," for such a program "is a moral act" he said.

It is a moral necessity to select, to buy from those stores and businesses, where one can buy with dignity and self respect. It is immoral to spend one's money when one cannot be treated with respect. He continued by "declaring that among other things, the sit-in movement was a revolt against the apathy and complacency of some Negroes." It is a revolt against those Negroes in the middle class who indulge themselves in big cars and ranch-style homes, rather than joining a movement for freedom. He concluded by saying, "This is an era of offensive on the part of the oppressed people. All peoples deprived of dignity and freedom are on the march on every continent throughout the world. These student sit-in movements represent just such an offensive in the history of the

Negro peoples struggle for freedom. These students have taken the struggles for justice into their own strong hands."

King's presence was significant to the conference because the students were using the philosophy of nonviolence in their demonstrations. And what better person could lead them.

During the sit-in demonstrations that followed, former President Harry S. Truman was quoted as saying that if anyone entered a store he ran to indulge in such a demonstration, "I'd throw them out."

While appearing on "Meet the Press" on NBC, King criticized Mr. Truman for expressing opposition to the demonstrations against segregation in public eating places. He called Mr. Truman's comment, "unfortunate." He said that in a sense it serves to aid and abet violent forces.

Mr. Truman also said while speaking at Cornell University that the student demonstrations were "engineered by Communists." Dr. King sent Mr. Truman a letter asking him to offer proof of his assertions and stated further that Truman's assertions affront and disappoint millions of Negroes, who are yearning for freedom. He received no reply.

IV

On May 16, a pre-trial was held to determine whether there was sufficient evidence to bring Martin Luther King, Jr. to trial. At the pre-trial, Reverend King, through his five attorneys, protested being put on trial in a segregated courtroom. His attorneys contended it would violate his constitutional rights. The defense attorneys also challenged the legality of Montgomery County's system of choosing prospective jurors and complained, now, of what it has been doing for years—systematically excluding Negroes from jury duty.

Since he was one of the five man commission that put names in the jury box, Judge Eugene Carter, promptly disqualified himself and called for the appointment of a special judge to hear all four pre-trial motions.

The pre-trial was held March 19. At this time, the special judge James Carter, rejected the defense attorneys claim of discrimination against Negroes as jurors in Montgomery, and refused to throw out the perjury indictment.

Judge Carter ruled that the defense attorneys had failed to show that the indictments against King were improperly drawn or that there was any reason to dismiss him. Dr. King was ordered to face trial the next week.

The trial began on March 25. The first witness for the prosecution was Lloyd Hale, a state tax auditor. He said that Dr. King owed the state $318.81, which King "promptly paid" and made no complaint about the additional taxes when informed, that he had not listed $7,000 in taxable income for 1956. He said the original return showed no taxes owed. His investigation showed that Dr. King's net worth increased from $154.01 to $3,199 from January 1 to December 30, 1956. An audit was ordered by the State Revenue Department and it showed that Dr. King had deposited in financial institutions in Alabama and Georgia a total of $16,182.46.

Assistant Solicitor Robert Stewart told the jury of twelve white men that while Dr. King's net worth had increased $3,044, he had listed taxable income of only $3,476 in 1956. "And what we want to know is where he got his 'spending money'," the assistant solictor concluded.

During the two days of testimony, Martin Luther King, Jr. was on the stand the majority of the time. He denied the state's charges of lying in the filing of his state income tax return. He said he had reported his income to the best of his knowledge and ability.

Dr. King said that many of the bank deposits had been made for reimbursements of expenses, for speaking engagements, and other repayments, that were not taxable and did not represent additional income.

Rev. King was questioned by the defense attorneys and William F. Thetford, the prosecutor. Mr. Thetford put him through a detailed examination of some of his financial records as he sought to show that King had failed to report all taxable income.

The defense contended that the state's audit of Dr. King's 1956 personal income tax return had been faulty. Defense Attorney William R. Ming, a Chicago tax expert, asserted in his closing argument that the state resorted to "fraudulent techniques" and a "mathematical trick," in an audit of the returns and that the prosecutor had carefully concealed the fact. Mr. Ming concluded: "The statute says the taxpayer must report his gross income and not the amount deposited in the bank. The state had completely ignored this hole in their case and they had fraudulently said that the taxpayers' gross income is the total of all the deposits when made in various banks in the year 1956. If you men in the jury go home and add up your bank deposits and want the state to consider that your total income which is taxable, then you will convict the defendant."

The Assistant Solicitor charged "that Dr. King was guilty of just plain lying!" He made gross misstatements of facts when he said his income was only $9,000, when it really was $16,000—a difference of $7,000. When summoning up, the Circuit Solicitor told the jurors that the Federal Government usually prosecuted tax cases "but, I would not expect the Federal Government to prosecute this defendant for any violation."

The jurors were asked by both prosecution and the defense attorneys to examine more than 1,400 exhibits. Finally, when the case was given to the jury, it deliberated for three hours and forty-five minutes before acquitting Martin Luther King, Jr.

King was emotionless when the verdict was read, but his wife, Coretta, and one of his attorneys, Hubert T. Delaney broke into tears. This was truly a memorable occasion. For a jury of twelve white men in Montgomery, Alabama, had acquitted Martin Luther King, Jr., a black man and an outsider, of "perjury charges."

Shortly after the trial Dr. King declared that his acquittal to his mind was a very significant verdict, not because he was involved, but because it offers a ray of hope for justice and understanding in the South. He concluded by saying, "This was Alabama's way and opportunity to say to the world and nation that a Negro can get a just trial in the state and the jury demonstrated this in a noteworthy manner." That while he felt there had been no miraculous conversion in Alabama, he was grateful for the white jurors. "Something happened to the jury: it said no matter how much they must suppress me they must tell the truth," said King.

Chapter Eleven

KING AND THE POLITICAL PARTIES

After the ordeal of the trial, King rested briefly and did not speak very much during the next three months. Since it was an election year, King declared that one of the main goals of the SCLC was to get Negroes in the South to register and to vote. The presidential election would be held two months from now and King was beginning to speak on this important issue.

Perhaps Martin Luther King, Jr. made his strongest references to the political parties on September 6, when he spoke at the Community Church, in New York City, as part of the annual convention of the National Urban League. Over 2,500 persons packed this small church to hear him, and the crowd was said to be the largest ever to have attended an event at the church.

Martin Luther King, Jr. began his speech by charging the Executive and Judicial branches of the Government with "a conspiracy of silence and apathy." He continued: "I must make it palpably clear, that the dearth of positive leadership from Washington is not confined to ONE political party—each of them has been willing to follow the long pattern of using the Negro as a political football." He asserted: "Both political parties have signed huge promissory notes in the strongest civil rights platform in their history, but we must not be contented with empty promises. We *must* demand implementation. We *must* make it clear that neither political party can deliver its platform promises alone. The job can be done through a sincere determined bipartisan effort." He concluded: "Both parties had missed a marvelous opportunity to demonstrate their good faiths, because they had not passed civil rights legislation in the post-convention session of Congress. Here we saw a vivid example of the same old game of hypocrisy, immoral compromises and political chicanery. The fact remains, however, that the issues of racial injustice cannot be successfully evaded, nor will it disappear with double-talk." He also reproved "White Northern liberals" who showed indignation about the lynching of a Negro in Mississippi, but who failed to be equally indignant about the rights of Negroes in the North. When the civil rights leader had finished, the audience applauded for several minutes.

After being in Atlanta about a week, on September 14, King announced at a news conference the formation of the "Nonpartisans to Register One Million Voters." Even though Martin Luther King, Jr. and the Southern Christian Leadership Conference put the crusade in operation, A Philip Randolph and Roy Wilkins also played a key role in its formation.

At the news conference King predicted that Negroes would vote by the merits of the candidates and on their stand on human rights. He also doubted that any religious issue would affect most Negroes as voters in the South and individuals who are anti-Catholic, are usually anti-Negro.

The late President John F. Kennedy's religion was an important issue in the election. He would be the first Catholic elected president of the United States.

I

While Martin Luther King was being lauded in the North, he was being harassed in the South. The Governor and other public officials had stated that King would be under constant watch and they were true to their words. While driving through DeKalb County, an adjoining county of Atlanta, he was arrested for driving without a Georgia driver's license and fined $25. Atlanta and the State of Georgia turned out to be no different from Montgomery and the State of Alabama.

On October 19, King and several college students, mainly from Morehouse College and Atlanta University, sought service in the eating places in Rich's Department Store in downtown Atlanta. King's main defense at the hearing was that Georgia's law under which he was arrested during the sit-in was unconstitutional. He also argued that the original twelve months traffic sentence was twice as long as the law allowed.

King's Attorney D. L. Howell immediately appealed for King to be released on bond. But, the judge said an appeal bond could not be obtained in a revocation of probation. Attorney Howell asked next for release of King on bond pending an appeal of the original traffic case. King was immediately taken to the Georgia State Prison at Reidsville, the state's largest prison, by the Georgia State Correctional Department.

This court went to the extreme to use all of the legal authority at its command to humiliate this Ghandian scholar, by even putting handcuffs on him. When King was being transported to the prison, he passed before a praying group of white Southern theologians from Northern schools on a mission of encouragement for sit-ins. The Mayor of Atlanta, William Hartsfield, made the following comment on the trial: "I have no desire to criticize the courts. But I have made requests of all the news agencies that in their stories they make it clear that this hearing did not take place in Atlanta, Georgia."

Peter Zaek, the Governor's executive secretary, revealed a somewhat contrary opinion of the trial when he said: "I think the maximum sentence for Martin Luther King might do him good, might make a law abiding citizen out of him, and teach him to respect the law of Georgia."

CORE called the sentence "a gross miscarriage of justice" and sent a telegram protesting the action to President Eisenhower and Attorney William P. Roger.

Martin Luther King, Jr. was taken from the DeKalb County jail about 4 a.m. and arrived at the State Prison about 8 a.m. There he was placed in "segregation," a prison term used for being alone in a cell pending assignment to prison duties.

Inmates of the state, like most Southern states, are segregated by race. Sheriff Robert Broome had asked King's transfer as soon as possible because he said his jail was overcrowded. Judge Mitchell's sentence had been that Dr. King serve in a public works camp, but the Corrections Department assigned him to the main prison.

One of the objects of the demonstration was to bring the whole issue of desegregation to the "conscience of Atlanta," declared King. Fifty-one demonstrators including King were arrested during the sit-in protest. Fourteen including King refused to post bond and went to jail. The demonstrators were held by the City Court and were to be tried by the County Court.

Meanwhile, the Negro leaders reached an agreement with Mayor William Hartsfield, to suspend for thirty days the sit-in protest. The agreement included promise to try for release of all jailed demonstrators, including Martin Luther King, Jr.

King, however, said he would refuse to post $500 bond proposed to him during his pending trial and would leave jail only if the charges were dropped. He remained in jail waiting on traffic charges revived by his arrest in the sit-in.

There was a hearing on the suspended twelve month sentence given on these charges. Judge Oscar Mitchell ordered the hearing saying that the sit-in arrest violated terms of the suspended sentence. These alleged terms were that King would not violate Georgia's law during the twelve months.

This time the state officials had King on a legal clause in the law. It was the first time Martin Luther King, Jr. had heard about the twelve month suspended sentence. King and his attorneys were caught completely off guard.

The hearing would be held despite statements that Rich's Department Store officials would not press charges against any of the 38 sit-in cases. This did not make any difference to the court. It had a stranglehold on Martin Luther King, Jr. and would not let go!

The hearing was held the next day at which time Judge Oscar Mitchell of DeKalb Civil and Criminal Court ordered the suspended sentence revoked. He ruled that Martin Luther King, Jr.'s participation in the sit-in demonstration had violated the terms of the suspended sentence in the traffic case. King was ordered to serve four months in prison.

His defense attorney argued that the original twelve months sentence was void because it was twice as long as allowed by law. The prosecution refused to concede this. King's attorney said the original suspended sentence could not be revoked because it was void.

The defense attorneys also argued that Rev. King's arrest in the sit-in demonstration had no bearing in the traffic case because the law under which he was arrested was unconstitutional.

Judge Mitchell refused the motion to set aside the revoca- tion of the sentence with a brief order carrying no explanation. Attorney Howell said a habeas corpus petition was to have been presented at the hearing that would have demanded Dr. King's release on the grounds that he had been sentenced illegally, but the transfer of Rev. King to Reidville made the habeas corpus action impossible.

Mr. Hartsfield, the Mayor of Atlanta, had been receiving many messages from people all over the world protesting Martin Luther King, Jr.'s sentence. Among them was one signed by the late Mrs. Franklin D. Roosevelt. It stated: "I wish to protest the imprisonment of Dr. Martin King and hope you will use your good office to correct this injustice." Mayor Hartsfield commented. "We wish the world to know that the city of Atlanta had no part in the trial and sentencing of Dr. King for a minor traffic offense. The responsibility for this belongs to DeKalb County and the State of Georgia."

II

The ordeal of her husband being in jail was almost un- bearable for Mrs. Coretta King. In fact the morale of the entire King family was very low. Even though the King family had received thousands of messages of encouragement, things still were hard to accept.

It appeared as if King's attorney had exhausted all of their legal remedies and there seemed to be no where else to turn when suddenly a new light with new hope shone through the clouds of darkness. Mrs. King received a call from Senator John F. Kennedy to express concern over the jailing of her husband.

"Senator Kennedy said he was very much concerned about the both of us," Mrs. King remarked. He told Mrs. King that this must be hard on her and he wanted her to know he was thinking about them and he would do all he could to help. Mrs. King told him she appreciated it and hoped he would help.

In Atlanta, it was reported that Republican headquarters had asked for some kind of a statement on the King case from Vice President Nixon, or for Republican campaign officials there to make some comment. Vice President Nixon, however, had no comment which later turned out that this was one of the most fatal mistakes that the Vice President and the Republican Party made during the Presidential election. It was the most single important movement that Senator Kennedy and the Democratic Party made during the election.

Martin Luther King, Jr. served only a day and a night in prison before he was released from jail on $2,000 bond. Judge Mitchell who ordered King's release indicated that Robert Kennedy, brother and campaign manager for Senator John F. Kennedy, had been among those who intervened in the case.

He said, however, the release was mandatory under Georgia law and not the result of any pressure put on him. The Judge explained that release on bond was required in an appeal of King's original suspended sentence of twelve months on a charge of driving without a license. He later said he had been under considerable pressure from both sides on whether to allow bond. He said some pressure came from a member of a presidential nominee's family. Asked which member, he said it was a brother. When questioned as to whether it had been Robert or Ted, he declared: "Well, I will say that I have heard of Ted's name being mentioned."

Martin Luther King, Jr. was released from Reidsville State Prison, about 200 miles south of Atlanta, in custody of his attorney. He was met at a private airport by a delegation of friends, his wife, their small son, and a niece. Waiting on the other side of the county border were about 400 Negro students from Atlanta University.

After the civil rights leader's release, immediate outcries came from the opposition. Four honorary colonels on the staff of Gov. Vandiver resigned in protest over Robert F. Kennedy's telephone call to a judge in King's behalf. The Lt. Governor also "violently disagreed" with the intervention of the Democratic Presidential candidate's brother and campaign manager.

The Governor also criticized Sen. Kennedy for telephoning Martin Luther King, Jr.'s wife while he was in jail. The

Governor said, however, barring unforeseen events, he would support the Democratic Party. He predicted that Georgia would go Democratic. "It is a sad commentary on the year 1960 and its political campaign when the Democratic nominee for the presidency makes a phone call to the home of the foremost radical in the country," the Governor said.

Sen. Kennedy may have lost a few votes from the "diehard" whites in the South, but he gained a new ally—the Negro. The Negro in the North and South voted overwhelmingly for former President Eisenhower and the Republican Party in the 1952 and the 1956 elections. The Negro was expected to play a "key" role in the 1960 election. In fact Martin Luther King, Sr. said he would vote for Sen. Kennedy because of the call to his son's wife. The elder King said he had planned earlier to vote against Kennedy because of his religion.[20] There is little doubt that thousands of Negroes voted for John F. Kennedy because of the call he made to Mrs. King. Atlanta, King's home town, a key Negro district, gave only a small 15 per cent of its votes in 1956 to Democrats. The percentage, however, rose to 42 percent in 1960, which is somewhat remarkable considering the fact that it did not show Kennedy's name on it. It did, however, have the names of electors known as segregationists.

At the climax of the election campaign the Justice Department finally prepared a statement for former President Eisenhower to issue on the jailing of Martin Luther King, Jr. The statement, however, was never issued. Just why it was not made public is not clear, but it seems beyond dispute now that some strong words coming from the President would have had a major impact on the Negro vote. The decision not to issue a statement may have been made by former President Eisenhower or his White House subordinate. It may have been made by Vice President Nixon's strategists. No one, however, would comment on who made the fatal mistake. Former President Dwight D. Eisenhower later remarked that a "couple of phone calls," had swung the Negro vote to the Democratic Party. In the election, the Negroes voted overwhelmingly for the late President John F. Kennedy and the Democrats.

Looking back at 1960, it was a year of decision. It was the year that Martin Luther King, Jr. returned to his home in Atlanta, became co-pastor with his father, and made his father's dream come true. It was the year that a "reign of terror" ran through Atlanta like it had never seen before. It was the year that King was tried and acquitted for perjury. And last it was the year that King was responsible for a large number of Negro votes for the late President Kennedy, and the Democratic Party.

Chapter Twelve

YEAR OF CRISIS

The Negro lunch counter demonstrations which began in 1960 had grown into a national protest movement against many forms of discrimination. The lowering of racial barriers at lunch counters in more than 125 Southern communities led the students and their adult supporters to turn to other fields of protest.

There have been stand-ins at theaters and kneel-ins at churches. Demonstrators have prayed on the steps of Southern capitols, paraded through the streets, picketed courthouses and City Halls. The civil rights advocates have also used "selective buying" as a weapon against businesses that practice discrimination.

The movement had more far-reaching effects than anyone dreamed possible. The movement spread as far as Capetown, South Africa. Northern chain stores have been boycotted because their Southern outlets discriminated against Negroes.

In all of the demonstrations the students used Martin Luther King, Jr.'s philosophy of nonviolence, and his suggestions for "selective buying." If Woolworth had only served the students a dime cup of coffee, they could have saved themselves and others millions of dollars and worries.

King's attorneys appealed his traffic to the Georgia Court of Appeals. The hearing was held March 6, 1961. At the hearing, the Court of Appeals upheld King's traffic conviction. The Court, however ruled that the twelve months sentence was excessive. Later at a hearing on April 6, Judge James Oscar Mitchell suspended the prison terms and placed him on probation.

I

In May 1961, a racially mixed group of bus riders were attacked by a white mob while traveling through Montgomery,

Ala. At least 20 of the riders were beaten. The mob, at times numbered about 1,000, attacked the white and Negro bus riders within minutes after the Greyhound Bus pulled into the downtown station from Birmingham, Ala.

The fighting broke out and subsided three times before the police, unable to restore order by other methods, tossed tear gas into the crowd. Some of the Negroes that were beaten by the mob had no apparent connection with the group that came to Montgomery on a trip into Alabama to challenge racial barriers at bus stations. The trip started at Nashville, Tenn.

Things were so tense in Montgomery that the federal government had to dispatch about 480 Marshals and other armed officers to restore order in areas that were plagued by racial violence. Attorney General Robert F. Kennedy said it was necessary to "guarantee safe passage in interstate commerce."

John Seigenthal, a representative of the Attorney General, was hit from behind as he struggled to help one of the Freedom Riders. He was taken to a hospital with a cut behind his ear. At least four out-of-town reporters and photographers were beaten as they attempted to take pictures of the rioting. Some reporters had their cameras taken away and smashed.

Things got out of hand and Alabama had to call on the federal government for help to put down a new eruption of racial violence in Montgomery. The State Director of Public Safety, Floyd Mann, asked the Justice Department to send any men it had because "this is an ugly situation." The state official changed his previous attitude of criticism of Federal intervention in the tense situation, as a mob gathered at a rally to hear Martin Luther King Jr. speak at the First Baptist Church.

The United States District Judge, Frank M. Johnson, Jr. granted a Justice Department request for an injunction against the KKK barring the group from interfering with the freedom of travel in interstate commerce. He later asked the Justice Department to protect him and his home from possible attack by the mob. Marshals were placed around his home. Rioting was becoming so uncontrollable that it prompted the governor to put the city of Montgomery under martial law. Steel-helmeted National Guardsmen with fixed bayonets, enforcing the governor's order, scattered a mob that tried to overpower the Federal Marshals protecting the church meeting.

The Negroes remained in the church and Rev. King began a scheduled speech that was more than two hours late. In his address he protested that the outbreaks of racial violence had "sunk to the level of barbarity, comparable to the tragic days of Hitler's Germany." The Negroes in the church sang, prayed and some moaned or screamed in panic as the howling of the mob drew near. One of the main concerns of most people who had attended the mass meeting was that their families would be worried. About 200 stood in line to use the phone and each was allowed only a minute to talk to his family.

As the mob became more uncontrollable, King and the Rev. Ralph Abernathy, pastor of the church, put in a call for more Federal Marshals. Martin Luther King, Jr. called Attorney General, Robert Kennedy, and told him, "They're moving in on the church. The Attorney General told him, "The Marshals will stop them." King left the phone and looked outside. He later returned and said, "You're right." The Federal Marshals had stopped the crowd.

Major General Henry V. Graham, in charge of the National Guard Troops, surrounded the church and told the people inside that they would be required to stay overnight. He offered to send in coffee and sandwiches, but most of the people in the church declined.

The earlier violence had prevented the people at the meeting from forming any plans about how to meet the racial problem in Montgomery. King had been outside the church only once since the meeting began and that was when he talked with General Graham. King told him that he had called the Attorney General and that 200 more Federal Marshals would be arriving soon.

Surely the nights of May 21 and 22 were the two "darkest nights" in Montgomery's modern history. The next day federal marshals evacuated the crowd from the church in buses.

As expected, the opposition made an unfavorable comment about the incident. The *Birmingham News* ran the following front page editorial:

"Mr. Kennedy: Why Aren't King Riders Held in Check?"
Mr. Robert Kennedy:

The people of Alabama and the people of the South want to
know why it isn't just as important to stop those who provoke
violence as it is to stop those who commit violence. This Mr.
Kennedy, is a direct question. We are sure you will want to answer.

"Martin Luther King flew in Montgomery. For what Mr.
Kennedy?" Why don't you put him under some control? Are
you pressing for an answer?

"The News understands that attempts were made to dissuade
King from going to Montgomery." He refused to heed them.

"Instead, he came into a city on the knife-edge of tension
and went through the heart of Montgomery in a motorcade which
was described by one observer—"Just like the President coming
to town."

The *New York Times*, however, gave a far different
comment. The editorial was headed, "ALABAMA AND THE
COLD WAR." It read:

In Birmingham and Montgomery the United States lost
another battle in the global cold war. The hoodlums, the screaming
women, the citizens who stood and watched, have done much to aid
the Communist cause throughout the world. . .

There has been much said and written about the prestige of
the United States in the last year or so. What price American
prestige of things can happen such as we and the whole wide
world have seen in Alabama.

II

The Attorney General of the United States called for a
"cooling off" period of the Freedom Riders, since violence
erupted everywhere they went. Even though some liberal
Southerners of both races joined moderates, and others in
declaring that the Freedoms Riders should be halted, Martin
Luther King, Jr. would not agree that the demonstrations had
damaged the cause of the Negro or that the methods had been
improper. He said despite a series of setbacks, the Freedom
Riders would resume "in full force" with the Southern capitol
of Jackson, Miss. remaining as the chief target.

King defended the demonstrators and their tactics by
asserting that "these are the pioneers who are making the
way possible for people of all areas to ride buses unmolested
by segregation, as well as to use the facilities of the bus
terminals without being segregated." He further implied that

he could conceive of no great social changes or progress without some individuals who were willing to take the blows and who were temporarily misunderstood, "In a democracy and a nation that is tied together by many strains as a federal union, can we call anyone an outsider? It is as much my obligation as one who lives in Atlanta to be concerned by what takes place in Mississippi as it is of a person who lives in Mississippi," the civil rights leader concluded.

The Attorney General withdrew all of the 566 Marshals from Alabama, leaving only 100 as part of his "cooling off" policies. Martin Luther King, Jr. immediately sent a telegram to the President of the United States, John F. Kennedy, asking that Federal Marshals not be withdrawn from Montgomery "at this crucial moment." For a perpetual reign of terror still existed in Montgomery.

The Attorney General also asked the Interstate Commerce Commission to adopt stringent regulations against segregation. Within months after Attorney General Kennedy asked the ICC to adopt regulations against segregation, it issued an order outlawing segregation in interstate travel. Almost overnight bus stations removed signs designating separated facilities.

The ICC also required that public carriers post signs stating that the passengers are to be seated regardless of race, color, or creed. The Freedom Riders, therefore, had accomplished one positive goal.

Even though Martin Luther King, Jr. was spending a great deal of his time in the South, he did find time to travel to New York City to be the guest of Governor Nelson A. Rockefeller and also flew to Albany with the governor. Governor Rockefeller said: "It was an honor indeed to welcome one of the truly great Americans, a man who has devoted his life to the realization of the American dream, not for just a few, but for all."

During this time Otto Preminger was producing and directing the screen version of "Advise and Consent" and had signed Martin Luther King, Jr. to portray Senator King of Georgia. King however, refused the role. He realized that this was his chance for stardom, but realized also that he was booked with speaking engagements for several years in advance, he just did not have the time. Besides, he was a minister, not an actor, and he felt that his obligations as a minister and president of the SCLC were far more important than going to Hollywood. Therefore, King diplomatically and apologetically declined the role.

While King was being acclaimed in New York and Hollywood, he was being threatened, attacked and heckled in other parts of the United States and abroad. When he was attending the National Baptist Convention in Kansas City, Missouri, September 9, 1961, a fatal riot broke out and a delegate was killed. Dr. J. H. Jackson, president of the National Baptist Convention, immediately accused Martin Luther King, Jr. of designing tactics that led to the riot. Dr. Jackson said King had "masterminded" the invasion of the convention floor which resulted in the death of a delegate.

Martin Luther King, Jr. spoke and encouraged the delegates to endorse a strong and immediate passage of all Civil Rights issues. Therefore, many delegates supported King and opposed Dr. Jackson who favored a slow approach to the Civil Rights issues. Consequently, the convention was in an uproar over the two opposing views. It was because of these views that the riot broke out.

Later when King spoke in Indianapolis he received word that he was to be assassinated. The police guarded him from the time he arrived in Indianapolis until he departed. King, however, just passed the threats off as pranks made by distraught men. There was one thing for sure everyone in Indianapolis did not want him there.

About the same time Martin Luther King, Jr. was also receiving some unfavorable comments from abroad. While he was speaking in London, a group of hecklers interrupted him and shouted, "Keep Britain White." There were also shouts of "Go back to your own country." In fact, the heckling became so vile, that the hecklers were ejected. They however, were few. At the end of the address Martin Luther King, Jr. received an ovation.

Martin Luther King, Jr. withstood most criticisms remarkably well. After going through the grave ordeal in Montgomery, he had learned to accept condemnation.

Chapter Thirteen

KING RETURNS TO ALBANY

In the past, the Southern Christian Leadership Conference had made little, but noteworthy progress, in its efforts to get Negroes to register and vote in the South. Therefore, a "new" approach was made in 1962 in an all out effort to revamp its program. The SCLC announced that it would make a "recruiting tour" into every state in the South as a full scale assault on segregation. Its president, Martin Luther King, Jr. would be its number one troubleshooter and voter "go-getter." He would go into the communities and talk to people on a person-to-person basis and get them to register and vote.

This person-to-person method had been used very effectively by politicians in securing votes and friends. Martin Luther King, Jr. however, was not seeking any public office. He wanted Negroes to register and vote for the candidate of their own choice—whether Democratic, Republican or Independent.

This assault began with a 70 mile trip through Mississippi "to enlist volunteers for the Freedom Corps." The "Freedom Corps" was divided into two units—volunteers for canvassing a Southwide voting area and volunteers for the "nonviolent Army." These two units traveled throughout the South making notable progress in getting Negroes to register and vote.

Voting registration drives were held in Louisiana, Atlanta, where the Georgia Voters League was organized. Similar leagues and associations were formed in other cities, including the Danville (Virginia) Christian Progressive Association and the Chatham County Crusades for Voters.

While Martin Luther King, Jr. was speaking in various sections of the South, his wife Mrs. King was also fulfilling some speaking engagements. She spoke at Abyssinian Baptist Church in New York.

Mrs. King said that Negroes had "a lot of running and catching up to do." She urged the government to subsidize training programs for Negroes, since "We have done as much as a group as any other group, and we cannot afford to wait much longer." Her speech was patterned after her husband's with the same emphasis on Christian love. She concluded: "America was founded on strong moral principles and prides herself on being both Christian and democratic. The paradox of it all is the treatment of Negroes. It is neither Christian nor democratic. The influence of America has been dimmed by her handling of race relations."

About a month later she was again taking part in world affairs. She and 49 women flew to Geneva, Switzerland, to impress the arms of "Women Strike For Peace" upon the delegates to the 17-nations disarmament conference.

Mrs. King had decided to make the trip because she felt the problem of human survival on this planet was so great that it should claim the foremost attention of every thoughtful citizen. The group of women left April 1, and returned April 7, 1962. The delegation included Mrs. Cyrus Eaton, along with a ballet dancer, a fashion merchandiser, a psychiatric researcher, and a woman who lived in Japan at the time of the atomic bombings of Hiroshima and Nagasaki. The group was a congenial one, and learned much from the conference.

II

At the request of the local Negro leaders, in December 1961, Martin Luther King, Jr. joined a mass demonstration in Albany, Georgia. While there, King was arrested and dramatically declared that he would stay in jail until Albany consented to desegregate its public facilities. Two days later, however, he came out on bail. The Albany Movement collapsed. But the Negroes in Albany continued to protest. On July 10, 1962, King and Abernathy came back to Albany for their trial.

Recorder A. N. Durden of the Recorder's Court found them guilty of having violated a street-sidewalk assembly ordinance by leading a street demonstration in December. Recorder Durden sentenced them to 45 days in jail or $178 fines. They repudiated the fines, refused to post bonds, and went to jail to await assignment to prison street gangs.

In December 1961, King was bitterly criticized for helping the Albany Movement to collapse. This time the civil rights leader realized his mistake; therefore, he went to jail and refused to leave. He assailed both the Albany law and the court that had convicted him. The Baptist minister called them unjust and said he would be "just as wrong if he paid a fine under the circumstances." Dr. King stayed in jail two days. Later the sentence was reduced to a $25 fine and six months probation.

An unidentified person paid the civil rights leaders' fines and they were released. They did not want to leave, because this was not their purpose, but they could stay no longer.

Rev. King suggested that the fines were paid by someone who did not want them to become martyrs. They were not seeking martyrdom nor publicity, as the city officials and others suggested, but merely expressing their convictions on the principles. Rev. Abernathy agreed and declared that someone had to break "for the sake of this and future generations."

Two Albany Negroes were convicted on the same charges, but received lighter sentences. Solomon Walker was given a choice of a $100 fine or 30 days in jail, and Eddie Jackson, a fine of $25 or 10 days. Walker gained freedom on bond. Jackson, however, served his time. They were among more than 700 arrested during December. The jailings provoked new Negro demonstrations in Albany and there were more arrests.

The Albany Movement was becoming so noteworthy that President Kennedy asked the Justice Department for a report on the cases to see if any civil rights were being violated. Later the Attorney General called the officials in Georgia and told them that the demonstrators release should make it possible for the citizens of Albany to resolve their differences in a less tense atmosphere. The city officials not only refused to listen to the Attorney General, but they also refused to sit down and try to come to any agreement with the Negro leaders.

Things were becoming so tense that Gov. Rockefeller was in fear of King's and his aides' lives. He sent a telegram to the Attorney General in which he said, "I consider it of utmost urgency that the Justice Department take immediate action to assure the physical safety of Dr. King and his companions, in view of reported threats of harassment, or worst, when they appear on the streets of Albany, Georgia, as members, of prison work gangs."

During the next few days King had several speaking engagements that would take him out of the city. He decided to remain in Albany. Meanwhile the opposition was active. They requested and got Federal District Judge J. Robert Elliot to issue a restraining order banning further demonstrations by the Negroes. Named as the defendants were: Martin Luther King, Jr., Rev. Ralph D. Abernathy, Rev. Wyatt Tee Walker, Mr. W. G. Anderson, Joseph Charles Jones, and Mrs. Ruby Hurley. The petition contended that "an atmosphere of tenseness and impending danger now looms over the city of Albany; which threatens to erupt in mass violence and the deterioration of the public peace."

Dr. King said that the city's action in obtaining the order "was like standing on the beaches of history trying to hold back the tide." Since the local authorities had consistently sought to block and ignore the legitimate aspirations of the Negroes, King declared that the only recourse the Negro had was through nonviolent demonstrations.

King and the leaders went to the City Hall and voluntarily accepted serving the restraining order from the Federal Marshals. Then they conferred for about 25 minutes with the Chief of Police and other city officials. King was asked whether the Negroes would comply with the court order and he replied that the injunction did not cover the people in the church. This was the reference to the rally then in progress at the Shiloh and Mount Zion Churches attended by hundreds of members of the Albany Movement. Negroes were urged at the mass meetings to prepare for a resumption of demonstrations, by W. G. Anderson, leader and President of the Albany Movement.

The Negroes in the churches left there and started marching to City Hall. The marchers, however, were stopped by the Chief of Police. Police Chief Lauerie Prichett told the marchers that they could not march without a permit. "I have no permit; we are going to march to the City Hall to pray," replied one of the ministers. The Chief told them that they were violating a city ordinance. Meanwhile King along with four or five men and women arrived in a station wagon, lined up before the Chief of Police, and told him they wanted to see the Mayor and the Commissioners. Chief Prichett replied that neither was in the City Hall.

"I am asking you to leave and go about your business," he replied. Mr. Anderson repeated the request. The Chief again asked them to leave and said that if they did not they would be arrested. At this point Dr. King asked Rev. Abernathy to lead them in prayer. Demonstrators who refused to get up off their knees were picked up and dropped into stretchers and carried off to jail. The demonstrators were booked on charges of parading without a permit and held in city jail pending transfer to the jail in the adjoining county.

The arrests only brought on another group of demonstrators. King and 25 other Negroes and one white person were also jailed. Mayor Asa D. Kelly, realizing that the federal government was vitally interested in the situation, telephoned the United States Department of Justice and informed them that Martin Luther King, Jr. had been arrested. The Mayor said that he thought that Dr. King was safer in prison than on the streets.

One of the key issues now was the demands that the charges be dropped against the marchers and that the police make no further arrests. If their demands were met, the Negroes would halt their demonstrations.

II

While Martin Luther King, Jr. was preaching nonviolence, violence erupted when a jeering crowd of 2,000 Negroes blocked the streets, hooted, laughed and threw bottles, bricks and rocks at more than 100 policemen and state highway patrolmen who marched down South Jackson Street behind the Chief of Police, who had ordered the night spots closed. The policemen, however, did not retaliate. They marched back to the police station.

"Did you see the nonviolent rocks?" Chief Prichett asked news reporters. He and the city officials said the violence had

117

confirmed their contentions that Negroes were responsible for the city's racial crisis. This incident prompted King to announce that if other incidents occurred the campaigning of mass protest against segregation here would be suspended.

King later said no persons active in the Albany Movement were involved in the rock-throwing incident. But he said we abhor violence so much that when it occurs in the ranks of the Negro community, we assume part of the responsibility for it.

The same night another rally was held and only 500 gathered at the Mount Zion Baptist Church. It appeared from the persons present that the long struggle had taken its toll. Speakers at the mass meeting pleaded in vain to recruit volunteers for a demonstration the next day. Only a few present, however, showed interest.

Charles Sherrod of Petersburg, Virginia, field secretary for the SCLC, even sought to shame them into participating, but with little success. He told the crowd, "They should be ashamed of themselves for sitting on their chairs while their leaders were sitting in a filthy jail. . ."

The next day, Attorney C. B. King, Jr. had gone to the Daugherty County Sheriff's office to see about obtaining medical aid for William Mansen, a white man who was arrested with 36 Negroes during a prayer protest.

Mr. King was talking with an official in the sheriff's office when Campbell told him to leave. He did not respond. The sheriff then hit him with a walking cane. Attorney King staggered from the courthouse with blood streaming from his head.

Sheriff Campbell later explained to the Mayor and Chief of Police, "he didn't get, so God damn it, I put him out." Mr. King immediately announced that he would press charges against Sheriff Campbell and the City of Albany. It was also reported that a Justice Department spokesman in Washington said agents of the FBI were conducting an inquiry of the attack.

The Negro leaders realizing that racial tension was mounting, called off the planned demonstrations. In fact things were so tense that Senator Jacob K. Javits of New York

118

also asked the Justice Department to intercede in behalf of King and others arrested in Georgia.

Meanwhile the arrested demonstrators, including King and Abernathy, refused food while in jail in keeping with their policy of fasting for 24 hours after having been arrested "unjustly."

During the same week Martin Luther King, Jr. was scheduled to appear on "Meet the Press," but he was in jail. He was replaced by Dr. W. G. Anderson.

Dr. Anderson was asked how long would they continue in Albany. He declared that the demonstrations would continue in Albany as long as segregation exists as it does at the present time. He recognized that complete desegregation could not be expected "overnight" in Albany. But he said he thought that Negroes had been "patient long enough," and in reply to one question said, "Why should we wait any longer for any of these constitutionally guaranteed rights?"

Dr. Anderson summed up the tension in Albany by saying a "Little Rock situation" might develop in the nonviolent movement if it were continually frustrated by the circumvention of law.

Meanwhile Federal District Judge Elliot denied a motion by the Negroes attorneys to dismiss the city's petition for a temporary injunction forbidding further racial demonstration. In explaining his position Judge Elliot said: "At the time I took jurisdiction of this case I felt this court had jurisdiction. To rule otherwise would be saying that the court has jurisdiction to protect minorities and their civil rights and not majorities and their civil rights."

The ban issued by Judge Elliot was lifted by Chief Judge Elbert P. Tuttle of the Court of Appeals for the fifth Circuit when he held that Judge Elliot did not have jurisdiction.

Judge Tuttle said the city had offered no evidence that Negro demonstrators had engaged in acts of violence, that the civil rights statutes cited were intended to protect the rights of individuals from infringement by state authorities and not vice versa, and that the city had failed to prove it had suffered damage of $10,000 or more. Such damages he said were necessary to establish jurisdiction in such a case.

From the position Judge Elliot had taken it appeared that an injunction would pave the way for the city to seek contempt citations on the ground that a ban on demonstrations issued by Judge Elliot on July 19 was violated by a mass protest march on City Hall two days later. King said if Judge Elliot issued a further ban on demonstrations he would abide by it.

The city officials and the demonstrations were now at a stalemate. Neither side would give an inch. Therefore, King said he would leave Albany if city officials entered "good faith" negotiations with the demands of the Albany Movement.

The Albany Movement had asked that charges against the demonstrations be set aside, that the city recognize the rights of Negroes to demonstrate peacefully and that a bi-racial committee be appointed to work out a timetable for desegregation of all public facilities in Albany. The Mayor said he would never negotiate with outside agitators (King, Walker, Abernathy) whose avowed purpose was to create turmoil through mass racial demonstrations.

During the same week President Kennedy was holding his weekly news conference. At the news conference, the President was asked about the demonstrations in Albany. He replied that "he believed that if the United States was willing to hold talks with Russia, the Albany City Commissioners should be willing to discuss social racial affairs with Negro leaders."

While in jail Martin Luther King, Jr. received an unexpected visit from his children and wife. This was the first time that the King's children had seen him in jail. They had not seen him in almost three months because of the desegregation program in Albany.

The Rev. George Lawrence, regional director of the SCLC for the New York area, along with more than 100 ministers requested that the president take a "positive official stand on the moral and ethical issues" in the struggle of the Albany movement to break down segregation of public facilities.

They suggested that there be a federal investigation of the jailing of Martin Luther King, Jr. and his colleagues for taking part in the demonstration on July 27, and that Attorney General Robert F. Kennedy make it directly from Georgia.

Rev. Lawrence acted as spokesman for the delegation that arrived at the White House without an appointment. They had written a week before but no appointment was promised. Therefore, they were not able to see the President. They were, however, received by Mr. L. C. White, who handled civil rights affairs.

After the White House visit, there was a brief "prayer vigil" on the sidewalk. The group called itself the Inter-Denominational Ministers March on the White House. Some of the ministers came from New York, Connecticut, Massachusetts, New Jersey, Pennslyvania, Maryland, and Virginia. In spite of the breakdown of informal talks the Negro leaders sent a delegation the next evening in hopes of finding a reconciliation.

III

Since negotiations were at a stalemate and neither side was making any progress, the Justice Department intervened in the Civil Rights struggle. The department filed a friend-of-the-court brief opposing the city's request for an injunction banning protest. It simply meant that the city had no right to impose segregation and strife. The government asserted that the city did not come into court "with clean hands," since it had not complied with the Federal Court rulings forbidding discrimination. This seemed to the Department of Justice to produce incongruous spectacles of laws adopted to protect the citizens from oppression by the state . . . being used to stifle the freedom of these defendants.

The Negro leaders planned two major demonstrations at City Hall. One was a three hours Mother's March, and the other was a "Prayer Pilgrimage." The spokesman said they were ready to go to jail to show their support of King and Abernathy.

However, "no permits were issued to parade," contended the Mayor, because of the tension in the city. Mayor Kelly also split with the six other members of the City Commission on negotiations with Negroes. The Mayor said that there should be some "lines of communication" with responsible, law abiding Negro leaders. The six other commissioners denounced any meeting.

The next day, King and Abernathy were freed after having served two weeks. Ander and Slater King also received suspended sentences. The demonstrations were called off to give the City Commission a chance to open good faith negotiations with local Negro leaders.

King left Albany to preach at his church in Atlanta. He had repeatedly said he would leave if it would pave the way for interracial talks on segregation. Dr. King, however, said he would be back on Monday for more demonstrations, unless plans for negotiations were being planned. He also said facilities would be tested to see if they could be used.

King returned the following Monday and changed his commitments to the Albany situation. He said he would remain with the problem for as long as two years if necessary. When he returned demonstrators were arrested day after day and tension continued to exist in Albany. King asked President Kennedy to serve as a mediator between the city commissioners and the leaders of the Albany Movement. He suggested that the discussion be held in Washington, D.C.

King also informed the President that 15 Protestant and Jewish religious leaders from among the 75 clergymen leaders in the racial demonstration remained in jail, and that they were fasting "in hope they will arouse the conscience of this nation to the gross violation of human dignity which is the rule in Albany."

The President later answered King's telegram and told him to see if the City Commission would meet with the leaders of the Albany Movement.

The leaders were seeking the following:

(1) Establishment of a bi-racial committee to work out a timetable for desegregation of schools, parks, libraries, lunch counters and other places of public accommodations.
(2) Recognition by the city that Negroes have the right to protest segregation peacefully under the United States Constitution.
(3) A declaration from the city that it will abide by the Interstate Commerce Commission's decision desegregating travel terminals.
(4) Desegregated operation of city buses if they resume service.
(5) "Fair and just disposition" of nearly 1,200 cases of arrested demonstrators and the exchange of surety bonds for $8,000 in cash bonds.

While the Negro leaders were holding rallies and mass meetings, the opposition was also holding meetings. The Ku Klux Klan held a mass meeting in Albany in a pasture, burned a cross and denounced the Negroes and the governor of the State of Georgia. The rally drew members from three states—Georgia, Alabama and Florida.

The Chief speaker at the meeting was Robert M. Shelton. He implied that Albany's racial trouble stemmed from a "Communist conspiracy." He said the solution was for the whites to discharge their Negro employees.

At the Albany Movement meeting Mr. Anderson said that on September 4, when the white public school opens, Negroes would seek enrollment. The next day, nineteen Negro students tried to enroll in a white school, but they were refused admission. The school officials said pupil assignments for the year had already been made. Once again desegregation was annihilated by legal sanction.

The same day sixteen clergymen were freed on $200 bond each. They were the last to leave prison of the group of 70 arrested. While in jail all of the sixteen fasted throughout the six day stay. Others refrained from eating periodically while those over 60 years of age ate for reasons of health. One group held communion in jail using "a baking powder biscuit and a bottle of grape soda pop" for the service.

Even though violence prevailed in Albany, it was not the only place that erupted. Mass arrests, police brutality, water hoses, police dogs and even bombings occurred in other parts of Georgia. In nearby Sasser, Georgia, two Negro churches were destroyed by fire. One of them had been holding weekly voter registration rallies.

Jackie Robinson happened to be in the area and went to visit the site of Mount Olive Baptist Church and announced on the spot that he would donate $100 to help rebuild the churches. He said he would be willing to serve as honorary chairman of the fund drive for this purpose.

The whole nation was horrified at such a shameful act. In fact, the President of the United States called the burning of the two churches "cowardly as well as outrageous acts."

The Department of Justice immediately sent FBI agents to investigate the burning of the churches. While in Georgia the FBI located three men and charged them with the burning. The men pleaded guilty and were given "light" sentences.

Martin Luther King Jr. and the Albany Movement received help and assurance from Northerners, mainly ministers, who formed nonviolent armies that would come to Albany at a moments notice.

IV

Later in the month the Southern Christian Leadership Conference held its Sixth National Convention in Birmingham. At the convention certain data were made available to the delegates. It was pointed out that in Albany and surrounding counties Negro voter registration had more than doubled from 2,400 to 4,900 mainly because of the efforts of the SCLC.

Martin Luther King Jr. in addressing the convention said supporters of former Marvin Griffin had blamed the "Negro block vote" for beating him in Albany in his "racist" bid for the governorship against Carl Sanders in the Democratic primary. He also mentioned the fact that Albany's Chief of Police called him after the primary and termed the election "interesting" and that he had voted for Mr. Sanders.

The president of the convention, went on to say the chief asked him if he ran for sheriff would the Negro support him. Dr. King replied that he had great admiration for him, if he kept growing. The chief also suggested that Rev. King could influence Mr. Sanders and wondered if an appointment as Director of the State Highway Patrol might be available. The chief immediately repudiated what King had said and replied that Dr. King must have misunderstood some of his inquiries.

At the convention King and Abernathy proposed a drive to admit Negroes to the segregated State University of Alabama and Auburn University, possibly with funds raised for scholarship.

King also met with about 60 persons from the Albany area to discuss ways of uniting forces for a full scale assault on the system of segregation in the city. One major outcome of the meeting was the formation of an Albany unit of the SCLC.

Everything was going along peacefully at the convention until the closing session when Roy James, a white man, rushed from the sixth row onto the stage, where Martin Luther King, Jr. was speaking, and struck him twice in the face. King suffered a bruised left cheekbone and a swelling near the ear. King, nor a half dozen of his associates, nor any of the 300 other persons present made any move to retaliate.

The assailant had been overcome with fury when Rev. King announced that Sammy Davis, Jr. would give a benefit performance for the conference at the Westchester County Playhouse in White Plains, New York. James asserted that Rev. King stood for "race mixing" and denounced Mr. Davis for having married a white woman.

Although Dr. King did not wish to press charges, the police took the assailant into custody and within three hours he had been questioned, taken to Recorders Court, found guilty of assault and battery, and sentenced by Judge C. H. Brown to 30 days in jail and a fine of $25 and costs.

The meeting lasted four days and 425 delegates came from all the southern states, except Texas. Dr. King was re-elected president of the conference. Now the SCLC had coordinated efforts of 75 affiliates. The conference adopted resolutions urging President Kennedy to employ all federal machinery as well as "moral persuasion" to insure equal justice for all citizens.

It declared that the dilatory tactics of the Federal courts in and around the Albany area needed to be investigated by the Federal Department of Justice. The convention also commended James H. Meredith on his efforts to enter the University of Mississippi.

V

Even though King had left Albany and had devoted his attention elsewhere, he did find time to come to New York to accept Premier Ben Bella of Algeria's invitation and have a one hour talk with him at his suite in the Barday Hotel.

At the meeting Mr. Ben Bella and Dr. King made it clear that they believed there was a direct relationship between the injustices of colonialism and injustices of segregation in the United States. The Premier also pointed out that the segregation problems in the United States were widely publicized in Algeria and in Africa.

King expressed great appreciation for the position President Kennedy had taken in speaking out for the independence of Algeria and for his forthright action in the Mississippi crisis.

King certainly tried to make it very, very clear to Mr. Ben Bella that one of the hopeful signs in the United States is that though this problem still confronts us, there is very great concern on the part of many people to solve it. He also pointed out too, that the government made it clear that segregation is unconstitutional and immoral.

The Premier apparently had been watching the struggle for integration in the United States, since he was deeply interested in the plight of the Negro and wanted to discuss it. Mohammed Khemisti, Algeria's Foreign Minister, and Algerian delegate to the United Nations were present at the talks. The delegates were Mohammed Sahnoun and Mohammed Bermebarek. The Premier also met with President Kennedy during the same week. Later during the month of November the question came up concerning the FBI's position in the Albany Movement. Martin Luther King, Jr. and his associates said that FBI agents in Albany, Georgia, sided with the city and the segregationists. And for that reason the FBI had not done an effective job of investigating, beatings and other intimidations of Negroes in the South. The Justice Department in Washington, however, declined to comment on Dr. King's remarks.

King implied that one of the great problems we face with the FBI in the South is that the agents are white Southerners who have been influenced by the mores of the community. To maintain their status, they have to be friendly with the local police. He concluded by suggesting that the federal government should consider assigning agents from outside of the South who are at least in agreement with the laws of the land.

A review of 1962, revealed that little, if any tangible progress occurred in Albany and many Southern cities. The public facilities and public schools showed only token integration. Nevertheless there were some notable achievements. For the first time Negroes voted in Albany and surrounding counties and let their voices be heard. And perhaps the most important was that Martin Luther King, Jr. and the Negroes learned a lesson in Albany. King later admitted his mistake. He said, "We attacked the political power structure instead of the economic power structure. You don't win against a political power structure where you don't have the votes. But you can win against an economic power to make the difference between a merchant's profit and loss."

The year 1962 was truly a year of mass arrests, demonstrations, and many whites along with Negroes went to jail by the hundreds. And they went with a new sense of dignity and understanding. So another chapter in the life and times of Martin Luther King, Jr. came to a close.

Chapter Fourteen
THE BIRMINGHAM MOVEMENT

After Martin Luther King, Jr. left Albany at the end of 1962, he announced early in 1963 that he would lead demonstrations in Birmingham, Alabama, until "Pharaoh lets God's people go."

Wyatt T. Walker explained the theory that governed King's planning: "We've got to have a crisis to begin with. To take a moderate approach, hoping to get white help doesn't work. They nail you to the cross and it stops the enthusiasm of the followers. You've got to have a crisis."

The Negroes and their leaders made their crisis, but it was not done overnight. It was carefully planned and carried out to military precision. Martin Luther King, Jr. went to Birmingham to conduct workshops in non-violent methods with other local Negro leaders. He requested and got 200 people who were willing to go to jail for the CAUSE.

The opposition was busy at work also, under the direction of the Public Safety Commissioner Theophilus Eugene ("Bull") Connor—a man who was somewhat a symbol of police brutality. Since Connor was running for mayor against a relative moderate, Albert Boutwell, the leaders of the Movement decided not to press the desegregation issue until after the April 2 election. Therefore, King decided to continue his speaking engagements. He made 28 speeches in 16 cities in the United States.

On April 5, King and his associates came to Birmingham and put their plans to work. Meanwhile, Mr. Connor lost the election, but refused to relinquish his power.

The leaders knew that Connor had sent his spies into the Negro community to seek information and fearing that their phones were tapped, King and his associates drafted a code. King was "JFK," Abernathy, "Dean," Shuttlesworth "Bull," and John Drew "Pope John." The demonstrators were called

"Baptismal candidates" and the whole operation was labeled "Project C—for Confrontation."

Day after day Negroes protested. And day after day they were arrested. The Negroes had created their crisis. And Connor had made it a success. President Kennedy later in a meeting with King said, "The civil rights movements owes Bull Connor as much as it owes Abraham Lincoln." Because of the methods Connor used in handling the demonstrators, his actions became front page news in all major newspapers.

On May 12, King was arrested and jailed for defying an injunction that prohibited the Negroes from demonstrating and for violating a city ordinance. While King was in jail, eight of Alabama's top white religious leaders issued formal statements calling the Birmingham demonstrations "unwise and untimely." King wrote a reply from his cell on pieces of toilet paper, the margin of newspapers and anything else he had at his disposal, since they would not allow him any writing paper. He secretly passed it out in bits through an aide.[21]

After President Kennedy and Attorney General Robert F. Kennedy had received telegrams urging them to end this "reign of terror" in Birmingham immediately, the President called about Martin Luther King, Jr.'s arrest. But there was no basis for federal intervention.

King's arrest brought violence to Birmingham. On several occasions some Negroes started hurling rocks at the policemen. The rock throwing was the most serious incident in all of the 12 days of the direct action campaign. After the rock throwing incident every volunteer was required to sign a commitment card that pledged him to nonviolence.[22]

To stimulate Federal intervention, some Negroes went to the Courthouse to register. They were told they could register, but they could not all go in like a parade. Another group of Negroes came to register and was seized and arrested. This was the only way they found to get the United States Department of Justice to intervene. Since Negroes were arrested for the violation of the 14th and 15th amendments, the Federal government sent troops to Birmingham.

On May 9, a full agreement on a limited desegregation package plan brought an end to the five weeks racial crisis.

A bi-racial committee finally met after repeated efforts by Burke Marshall, Chief of the U.S. Justice Department Civil Rights Division.

Most of the details of the agreement were announced in a news conference by Rev. Fred L. Shuttlesworth, President of the Alabama Christian Movement for Human Rights, an affiliate of the SCLC. His announcement, along with statements by Dr. Martin Luther King, Jr., and the Rev. Ralph D. Abernathy, indicated the terms of the agreement reached with white business and civic leaders. Briefly this agreement concerned public accommodations hiring Negroes, legal treatment, and other aspects of human dignity in general.[23]

II

Following the long months of violence in Birmingham, Dr. King dropped from the public view for a time. While he was preaching non-violence, violence was erupting everywhere — Jackson, Miss.; Cambridge, Md.; Danville, Va.; and CORE's lonesome "freedom walker," William Moore, was shot and killed on April 23 near Attalla, Ala.

While Martin Luther King, Jr. was traveling around the country making quiet speeches, he was also working on *Why We Can't Wait,* a book about Birmingham and the failure of integration there and elsewhere. King narrates the whole strategy of Birmingham and reviews the progress of the Negro since Reconstruction. He shows how completely irrational it is to expect the Negro to derive hope from past events. He discusses the question "Why 1963?" and concerns himself with the effects of the Church, civil rights organizations, and the Black Muslims.[24]

The concluding sentence in the book is the most significant of all. It states Martin Luther King, Jr.'s philosophy: "Nonviolence, the answer to the Negroes' need, may become the answer to the most desperate need of all humanity." [25]

III

Mississippi's NAACP leader, Medger Evers, was assassinated outside his home in Jackson, Miss., on June 12. Ironically the assassination happened the day before the late President John F. Kennedy delivered his Civil Rights message to the country on nation-wide television. The address was one of the most important documents about the Negro ever delivered by a President.[26] The message was also significant because some of the same points the President mentioned, Martin Luther King, Jr., had talked about for years.

Chapter Fifteen

THE MARCH ON WASHINGTON

On July 2, the major Negro organizations: NAACP, SCLC, SNICK, National Council of Negro Women, NAACP Legal Defense and Education Fund, Brotherhood of Sleeping Car Porters, met at a luncheon at the Roosevelt Hotel in New York and agreed to coordinate their planning and activities for "racial desegregation and equal opportunity."

After a meeting of the Leadership Conference on Civil Rights, these organizations met and announced the march on Washington. The march was suggested by Asa Philip Randolph. Back in January he suggested a march on Washington to dramatize the plight of unemployed Negroes, but nobody was listening—except a few students and militants. Then came the Birmingham Movement, mass arrests, demonstrations, and the leaders remembered what Randolph had done in the past and what he wanted to do in the future. Consequently, they chose him as the Director of the march and he named Bayard Rustin as his deputy director.

To the strange dismay of some, there was some opposition to the march. One of the most noteworthy was Arthur Spingarn, white, and President of the NAACP. Mr. Spingarn had serious doubts about the wisdom of the march. He felt that instead of influencing senators to help break a filibuster, it might alienate them. Representative James A. Halsey (Democrat of Florida) said the march could touch off an ugly, blood-letting riot accomplished, perhaps, by killings. Even Representative Emmanuel L. Cellar of New York, said the march might cause uncommitted legislators to turn against the Civil Rights Bill.

Powerful politicians and men in labor and business urged the leaders to abandon the march; it was unwise, imprudent, unnecessary and perhaps illegal, they said. President Kennedy, however, backed the march. As planned this will not be a march on Washington. He said: "Rather it is the great tradition of peaceful assembly for a redress of grievances, said the President. I'll look forward to being here. I am sure members of Congress will be here." He concluded by saying, "We want citizens to come to Washington if they feel that they're not having their rights expressed."

I

The leaders met again in New York and over 1,500 organizations were contacted and regional directors were named. The leaders distributed a manual of instructions to the organizations that had expressed an interest in the march.

The booklet was entitled, "Organizing Manual No. 1." It was intended to ensure an orderly, efficient, self-disciplined demonstration, reducing the risk of violence to the minimum. Mr. Randolph had stressed two points that the leaders were to follow during the march. One was that the organizers for the most part would be churches, since they would be playing a leading role in recruiting the marchers and arranging for their food and transportation to and from the Capitol.

The second precaution emphasized by Mr. Randolph was that the marchers would go directly to one of 51 designated assembly points when they arrived in Washington. The second plan, however, was abandoned.

After the first three meetings, CORE joined the other organizations and later four more persons were named as march leaders: Walter Reuther, head of the United Auto Workers; the Reverend Dr. Eugene Carson Blake of the National Council of Churches; Rabbi Joachim Prinz, head of the American Jewish Congress, and Walter Ahmarin of the National Catholic Council for Interracial Justice.

It was estimated that 100,000 persons would come to Washington and that the march would exceed $65,000. Most of the expenses to be shared by the seven organizations.

As the date of the march drew near, the leaders went to extraordinary lengths to insure a peaceful demonstration. At first it seemed that the event would be a failure. Newspapers reported that the public was not showing a general interest. They reported that sponsors were having difficulties in filling

chartered buses and other means of transportation. As it
sometimes happens, the press was wrong. Near the end of
August, the march headquarters was receiving requests from
organizations who wanted to be part of this mammoth event.

In fact hundreds of Americans in Europe went to their
embassies and registered their support for the march on Washington.

The petition read:

> I cannot physically participate in the march on Washington
> but I _____ have been
> tremendously stirred by so disciplined an exhibition of dignity
> and courage and persistence, and would like to associate myself
> with it.

At first it was reported that about 25,000 from New York
would participate. Later this figure rose to 40,000. It was also
estimated that over 100,000 would come to Washington from all
over the United States.

Organizations all over the country were busy staging
benefits to raise money to send people to Washington. Johnny
Mathis appeared at Miles College in Birmingham for a benefit
performance. Paul Newman and Marlon Brando, the actors,
took part in a performance to raise funds for the march at the
Apollo Theater in New York. A crowd of 2,000 turned out
for the show. Funds came from various places. The American
Jewish Committee gave $1,000. Bishop Bryan J. McEntegart
of the Brooklyn Diocese of the Roman Catholic Church donated
$5,000.

All financial efforts were not successful. One of the most
disappointing rallies was held at the Polo Grounds in New York
and sponsored by the 50,000 members of the New York Association of the Elks and Improved Benevolent Protection Orders of
the Elks of the World. Only 2,000 persons attended the Polo
Grounds that will seat over 50,000 persons.

The sponsors attributed the poor attendance to a lack of
support from the Civil Rights groups and also to ineffective
publicity and advertising and a lack of door-to-door promotion.

Large buttons, one and a half times the size of a silver
dollar were to be worn by the marchers. The button, black on
white, showed a white and black hand clasped in friendship.

From the top to bottom, the legend read: March on Washington for Job and Freedom, August 28, 1963.

Weeks before the March, Jay Hardo, an 82 year old man left Dayton, Ohio, on a bicycle for Washington. A week later Ledger Smith left Chicago on roller skates. As Monday came, things were looking as if the march was going to be a success. Many persons were leaving now from Vermont, Connecticut, Oregon, Nevada, Washington, California and North Carolina.

The day before the March, August 27, the tempo began picking up. In New York City 80,000 lunches were made by volunteers of all faiths for the Capitol rally. By Tuesday night, most of the ten leaders were at the Statler Hotel making last minute arrangements.

II

During the night, special buses, trains and airplanes began moving into Washington from all parts of the United States. Some of the early arrivals went to picket the Justice Department. As of 7 a.m. there were more policemen than marchers on the assembly grounds around the Washington Monument. About 1,000 marchers had assembled by 7:30. Slowly the crowd continued to build and near 9:45 there were about 40,000 people. Throughout the following hours crowds constantly streamed into the nation's Capitol. At 11 a.m. there were about 95,000 on the slopes of the Monument.

The march from the Washington Monument to the Lincoln Memorial, a distance of about 8/10 of a mile, had been scheduled to start at 11:30 a.m. But at 11:15, fifteen minutes ahead of schedule, the march began when a group of Negroes started strolling away from the Monument grounds on the way to the Memorial. Hundreds, then thousands, and tens of thousands followed. Constitution and Independence Avenues were transformed into an oasis of placards and banners.

At the Lincoln Memorial, the marchers regrouped on both sides of the pool and elms and oaks stretched almost a mile to the east and stood around the steps of the Memorial where the speakers were seated.

At the Memorial, the marchers were first entertained by well-known entertainers. Singers Joan Baez, Bobby Darin,

Josh White, Odetta, Bob Dylan, Peter, Paul and Mary, Lena Horne, rendered hymns, songs, and civil rights songs. Josephine Baker flew to Washington from her Paris home. Author James Baldwin, actors Paul Newman, Charlton Heston, Burt Lancaster and Sidney Poitier made appearances. Actor Marlon Brando brandished an electric cattle prod of the kind sometimes used by policemen against civil rights demonstrations.

Hall of Famer Jackie Robinson and his son David were present. Sammy Davis, Jr., Wilt Chamberlain and Julnius Kellog, Dick Gregory were also there. Marian Anderson was tied up by traffic, arrived in tears and too late to sing the National Anthem that began the ceremonies at the Lincoln Memorial. It was sung by Camilla William. Miss Anderson, however, later sung one of her most beloved spirituals, "He's Got The Whole World In His Hands."

But entertainment was not what the marchers had gathered for around the Memorial. Finally, the formal program began. Speaker followed speaker to the platform. Each was supposed to talk for four minutes, but each spoke longer. James Farmer, who was in a Louisiana jail, had his speech read by Floyd B. McKissick.

For almost three hours, the crowd listened to speakers who emphasized the . . .

GOALS OF RIGHTS MARCH

(1) A comprehensive civil rights bill from the present Congress, including provisions guaranteeing access to public accomodations, adequate and integrated education, protection of the right to vote, better housing, and authority for the Attorney General to seek injunctive relief when individuals constitutional rights are violated.
(2) Withholding of Federal funds from all programs in which discrimination exists.
(3) Desegregation of all public schools in 1963.
(4) A reduction in Congressional seats in states where citizens are disenfranchised.
(5) A stronger Executive Order prohibiting discrimination in all housing programs supported by Federal Funds.
(6) A massive Federal Program to train and place unemployed workers.
(7) An increase in the minimum wage to $2 an hour. The Federal minimum covering workers in interstate industries.

(8) Extension of the Fair Labor Standards Act to include exempted fields of employment.

(9) A Federal Fair Employment Practices Act barring discrimination in all employments.

Of all the participants seven were distinguished: Asa Philip Randolph, the Director and Father of the March, saying that this was the beginning and the ending and that "wave after wave" would come back to Washington if immediate changes were not made in American life; the Reverend Dr. Eugene Carson Blake of the National Council of Churches, indicting American Christians and saying repeatedly: "We come . . . late . . . we come . . . but we come;" Rabbi Joachim Prinz, recalling the downfall of Germany and saying that the basic problem is not evil, but silence; Roy Wilkins, introduced as "the acknowledged leader" of the Civil Rights Movement, warning that the President's proposals represent too moderate an approach that if any part is weakened or eliminated, the remainder will be little more than sugar water; John Lewis calling for a real and "serious revolution;" Mahalia Jackson singing a gospel song that sent a spasm through the crowd; and Martin Luther King, Jr., electrifying the multitudes and providing the highlight of the day with his blueprint of a dream big enough to include all men and all children and all America.

When Martin Luther King, Jr. came to the lectern, his introduction was drowned out with thunderous applause by the cheers of those who saw him heading toward the speakers' platform. Even though he had spoken before thousands, he did not want to take any chances of forgetting what he had intended to say, therefore, he read for a time from a prepared manuscript.

He was full of the symbolism of Lincoln and Ghandi and the cadences of the Bible. He would occasionally look down at his manuscript, and then he would expound into a flight of pungent language and speak of a dream big enough to include all Americans and mankind.

"I have a dream," King cried over and over again, and the audience began cheering, but King never pausing, brought silence as he continued.

"I have a dream," he went on "that even the state of Mississippi, a state sweltering with people's injustices, sweltering with the heat of oppression, will be transformed into an oasis of freedom and justice."

"I have a dream," he went on, "that my four little children will one day live in a nation where they will not be judged by the color of their skin but by the content of their character." [27]

When he finished, the marchers screamed, cheered and cried; then caught themselves and wondered what had happened to them as they sat down quietly.

After King's speech, there were some final speeches and ceremonies, but for all intents and purposes the day was over. Later in the afternoon, the leaders met with President Kennedy at the White House.

The President told them: "We have witnessed today in Washington tens of thousands of Americans — both Negroes and white — exercising their rights to assemble peaceably. The cause of 200,000 Negroes has been advanced by the program conducted so appropriately before the nation's shrine to the Great Emancipator, but even more significant is the contribution to all mankind . . . ."

By nightfall the marchers had left Washington by whatever way they had come. And they knew that if the march did not change any votes in Congress or any opinions in America that it had changed them!

The mammoth march on Washington was eminently successful. Despite widespread apprehension and fear of violence, the march was orderly and peaceful. Over 200,000 Americans, Negroes and Caucasians, petitioned their government to pass Civil Rights legislation, create more jobs and eliminate discrimination in employment.

For a short time it appeared that there were more whites than Negroes. Soon the Negroes became the predominant group at an approximate ratio of 3 to 1.

The March on Washington was covered by all the major television networks and newspapers and it was acclaimed a success the world over. It was praised in Bonn, Paris, Cairo, Algiers, Ghana, Hong Kong, and Ottawa, as well as, by the United Nations.

The March made an immeasurable impact on Congress, which later passed a Civil Rights Bill. The march impressed millions of people the world over. It moved men and women as they had never been moved before. The March made clear all that had gone before in the year of the Negro Revolt.

The leaders, perhaps, best expressed the triumph of the march: "We have subpoenaed the conscience of the nation," said Martin Luther King, Jr. "We have developed a new unity among the leadership of the civil rights movement," said Asa Phillip Randolph. "It is the first step in the building of a coalition of conscience," declared Walter Reuther. "It did something for Negroes to see white people there with them and not in any condescending relation," said Roy Wilkins.

No one who saw the march or participated could come to any other conclusion than that those thousands of Marching Negroes were not able to accept the responsibilities of first class citizenship.

August 28, 1963 will go down in history as being the greatest demonstration for Civil Rights.

III

Three months later, on November 22, 1963, President John F. Kennedy was assassinated in Dallas, Texas. The slaying of the President shocked the United States and the world more than any single event in modern times.

Men and women across the country were sobbing everywhere, and they did not have to explain why. It touched all men directly, but some more than others. Government leaders of most nations and private citizens throughout the world sent messages of grief and sympathy to Washington. Even in Russia, press, radio and television praised the late President. Premier Nikita Khrushchev and his wife sent personal messages of sympathy.

"The assassination of President Kennedy killed not only a man but a complex of illusion. It demolished the myth that hate and violence can be confined to an airtight chamber to be employed against but a few. Suddenly, the truth was revealed that hate is a contagion; that it grows and spreads as a disease; that no society is so healthy that it can automatically maintain its immunity," declared Dr. King.

"No President except perhaps Lincoln had ever sufficiently given that degree of support to the Negro's struggle for freedom to justify the Negro confidence and endorsement." King had to conclude that the then known facts about Kennedy were not adequate to make an unqualified judgment in his favor. And yet had Kennedy lived, Dr. King would probably have endorsed him in the 1964 Presidential election. King was impressed by Mr. Kennedy's qualities, many elements of his records and by his program. Dr. King had learned to enjoy and respect his charm and incisive mind. Martin Luther King, Jr. expressed his respect and admiration for the late President John Fitzgerald Kennedy in Epitaph and Challenge.[28]

Martin Luther King, Jr. reached a major milestone in his illustrious career when he was selected *Time*'s Man of the Year for 1963. King made it as a man and not as a Negro, even though there had never been a Negro selected until that year. Being the person who had dominated the news thereby making an indelible mark on history, King met all the requirements for *Time*'s selection.

Another chapter comes to a close in the life and times of Martin Luther King, Jr. It was one of the most tragic and noteworthy years in America's history!

Chapter Sixteen

TARGET – ST. AUGUSTINE

The year 1964 was a triumphant one not only for Martin Luther King, Jr., but for Negroes in general. It was the year that the most significant Civil Rights legislation was passed since Reconstruction. There is little doubt that Negro people praised Dr. King for his help in getting it enacted. It was the year that Negroes made more gains in employment, housing and school desegregation, than any other. More riots, however, occurred than any other year and more people, both whites and Negroes, were killed or injured than before, because of the civil rights movement.

It was an illustrious year for Martin Luther King, Jr., in that he received the John F. Kennedy Award; met Pope Paul VI; and reached the apex of his career, when he won the Nobel Peace Prize.

I

In early January, President Johnson telephoned Dr. King and invited him to the White House to discuss his campaign for the Civil Rights Bill and poverty program. The purpose of the meeting was to have King along with Roy Wilkins, Whitney Young and James Farmer to act as consultants and advise him in the future on civil rights matters.

One of the chief items discussed was the pending message that the President would use to cope with the poverty problem. The President shared their hope that the House of Representatives would debate the Civil Rights Bill on the floor before February.

The meeting proved to be fruitful for both the President and the leaders. First, the President realized that the Civil Rights Bill and the poverty program were vital issues that concerned the entire nation. Secondly, the leaders knew the President's crusade against poverty was depended upon improvements in education, both general and vocational, and that they were tied to the Civil Rights issue. Thirdly, the leaders were convinced that the President would do all in his power to see that the Civil Rights Bill and Poverty program would be approved by Congress.

There were some speculations that the President had called the leaders to the White House to discuss a compromise, however, such was not discussed. King summed up the feelings of the leaders when he said, "We feel that this bill should not be watered down any further. We are not prepared to compromise in any form."

The world was aware of King's desires and struggles as evidenced by eight Swedish members of Parliament who nominated him for the 1964 Nobel Peace Prize. In a letter to the Norwegian Nobel Committee, they said, "the Reverend Dr. Martin Luther King, Jr., who has led American Negroes in their fight for equality since 1955, had succeeded in keeping his followers to the principle of nonviolence. And without Dr. King's confirmed and effectiveness of this principle, demonstrations and marches could easily have become violent and ended with the spilling of blood."

Dr. King was deeply honored over the nomination and thrilled at the thought that he had been selected as a possible recipient of the Nobel Peace Prize. Even if he did not win, King was aware that, now, the principle of non-violence was being recognized the world over and that people must continue to use it.

Speaking engagements, nominations and awards were constantly pouring into King's office and it was a hard job to select any one speaking engagement or award. King, however, felt that he had to speak to the 2,500 members of the United Federation of Teachers at their spring luncheon in the Americana Hotel in New York City.

At the luncheon, King predicted there would be enormous civil rights demonstrations throughout the country and that they would be non-violent. Violence, he said, "would play into the hands of many opponents in the South who would be happy if we turned to violence."

In his speech, he said that race relations had reached a crisis but he was certain that "the white majority was willing to meet the Negro halfway." King's stand on non-violence was in direct opposition to that taken by the late Malcolm X, leader of the Black Nationalists. Malcolm X believed that violence was the only language the white man understood. He made a statement that Negroes should arm themselves. King, however, said that Malcolm X's "call to arms" was ineffective and immoral.

Dr. King concluded his speech by saying poor quality and segregated education would not be overcome without some cost to the white majority. "It would be pleasant if it could be painless, but there are no miracles. Many people who object to necessary changes are inherently against desegregation. However, many others who have opposed change are not for segregation. They are too inconvenient for their children," he said. While at the luncheon, Dr. King received the John Dewey Award, which is conferred annually to the outstanding citizen who has aided education.

II

In the spring, the Southern Christian Leadership Conference selected St. Augustine, Florida, as the prime target of its "long hot summer" campaign for civil rights demonstrations. There were several reasons why this city was chosen. First, it is the oldest city in the United States and one of the most segregated. Secondly, the Conference was determined that this city would not celebrate its quadricentennial as a segregated city. It was reasoned that if the oldest and most segregated city could be desegregated, the other cities could be also. That was not, however, entirely true, but a start had to be made.

On May 25, King and the Conference moved their forces into St. Augustine. After consulting with the local Negro leaders in advance, the Conference began asking the Negro community for help. Most of the Negroes, however, feared losing their jobs and would not take part in the movement. This made it necessary for Dr. King to make an appeal to "men of conscience" to join the anti-segregation drive in the nation's oldest city. He sent telegrams to chaplains at Yale and Boston Universities, Smith College, Andover-Newton and many others.

Demonstrators came from other states to lend a hand and in two days the number reached over 200. On May 28, the 200 demonstrators marched at night from the Negro section of the city to the downtown. The police and St. John's County sheriff's deputies had moved in to prevent attacks on the marchers. White attackers, however, still knocked some of the marchers down, before the police could move in. Actually, some of the officers acted rather slowly in protecting some people involved in the march. The police did, however, escort the marchers back into the Negro residential section of the city.

The marchers held another meeting at the New St. Paul's African Methodist Episcopal Church that night. Later the authorities came to the church and told the leaders they could not hold further mass marches without a permit. They were warned that if they marched without a permit, they would be arrested.

The next day fifteen Negroes attempted to obtain service at local motels and restaurants and were arrested. They were held in lieu of $500 bonds in the St. John's County jail on charges of conspiracy, being undesirable guests and trespassing.

The Negro leaders tried to meet with the white community leaders to discuss their demands for desegregation of motels, hotels, restaurants and for better jobs. Neither officials or business leaders, however, indicated any willingness to discuss the Negro leaders' demands.

The following two nights the demonstrators marched into the downtown area again. On the second night, they were met by about 80 Klu Klux Klansmen and other whites armed with bicycle chains, clubs, tire irons, knives and firearms. The marchers went back to the Negro section of the city because they did not want any violence.

The business leaders should have realized what all the bad publicity was doing to the city. St. Augustine is an East coast tourist and fishing center. The city got 80 percent of its income from tourists. According to the National Park Service, visitors to the Old Spanish Fort declined about 45 percent during the first ten days in June compared to the same period in 1963. The officials should have realized that of the 15,000 persons in St. Augustine, 23 percent of the population were Negroes and that they wanted better jobs and a voice in the city government. The officials pointed out that all city-owned or supported facilities were desegregated. That was, however, in theory only, not in fact.

<h1 style="text-align:center">III</h1>

Dr. King and his aides were constantly meeting with the Negro leaders in the community. At each meeting Dr. King asked the leaders to urge the marchers to leave all firearms, knives and weapons home and to be non-violent.

Of all the people that came to St. Augustine in answer to Dr. King's appeal, Mrs. Malcolm Peabody was probably the oldest and most celebrated. Mrs. Peabody, 72 years old, and the mother of the Governor of Massachusetts was even arrested. She was arrested as she was preparing to sit down with a bi-racial group in the segregated dining room of the Ponce de Leon Motor Lodge.

She was charged with trespassing, being an undesirable guest, and conspiracy, after a warning, and jail under a $450 bond. Taken into custody with Mrs. Peabody were Mrs. Donald J. Campbell, wife of the dean of the Episcopal Theological Seminary at Cambridge, Massachusetts; Professor J. Lawrence Burholder, a Harvard Divinity School professor; Mrs. Nellie Mitchell; Mrs. Lillian Robinson; Mrs. Georgia Ann Reed; Miss Kuter Ubanks; and Mrs. Rosale Phelps.

Until Mrs. Peabody's arrest, L. O. Davis, Sheriff of St. John's County, had refused to accept anything but cash bonds for the marchers, and few of them made bond. Mrs. Peabody announced that she would not leave jail if she had to pay cash. Ironically enough, the Sheriff accepted bonds signed by professional bondsmen. Mrs. Peabody's presence, therefore, served one useful and immediate purpose.

While Dr. King was in St. Augustine, he received many threats on his life. He appealed to the Federal Government to protect him and the demonstrators. He advised the White

House that there was a breakdown in local law enforcement. He was assured that Federal and state authorities would see that he and the demonstrators were protected.

At the same time Dr. King tried to reason with the white leaders and told them that they could prevent a resumption of widespread demonstrations by making "good faith" moves toward ending discrimination. The white leaders, however, turned deaf ears.

Embittered by months of demonstrations, the white leaders blamed Dr. King and his aides for the trouble. The leaders said that they were there to stop the city's 400th anniversary celebration next year.

Day after day tension was growing greater and greater. Governor Farrie C. Bryant was silent on the situation in St. Augustine and refused to intervene. Things were getting so bad that King and his aides declared: "That they have worked in some difficult communities, but they have never worked in one as "lawless" as St. Augustine." After months of demonstrations, the Governor finally sent about 75 State patrolllmen to St. Augustine and said he would do whatever was necessary to protect the demonstrators.

Everyday more and more people, both local and out-of-towners would participate in the demonstrations, until the number rose well over 500. When this occurred the Negro leaders knew that now was the time to march, like they had never marched before. Shortly, the 500 or more demonstrators assembled in the New St. Paul's African Methodist Episcopal Church for a rally. After the rally the demonstrators left the church and started walking downtown. When they reached the town square a mob of about 70 whites was in a small park that lies in the center of town. Hundreds of townspeople lined the streets and watched. The State troopers, accompanied by the Sheriff's deputies, made a line alongside the marchers as they rounded the Old Slave Market. At this point a state trooper with dogs ordered the mob to disperse. When they refused, he threw a tear gas bomb in the midst of them. This, however, stopped the mob for only a few minutes. They picked up bricks from the flower gardens and threw them at the policemen. It took more tear gas and threats to break

146

them up. The crowd finally dispersed and the marchers returned to the church.

Sheriff Davis finally arrived after the violence had begun. He declared that the Negro leaders had failed to live up to an agreement to inform him when they planned to march. "We were unprepared," he said.

After continuous turmoil the city officials still would not yield to the Negroes demands. King felt that some dramatic incident must occur to show the nation and the world how segregated St. Augustine really was. Therefore, after meeting with his associates and the local Negro leaders, he announced that he would go to jail. Most of the Negro leaders felt that if King were arrested, he would be playing into the officials' hands. King's reasoning, however, was two-fold in purpose. First, if he went to jail he would be dramatizing discrimination against Negroes in the city. Secondly, if he showed the local Negro community that he did not mind going to jail, more would participate in the movement. At this point, the movement had gained too much momentum for any one person to stop it.

The following day King and eight companions went to the Monson Motor Lodge Restaurant to seek service. They were, however, stopped on the doorsteps by the president and general manager, James Brock.

Mr. Brock told Reverend King that he and his party were not wanted. Reverend King asked Mr. Brock if he understood the "humiliation the Negroes have to go through." Mr. Brock said he would integrate his business if the substantial white citizens of the community asked him to or if he were served with a Federal Court order.

"You realize it would be detrimental to my business to serve you here," he said. Then Mr. Brock turned to the television camera on the scene, smiled and said, "I invited my many friends through the country to come to Monson's. We expect to remain segregated."

After a twenty minute discussion, the Sheriff and his deputy finally arrived and took King and his companions to jail. Dr. King stayed in jail for several days and the demonstrations continued.

147

After Dr. King's arrest several incidents occurred that proved to be turning points and broke the stalemate in the movement and gave it another energizing whiff of legal oxygen. First, in Jacksonville, Florida, Federal District Judge Bryan Simpson said in a court order that there had been a deliberate attempt by the law enforcement officers in St. Augustine to break the civil rights movement by punishing those arrested. He, therefore, ordered bonds for the defendents in sit-in cases reduced. He also ordered Sheriff Davis to stop putting prisoners in an outdoor pen in the open sun and in padded cells.

"More than cruel and unusual punishment has been shown. Here is exposed in its raw ugliness, studied and cynical brutally deliberated and contrived to break men, physically and mentally," Judge Simpson said in his order.

Busloads of Negroes came from other states to give impetus to the movement. Demonstrators came from Savanah, Georgia, Gadsden and Birmingham, Alabama, New York and Massachusetts.

Later during the same week a grand jury began investigating the racial situation. Dr. King was brought from the jail to the county Court House at the request of the jury and testified for three hours. At the hearing Dr. King explained the Southern Christian Leadership Conference's role in the movement. After the session, he was placed in the back seat of a police car alongside a large German shepherd dog and returned to jail.

While Dr. King was in jail, the Sheriff's department received many threatening calls on Dr. King's life. The Sheriff realizing that he could not afford to let any harm come to King, slipped him out of town at night, under heavy guard. He was taken to the Duval County jail in nearby Jacksonville.

J. B. Stoner, an Atlanta lawyer, who represented the klansmen in court, arrived in St. Augustine and organized a march in opposition to King's campaign. Waving a Confederate flag, Mr. Stoner stood in the Old Slave Market and told a crowd of about 350 whites "tonight we are going to see if white people have any rights." The "coons" have been parading around St. Augustine for a long time, he said. He also called Dr. King a long-time associate of communists and referred to the Jew-stacked communist-loving Supreme Court.

The same night 200 whites, led by J. B. Stoner and more than 100 uniformed policemen, several police dogs and about 20 newsmen marched silently through the Negro section of the city without an incident, to the surprise of many.

"Why St. Augustine did not make progress in race relations was because of the St. John County Chapter of the Florida Coalition of Patriotic Societies," according to Charles Arnade, professor of history at the University of South Florida. Dr. Arnade said, "St. Augustine was dominated by a small, narrow-minded power structure which cannot see anything." And that they were years behind in everything.

Moderate whites said it was difficult to begin negotiations of the city's racial problem under the present atmosphere. Both Negro leaders and city officials, however, began putting out feelers for the appointment of a bi-racial committee to arrange a truce.

The city received another disappointing blow in addition to the continuing decrease of tourists, when it went into the Federal District Court at Jacksonville and asked Judge Simpson to amend his injunction on a police ban against night marchers. The Judge declined to alter the injunction. Attorney General James W. Kynes told the Federal Judge that evidence of clear and present danger had arisen since he issued his order earlier that week. Judge Simpson said violence could be prevented by better law enforcement.

IV

After spending two days in jail Dr. King was released under a $900 bond. He left St. Augustine once again and immediately went to Atlanta and then to Springfield, Massachusetts.

Dr. King spoke at the 78th annual Springfield College commencement. In his address, he told the students that too many Americans were sleeping through the "great civil rights revolutions like Rip Van Winkle's." Too many people find themselves living in a great period of social change but fail to adopt a new attitude necessary for that change. Dr. King concluded his speech by pledging to return to St. Augustine and stay there until the problem of segregation was solved.

The next day he received a standing ovation from 10,000 persons at Yale University's 263rd commencement and an honorary doctor of law degree.

Dr. King was among 12 other recipients of honorary degrees. He was cited for an "eloquence that has kindled the nation's sense of outrage" and for having displayed a "steadfast refusal to countenance violence." Dr. King's citation read:

> When outrage and shame together shall one day have vindicated the promise of legal, social and economic opportunity for all citizens, the generations of Americans yet unborn will echo our admiration.

Later during the week Dr. King returned to St. Augustine, after a brief stop in Atlanta to answer some of his overflowing correspondence.

After months of demonstrations, Governor Bryant finally named an emergency committee to "restore communications" between white and Negro leaders. Dr. King believed personal intervention by President Johnson had moved the Governor to appoint the committee. Dr. King had called the White House and the Justice Department several times during the campaign, and asked for Federal Marshals. Dr. King said the Federal Government played a chief role in getting the bi-racial committee organized.

Earlier in Tallahassee, Governor Bryant said he had informed the White House law and order would be maintained. The committee served until a permanent one could be named by the special grand jury. Since it opened the channels of communication, the formation of the committee was the first step toward the solution of the problem.

After the appointment of the bi-racial committee, King felt that the Governor was displaying good faith, and, therefore, called off further civil rights demonstrations. He did not leave St. Augustine, however, until a meaningful resolution of the conflict had been worked out.

King and his associates' next project was testing the Civil Rights Bill after President Johnson signed it. The group met around the clock until finally they agreed on a two-phrase program that would be executed by the Southern Christian Leadership Conference.

The first phase was called Operation Dialogue. Local affiliates of the Conference would sound out business and community leaders all over the South and seek to persuade them to announce their compliance with the law.

Then after about a week, the second phase, called Operation Implementation would be executed. This was the actual testing of hotels, restaurants, motels and other businesses, to determine whether they would serve Negroes. Those who turned Negroes away would face lawsuits in the Federal Courts.

Six deep Southern cities had already indicated that they would not obey the law and those cities would face massive direct-action programs similar to that staged in St. Augustine. The six cities listed were Birmingham, Tuscaloosa, Montgomery, Selma, and Gadsden, all in Alabama, and Albany, Georgia.

President Johnson signed the Civil Rights Act of 1964 about five hours after the House of Representatives had completed Congressional action on the bill. It was the most far-reaching Civil Rights law since Reconstruction days. The President announced steps to implement it and called on all Americans to help eliminate the vestiges of injustice in America. The President signed the Bill in the East Room of the White House before television cameras.

Martin Luther King, Jr. was among the invited guests on hand for the ceremony and was among the first to receive one of the pens used by the President to sign the bill. That pen was one of Dr. King's most cherished possessions. He wanted several pens to give to some of his associates who played a major role in helping get the bill passed, but the pens were limited.

It has become self-evident, now, that without Martin Luther King, Jr.'s help the Civil Rights Bill of 1964 would not have been passed. There is little doubt that the historical

1963 March on Washington also played a major role in the Bill's enactment.

VI

While Negroes were demonstrating in the South, Negroes were rioting in the North, specifically in Rochester, New York; Jersey City, Paterson and Elizabeth, New Jersey. A teenage Negro boy was shot and killed by an off-duty white policeman in New York City. Thousands of Negroes rioted in central Harlem protesting the shooting of the youth. Stores were looted, cars turned over, windows smashed, home-made bombs were thrown at policemen and tension was great.

Local Negro leaders who spoke against violence were called "Uncle Toms." Jessie Gray, a local Negro leader, called for "guerilla warfare" and 100 black revolutionaries to counter police brutality.

Things were so tense in New York City that Mayor Robert Wagner invited Martin Luther King, Jr. for a consultation. On July 27, Dr. King left Atlanta on his "peace mission" to New York City. Upon his arrival 69 Harlem groups held a meeting to form the Unity Council of Harlem Organizations. Because of a news conference and meeting with the Mayor, Dr. King could not attend the meeting, and this omission caused some resentment. Resentment was also strong from New York Negro leaders, including Adam Clayton Powell, because Dr. King came to New York in the first place. In fact the Negro leaders were mad as "hell" at Mayor Wagner for importing Dr. King from Atlanta to discuss problems of Harlem.

Dr. King made it clear to the Mayor that the city must deal with Harlem leaders in attempting to solve the city's race problem. And that he had not come to New York "to subvert the local leaders."

Nothing really happened at the meetings with the Mayor, since no major statement was issued other than that the meetings had been "informative." Dr. King, however, tried to interpret for the Mayor the aspirations of the Negro people throughout the nation—aspirations whether expressed in Birmingham or New York. He came away with the feeling that the Mayor had gained new insight on the Negro's problems.

King did accomplish one thing while in New York. He met with Roy Wilkins, Whitney M. Young, Jr., A. Philip Randolph and they signed a statement urging the members of their organizations to observe a "broad curtailment if not total moratorium" on all mass demonstrations until after the November 3 Presidential election.

The statement also was critical of Senator Barry Goldwater. It said, "We believe racism has been injected into the campaign by the Goldwater forces. The Senator himself maintains his position that civil rights matters be left to the states is clear enough language for any Negro American."

James Farmer and John Lewis attended the meeting, but did not sign the statement to halt demonstrations. Farmer and Lewis agreed personally with the statement, but withheld signing it pending meeting of their steering committees.

Later Lewis declared, "Demonstrations must continue. The pressure must be kept on. Demonstrations must be played by ear. If we need to, we will demonstrate in connection with voter registration." As far as Farmer and CORE were concerned, there were no moratorium.

Dr. King endorsed Mr. Goldwater's sincerity, but said that the Senator "articulates a philosophy that if followed in international affairs could plunge the world into an abyss." King forecast a "dark night of social disruption" in the United States if Senator Goldwater were elected President.

Chapter Seventeen
KING WINS NOBEL PEACE PRIZE

Dr. King and his associate, Rev. Ralph D. Abernathy, flew to West Berlin to the Cultural festival at the invitation of Mayor Willy Brandt. The correlation of races and the interdependence of African and Europeans culture was the theme of that year's event in the field of drama, music, ballet and art.

While in West Berlin, King was asked his views on Senator Goldwater. He told the press that he was convinced that the discontent, frustration and despair of disinherited poverty-stricken groups would then erupt into "violence and riots," the like of which we have never seen before, if Senator Goldwater were elected President. Dr. King concluded: "It is important for all responsible persons to see that Mr. Goldwater is defeated." He saw "danger signs of Hitlerism" in the program of the Republican candidate.

King attended Protestant functions in East and West Berlin. He was surprised at the religious freedom that was allowed in East Berlin. He also preached in East Berlin's downtown Marienkirche.

King addressed 25,000 West Berliners at a church rally in Waldruehne Stadium. This was one of the largest crowds to hear an American minister. He spoke for nearly an hour and concluded his speech by saying American Negroes were following the call "to be the conscience of the nation."

Reverend King heard German Church leaders and Christian believers pledge their support of the civil rights movement in America. Bishop Otto Dibeluis, head of the Protestant Church in Berlin, declared "the whole of Christianity will be at your side in your struggle of nonviolence." The Theological School of the Church conferred an honorary degree on King. One of the other highlights of his visit was the joining of Mr. Brandt at the Berlin Philharmonic Hall to pay homage to the late President John F. Kennedy.

I

Dr. King and Rev. Abernathy left Berlin and continued their overseas tour by going to Rome to see Pope Paul VI. The papal audience was arranged by the Most Reverend Paul J. Hallman, Catholic Archbishop of Atlanta, Georgia.

Having an audience with the Pope was quite an honor for a non-Catholic. King had great admiration for the Pope and he knew some of his views. Reverend King and Reverend Abernathy saw the Pope for 25 minutes in the Pope's private library, at the Vatican's Apostic Palace. After the meeting Rev. King said the Pope made it palpably clear that he is a friend of the Negro people and asked him to tell the American Negro people that he is committed to the civil rights movement in the United States. King said he believed that the civil rights movement had received the "endorsement" of the most influential religious leaders in the world and the head of the largest Church in Christiandom.

In the meeting King and Abernathy told the Pope that the Negroes in the United States were making "significant strides" in their struggle against segregation and discrimination. They reported to the Pope that the Civil Rights Act of 1964 was being implemented all over the South, and that they were surprised at the degree of compliance in Southern communities.

King told the Pope, however, that Negroes in large urban areas in the North were confronted with difficult discrimination problems in housing and other fields, and in those counties the Catholic Church is very strong and a reaffirmation of its position on civil rights would mean much.

Pope Paul showed himself well informed on race relations in the United States and the world. The Pope said he was remembering the Negro people daily in his prayers and promised to issue a public pronouncement of his views on interracial problems.

The civil rights leader was deeply encouraged by his meeting with the Pope. With a smile he observed, "that I think new days have come when a Pope meets a fellow who happens to have the name Martin Luther."

The Pope presented Reverend King and Reverend Abernathy with silver medals commemorating the present Ecumenical Council in the Vatican. King and his associate flew to Madrid for a two day "holiday" and later visited London before returning to the United States.

II

The Southern Christian Leadership Conference held its eighth annual convention in Savannah, Georgia, on September 28 and pledged an all-out endorsement of President Johnson. This was the first official endorsement of the President by the Conference. That announcement was an expanded course for the Conference and it moved the organization into a new sphere of civil rights activities. Up to this point the organization was non-political in scope. Maintaining that the Republican nominee, Senator Barry Goldwater, must be defeated, King announced that he would put the Conference behind President Johnson.

Dr. King said that Negro voting registration in the South had nearly doubled since the Presidential election of 1960. He said that about 2 million Negroes were registered in the South compared to 1.1 million in 1960. "This could mean the balance of power in the upcoming election," said King. He declared that he would speak and campaign for the President, wherever and whenever, necessary.

The Convention was held at the Manager Hotel. Over 500 delegates from 25 states representing 210 Conference affiliates attended the four day convention. At the opening session, Dr. King made an hour-long 5,000 word annual report before the Convention. He pledged a program of broad political action and political reforms to fight basic social and economic problems of the Negro. "Demonstrations can call attention to evil, arise the conscience of the community," Dr. King said to the delegates, "but such demonstrations are not a program for removing evil itself."

"Such a program calls for political action because it is necessary to create a political power to induce Congress to appropriate billions of dollars. We must add our political power to that of other groups, the religious communities,

156

Catholic, Protestant and Jewish, to labor, to the liberals and intellectuals, in order to create a broad and strong political force to insure positive action," said Dr. King.

At the close of the Convention, King emphasized that perhaps the greatest contribution the Conference could make to American democracy and the civil rights movement was to "reject rigidity, renounce the rehearsed repose and remain eternally open to new ideas and new tactics and strategies."

While the Conference was in session no racial incidents were reported. In fact, city officials and the white community courteously welcomed the delegates without formal ceremony. It was not unusual to see a white motorist direct a visiting delegate to the Manager or De Soto Hotel, the city's two leading hotels.

Police Chief L. B. Ryan was reported as saying, "We've had many conventions in this town and I can truly say that this has been one of the most orderly . . . to my knowledge we did not have one unpleasant incident."

Savannah had made progress since that time last year (1963) when demonstrations were being carried on against the city. In fact, the city completely dropped all barriers in places of public accommodations. It has in integration matters moved in a very reasonable manner and is one of the most desegregated cities in the South.

III

After going many months with little sleep and rest, King was beginning to feel tired and run down. He therefore decided that he would have a checkup and get some much needed rest. On October 14, he checked into St. Joseph's Infirmary in Atlanta. While there, his wife, Coretta called and told him that he had just won the Nobel Peace Prize. He was resting and not fully awaken. For a while he thought it was a dream and then he realized that it was true.

Dr. King also realized that the Nobel Peace Prize was in effect a tribute to millions of Americans who followed the precepts of nonviolence.

"I was deeply gratified to hear that I had been chosen for the most significant award," he said, and "I will certainly receive it with great humility and profound appreciation."

157

His wife, Coretta, perhaps best summed up the feeling of the entire King family when she said, "For many years we have had to contend with the other side. For something like this to happen makes it all worthwhile."

King immediately announced that "every penny" of the prize money, which amounted to $54,600, would be given to the civil rights movement. Since he received the Nobel Peace Prize without any direct action on his part, it was exempt from income taxes.

"I do not consider this merely an honor to me personally," said Dr. King, "but a tribute to the disciplined, wise restraint and majestic courage of gallant Negro and white persons of good-will who have followed a nonviolence course in seeking to establish a reign of justice and rule of love across the nation."

Dr. King felt gratified in knowing "the nations of the world, in bestowing the prize on him, recognized the civil rights movement in this country as so significant a moral force as to merit such recognition." He saw no political implications in the award. "I am a minister of the gospel, not a political leader," Dr. King said.

Reactions to the award ranged from applause to bitter criticism. The news was greeted warmly by the Vatican, the White House, Dr. Ralph J. Bunche, the first Negro to win the Nobel Prize, the Right Reverend Arthur Lichtenberger, Presiding Bishop of the Protestant Episcopal Church, Richard Cardinal Cushing, Roman Catholic Archbishop of Boston, the Reverend Aubrey Brown, editor of the *Presbyterian Outlook,* former Attorney Robert F. Kennedy, Mayor Ivan Allen of Atlanta and many thousands.

As expected bitter criticism came from segregationists Eugene Conner, former Police Commissioner of Birmingham; Leander H. Perez, Sr., prominent segregationist of New Orleans; Police Chief Virgil Stuart of St. Augustine, Florida, and many more.

Upon learning of Kings award, Dr. Bunche said, "this announcement by the Nobel Peace Prize Committee is a striking international recognition of the cause and struggle of the American Negro for full participation in the mainstream of American life."

The Right Reverend Lichtenberger hailed Dr. King as "one of the great men of our times." Richard Cardinal Cushing said that "all friends of liberty and peace" would rejoice. Reverend Brown declared, "the South ought to thank God every day for him. With his power and influence he has been able to direct into constructive channels what otherwise might have become irresponsible action and brought terrifying result."

Former Attorney Kennedy sent Dr. King a message stating that the prize was "richly deserved" and that his life and work symbolized "the struggle of mankind for justice and equality through nonviolence means."

In Atlanta, Mayor Ivan Allen, in extending his city's congratulations, declared, "He has displayed remarkable leadership at both national and international levels to the 20 million American Negro citizens and has been instrumental in bringing full citizenship to them."

Mr. Connor, however, at first declined to comment on the award. "I don't care enough about it to say anything," he remarked. "It's awarded over there (Norway) and not here. They don't know him." Then he added: "They're scraping the bottom of the barrel when they pick him. He's caused more strife and trouble in this country than anyone I can think of."

Mr. Perez said of the award: "That only shows the Communist influence nationally and internationally. Shame on somebody."

Police Chief Stuart declared, "I consider it one of the biggest jokes of the years. How can you win a peace prize when you stir up all the trouble he did down here (St. Augustine, Fla.)."

Newspapers all over the world also paid tribute to Dr. King. *The New York Times,* on its editorial page for October 15, praised Dr. King.[29] However, there were some dissents from Southern newspapers. *The Post Herald* of Birmingham, Ala., said in an editorial: "The people in the South know that violence and conflict followed his trail."

The majority of the reactions were favorable to Dr. King. He was sincerely grateful for all people who had confidence that he would win the Nobel Peace Prize. He was the 12th American to receive the Prize and the youngest. The award would be made in Oslo, Norway, December 10.

In October Dr. King also received another unexpected award. The John F. Kennedy Award for his efforts in furthering race relations. The award was made by the Chicago Interracial Council.

IV

After King got over the fanfare of winning the Nobel Peace Prize, he continued campaigning for the Democratic Party and President Johnson, as he had pledged. He traveled through the backwoods of Alabama, red hills of Georgia, and the Delta of Louisiana, encouraging Negroes to get out and vote. He was campaigning so vigorously, one would have thought that he were running for office.

On November 4, President Johnson won by a landslide over Senator Barry Goldwater. Dr. King sent congratulations to the President on winning the election and urged him to call a conference on methods by which he and other civil rights leaders could help implement the 1964 Civil Rights Act and aid in programs to give Negroes more economic opportunities.

Dr. King and the Southern Christian Leadership Conference were planning to engage in more civil rights demonstrations soon in Alabama and Mississippi.. King was of the opinion that the landslide vote given President Johnson in the election should convince him that he had a "definite mandate from the American public" to support such demonstrations.

The Civil Rights leader said: "Now that the election is over we will naturally move back into some of the area where we have been working to be sure that the Civil Rights Bill has been implemented in all its dimensions. We will probably have demonstrations based around the right to vote. We hope that through this process we can bring the necessary moral pressure to bear on the Federal Government to get Federal registers appointed in those areas as well as to get Federal Marshals in those places to escort Negroes to the registration places if necessary."

Chapter Eighteen

THE KING–HOOVER DISPUTE

After campaigning many weeks for the Democratic Party, Dr. King decided he needed a "vacation." He therefore went to the Bimini Island, off the coast of Miami Beach, Florida. While on the Bimini Island, he began drafting his acceptance speech for the Nobel Peace Prize. King was fully aware that this speech was to be one of the most important he would ever deliver, therefore, he wanted to be uninterrupted as little as possible, while writing it.

While Dr. King was on the Bimini Island, J. Edgar Hoover, director of the Federal Bureau of Investigation, who rarely holds open-forum press conferences, all of a sudden, agreed to talk over coffee cups with a group of Washington newswomen. Just why Mr. Hoover decided to talk to the newswomen at that time was a mystery. At the news conference, he denounced the Warren Commission's criticism of his bureau for not warnnig the Secret Service that Lee Harvey Oswald was a potential threat to the late President John F. Kennedy. He called the criticism "unfair and unjust" and a "classic example of Monday morning quarter-backing."

The Commission's recommendation for better communication between the Federal Bureau of Investigation and the Secret Service did result in the Bureau sending thousands of names to the White House security details each time the President journeyed out of town.

Mr. Hoover's blast against the Warren Commission was relatively mild compared to the one he made against Martin Luther King, Jr. "I remember," said Mr. Hoover to the newswomen, "the notorious Martin Luther King making a speech in the South some months ago when he advised the Negroes not to report any violations to our Albany, Georgia, agents because they were all Southerners and they would do nothing." Then Hoover delivered the line that rang around the world.

He said of Dr. King: "He is the most notorious liar in the country."

The newswomen were so shocked at what they had considered a major scoop, that they asked if they could quote him on that. "Yes the newswomen could," said Mr. Hoover. The next day, however, one of his aides entered some qualifications. "He didn't say everything King said was a lie, just the specific point on Albany," said the agent.

Mr. Hoover charged at the news conference that "red-necked sheriffs" in Mississippi and members of the Ku Klux Klan had precipitated racial violence. He repeatedly stressed that the Bureau does not protect anyone. He said that included the President and "those who go down to reform the South."

Dr. King could not be reached to comment on Mr. Hoover's statement. Later, however, Dr. King released a statement (to the press) through the Southern Christian Leadership Conference in Atlanta.

> I cannot conceive of Mr. Hoover making a statement like this without being under extreme pressure. He has apparently faltered under the awesome burden, complexities and responsibilities of his office. Therefore, I cannot engage in a public debate with him. I have nothing but sympathy for this man who has served his country so well.

King also stated his case thoroughly in a telegram to Mr. Hoover.[30] "I have never advised Negroes in Albany not to report to the FBI. On the contrary we reported every incident. But we were dismayed by the fact that nothing was ever done. The fact that no arrests have been made in the brutalities at Albany, the murder of the three civil rights workers in Mississippi, and the bombing of a church in Birmingham, Alabama, has left us all discouraged," declared King.

Dr. King said that he had never made a blanket criticism of the FBI and its agents. He actually believed a Southerner dedicated to his job could be as effective as one from the North. Dr. King was of the opinion that Mr. Hoover would not have made such a vicious accusation without being under extreme pressure. "This pressure has come on the racial front and from the Warren Report, raising serious questions about the effectiveness of the FBI," said Dr. King.

Leslie W. Dunbar, executive director of the Southern Regional Council, said it was difficult for the agents to "act contrary to the interest of the local law people." In Albany, Mr. Dunbar said, the record of the whole Justice Department was poor . . . it did everything wrong. He also inserted, "The main drawback to vigorous enforcement of civil rights by the FBI is their organizational approach of working very closely with local law enforcement authorities."

I

The following day a group of civil rights leaders met with President Johnson at the White House and told him they all supported Dr. King against the attack made by Mr. Hoover. The meeting had been arranged before Mr. Hoover had held his news conference with the newswomen. The Hoover interview was the major topic at the meeting. Roy Wilkins of the NAACP acted as spokesman for the group.

The Negro community agreed with Dr. King's statement that they were not getting adequate protection from the FBI, Roy Wilkins said: "It's not a matter of where FBI men were born. The Negroes feel they are not getting adequate protection whether the agents were born in Mobile or Minneapolis."

A. Philip Randolph, Whitney Young, James Farmer, Mrs. Dorthy Height, and Jack Greenberg were at the meeting. Acting Attorney General Nicholas Katzenbach and Burke Marshall, his civil rights chief, were also present. Dr. King had been invited but was out of the country.

Mr. Hoover received criticisms from many people and organizations. In a statement CORE charged that Mr. Hoover's criticism of Dr. King was "both intemperated and unfortunate." The statement inserted "that although the FBI's activity in the civil rights field had "significantly increased" in the last year, it must be remembered that for many years prior to the present civil rights crisis the FBI had been extremely lax in implementing existing legislation and protecting the civil rights of Negroes and CORE workers throughout the nation."

The Lawyers Constitutional Defense Committee, an organization of civil rights lawyers, sent a telegram to President

163

Johnson expressing its "outrage at Mr. J. Edgar Hoover's slanderous attack." They also urged Mr. Johnson to "publicly censor Mr. Hoover for his vilification of a highly respected American."

John de J. Pemberton, Jr., executive director of the American Civil Liberties Union, said that Mr. Hoover's remarks about Dr. King were "terribly unfortunate."

Bishop James K. Mathrews of the Methodist Church in a message to President Johnson said:

> May I respectfully register a protest against J. Edgar Hoover's unwarranted and slanderous attack on Dr. Martin Luther King, Jr. Surely public retraction and an apology are called for. This outburst, together with Mr. Hoover's other observations, would appear to justify his retirement at age 70, with recognition of his many years of services to our country.

The Southern Regional Council, a biracial group, whose stated purpose is to seek equal opportunity for all people in the South, adopted a resolution at its annual meeting expressing "unreserved faith" in the Reverend Dr. Martin Luther King, Jr. as a nonviolence leader of Negro aspirations.

The resolution said:

> On the basis of our first hand knowledge of the character and work of Martin Luther King, now under attack from many sources, we express our unreserved faith in his integrity, high sense of honor and unswerving commitment as a person and as a leader in the nonviolent struggle for obedience to the law of the land as interpreted by the Supreme Court of the United States toward the fulfillment of our Judeo-Christian heritage and the American dream.

The Chicago Catholic Interracial Council said it was "greatly disturbed" by Mr. Hoover's statement about Dr. King.

Newsweek reported that the President had begun to look for a successor to Mr. Hoover. But the White House denied that report, even though the information came from a highly placed source within the White House. *The New York Times* in an editorial said " . . . Unquestionably the strain put upon the FBI Chief by the controversy over the agency's role in the Kennedy assassination and the handling of civil rights cases in the South have been unsettling for one accustomed to nothing but praise. Under the circumstances it would be wise to let the mandatory provisions of the Federal retirement law take effect on Mr. Hoover's 70th birthday."

The New York Herald Tribune in an editorial said the FBI Director had shown "a cavalier reckless with fact and fancy." *Time* magazine said undoubtedly there will be vastly increased pressure on the White House from now on to boot the old fellow out of his job.

Mr. Hoover, who was 70 years old January 1, 1965, would ordinarily have had to retire on his birthday. Mr. Johnson, however, waived the compulsory retirement age to permit Mr. Hoover to remain as director past the age 70.

All of the criticisms of Mr. Hoover and the FBI did get some immediate results. A few days after the King-Hoover affair, the FBI announced that it knew the identities of the slayers of the three civil rights workers in Mississippi.

The FBI said it was making an intensive investigation of the Birmingham church bombing and would continue the investigation. The spokesman's report on the Philadelphia, Mississippi, case was made in response to a request by the *Washington Star* for comment on complaints about the FBI by Dr. King.

In reviewing the FBI's work in other Southern civil rights cases, the spokesman cited the following actions:

> Arrests of five present and former law enforcement officers in Philadelphia, Mississippi on charges of police brutality.
>
> The arrests of a deputy marshal in Sasser, Georgia, 20 miles from Albany, on charges that he had cursed voter registration workers and fired at the tires of their cars.
>
> Arrests and convictions of four white men who burned a Negro church near Leesbury, Georgia.

The spokesman also challenged Dr. King's statement that he had always made himself available to agents in the Atlanta FBI office.

Later during the week James Farmer, Whitney M. Young, Jr., Roy Wilkins and Charles Evers, demanded that Mr. Hoover either resign as director of the FBI or reconsider his position. Dr. King, however, did not urge Mr. Hoover's removal.

Mr. Hoover received support from Governor Paul B. Johnson of Mississippi. Mr. Johnson said at a news conference that he agreed with Mr. Hoover that Dr. King was a "notorious liar," as do thousands of people. He said that Dr. King "has left a trail of blood and bitterness." Rather than a man of peace, he is a man of division and dissensions. Fifty business and professional men of Mississippi signed a resolution also supporting Mr. Hoover.

Mr. Hoover declared that he did not enjoy a controversy and he didn't go looking for one. "I tried for years to avoid public disputes. But I cannot let attacks on the FBI go unchallenged when they are not justified. If I didn't speak out in defense of my agents, I would have no morals left in this organization," said the FBI director.

II

Dr. King made arrangements to see Mr. Hoover to discuss the whole problem and especially to express his concern for the future of Negroes in the civil rights movement in the South. The next day the two men met in the Justice Department's Washington office. After the meeting, King reported that J. Edgar Hoover informed him there would be arrests "in the next few days" in the murders of the three civil rights workers in Mississippi.

King also said that the meeting had been quite amicable and he was pleased with the outcome. Furthermore, he realized that civil rights leaders must seek to maintain open channels of communications with all who are in a position to help the disadvantaged Negroes in the South.

"I sincerely hope we can forget the confusion of the past and get on with the job that Congress, the Supreme Court and the President have outlined, the job of providing freedom and justice for all citizens of this nation," said King.

Mr. Hoover told Dr. King that the FBI had infiltrated the Ku Klux Klan and other extremist groups. Mr. Hoover commented on the good work of Negro FBI agents. He also pledged to take action against any FBI agent guilty of discrimination or injustice. Hoover told King that the FBI could not act as a national police force, but it would do all that it could, legally, to protect civil rights workers.

Dr. King expressed the Negroes' appreciation for what the FBI had accomplished in the South and said it had overcome many obstacles there. Both King and Hoover wanted to ease tension and their meeting did make some progress toward this end.

Within a few days the FBI arrested the Neshoba (Philadelphia, Mississippi) County Sheriff, his deputy and 19 other white men in connection with the murder of the three civil rights workers. The bureau said the murders had been plotted by the Ku Klux Klan. The defendants were charged under the United States Code (Title 18, Chapter 13, Civil Rights Section 211) with conspiracy to violate the constitutional rights of the deceased men.

As the sheriff was taken in custody by the FBI agents, Vernon Gamblin, Vice President of the Citizens Bank, was overheard to have said the arrests proved that "the whole country is taking orders from Martin Luther King, Jr." Most Philadelphians, however, were relieved that the FBI had finally made the arrests.

Jack Tannehill, editor of the *Neshoba County Democrat*, ran a front page editorial pleading for obedience to the law: "We must plan and make arrangements to live with it the best way possible," he said. "We must not cut off our noses to spite our faces. It means too much to our community to say that we won't obey the law to the best of our ability," Mr. Tannehill declared.

Most of the civil rights leaders applauded the arrests of the defendant. They, however, expressed doubt that convictions could or would be obtained in Mississippi. Roy Wilkins of the NAACP said, "the FBI had done its job of gathering the evidence, detecting and arresting the suspects and it is up to Mississippi to do the rest." He continued, "We may be sure that the evidence is of a kind which, in any normal jurisdiction, would justify indictment by a grand jury. Mississippi, however, is not a normal jurisdiction, as far as the lives and rights of Negroes are concerned. The record to date shows that its white people can kill Negroes without fear of punishment in a judicial process." He concluded by saying that "the state now has another chance to make a new kind of history."

Whitney M. Young, Jr., of the Urban League declared, "This is the kind of outstanding effort to protect the civil liberties and freedom of American citizens which one expects of the FBI. The agency and all its officials who worked to bring the accused to the bar of justice deserve the congratulations of the entire nation."

James Farmer of CORE said, "I will not prejudice the case, but I understand the evidence against the accused is very substantial. The investigation has been painstaking; the prosecution must now be diligent and vigorous. We want the defendants to have a trial that is fair in every regard; the guilty must be convicted for the sake of justice, not vengeance. In one sense the jury system will be itself on trial."

Martin Luther King, Jr., while stopping in New York on his way to Oslo, said, "I must commend the FBI for the work they have done in uncovering the perpetrators of the dastardly act. It renews again my faith in democracy."

He went on to say, "I sincerely pray that justice reign in this situation and that the State of Mississippi find its conscience and forthrightly declare that murder, even if it be the murder of a black man, is a crime in every state of this great Union of ours, even in the State of Mississippi." Reverend King believed that even if the men arrested were not convicted, "they would stand before the world as those who have committed the world's greatest crime."

Chapter Nineteen
KING GOES TO OSLO

Dr. King and his group of 30 left New York City and flew to London. They stopped there for a three-day delay en route to Oslo, Norway. The group included: Dr. King's parents, Reverend and Mrs. Martin Luther King, Sr.; Dr. King's sister, Mrs. Christine Farris; Dr. King's brother, Reverend A. D. King; Dr. King's associates, Reverend and Mrs. Ralph Abernathy, Reverend Wyatt T. Walker, Bayard Rustin, and Reverend Andrew Young; Reverend Bernard Lee; Professor Lawrence D. Reddick; Dora McDonald, Attorney and Mrs. Harry Wachtel; Mrs. Martin Logan; Reverend Richard Dixon, Jr.; Dorothy Cotton, Mrs. Nina Miller, Mrs. Septima Clark, Reverend Logan Kearse, Attorney Chauncey Eskridge, Reverend Charles Wallace, Reverend O. M. Hoover and his daughter, Carole. Many that accompanied Dr. King borrowed money from relatives, banks, or churches to sponsor their trip. A few went on the travel-now, pay later plan. Only Dr. and Mrs. King were official guests of the Norwegian government.

While Dr. and Mrs. King were in London, he and his companions met some members of Parliament. They also talked with officials and were guests of the British Council of Churches. Reverend King was invited to speak at St. Paul Cathedral by Canon John Collins. Over four thousand Britons packed the Cathedral to hear him. Reverend King was the first non-Anglican to deliver an evening sermon.

Reverend King spoke on the theme, "The Three Dimensions of a Complete Life; Length, a Healthy, Rational Self-Interest: Breath, Honor Thy Neighbor and Height, Love of God."

He devoted his sermon largely to noncontroversial themes. He did, however, plead for moderation in the civil rights struggles. His plea was directed at the activities of the late

Malcolm X who spoke on television in England the night before King arrived. Malcolm X warned that the patience of the American Negro was wearing thin in the fight for equal rights. He implied that violence was near at hand.

King said, "The doctrine of black supremacy is as great a danger as the doctrine of white supremacy." He continued, "All over the world, as we struggle for justice and freedom, we must never use second-class methods to gain it." He added, "We must not seek to rise from a position of disadvantage to one of advantage, substituting injustice of one type for that of another. We must not substitute our oppression for another kind of oppression."

During the sermon, Dr. King recalled the parable of the Good Samaritan, who helped a stricken man on the road between Jericho and Jerusalem. He asked why a priest had passed by without stopping. The priest may not have noticed the stricken man or he may have been afraid to stop. Then again suggested Dr. King, "He might have been rushing off to form a Jericho Improvement Association." This drew a murmur of amusement from the congregation.

After the sermon, the congregation stood and sang a hymn that began:

> Once to every man and nation
> Comes the movement to decide
> In the strife of truth with falsehood,
> For the good or evil side.

A news conference was held after the sermon. The press asked King to comment on the racial situation in America and how much influence the black supremacy groups assert on American Negroes. "Negroes in the United States are more in line with integration," King said. He added that only 75,000 out of 22 million Negroes in the United States, "joined groups supporting black supremacy."

I

After three days delay, Dr. King and his group flew to Oslo, Norway, and arrived there a day before he received the Nobel Peace Prize.

Martin Luther King, Jr. was greeted at the airport by hundreds of Scandinavians, including many teenagers, who shouted, "Welcome, Dr. Martin Luther King, Jr." Dr. King delighted the crowd by breaking away from escorts to shake hands and sign autographs. Then he and his entourage were loaded into U.S. limousines and taken to the Grand Hotel where a three-room suite had been provided for the Kings' use.

Later a news conference was held and Dr. King said, "We are not finished. The struggle will take on a new dimension. It will not be a battle to integrate lunch counters, but a problem of dealing with de facto segregation in schools, jobs, housing and other such areas." The next step in the movement would be "work in the field of political action reform," he declared.

King was well aware that American Negroes did not have sufficient power to take the struggle for civil rights beyond the lunch counters. Therefore, he reiterated that the movement would have to depend on a constructive alliance.

Dr. King was asked if he had tried to persuade the United States Government not to take part in the recent Congo action with Belgian paratroops in Stanleyville. "No, I have not gone that far. But the Congo civil war will not be resolved until all foreign elements are withdrawn. The Congo was reaping the violent harvest of injustice, neglect and man's inhumanity to man across the years."

The same day Dr. King arrived, he received the prize money. At the news conference he held up the large yellow check for 273,000 Swedish crowns, worth about $54,600.

After the news conference, on the day of his arrival Dr. King and his party attended an informal buffet that was arranged for them by the American Ambassador, Miss Margaret Joy Tibbetts. The buffet was held at the elegant American Embassy.

II

On the morning of the ceremony, King Olva V sent his personal limousine to the Grand Hotel and Dr. and Mrs. King were taken to the Royal Palace for a 30-minute audience with the King and his family.

Later that day Martin Luther King, Jr. accepted the Nobel Peace Prize on behalf of the civil rights movement. He was hailed by Dr. Gunnar Jahn, chairman of the Norwegian Parliament's Nobel Committee, as an "undaunted champion of peace," and the first person in the Western world to have shown us that a struggle can be waged without violence."

Dr. Jahn spoke for forty-five minutes describing Dr. King's background and his fight for civil rights. He said that though Dr. King "has not personally committed himself to the international conflict, his own struggle is a clarion call for all who work for peace." He continued, "Dr. King never abandoned his faith in the unarmed struggle he is waging, who has suffered for his faith, been imprisoned on many occasions, whose home has been threatened, and who nevertheless has never faltered."

At the close of his speech, Dr. Jahn presented the Nobel medal and diploma to Dr. King before an audience which included King Olva of Norway, Crown Prince Harald, and other government and diplomatic officials.

Rev. King delivered a sermon-like acceptance speech. He spoke for ten minutes in a slow, deep voice that filled the marble hall of Oslo University. Dr. King said that he had come to Oslo as a "trustee" for the "humble children" of the civil rights movement "who were willing to suffer for righteousness sake." He concluded by saying: "I think Alfred Nobel would know what I mean when I say that I accept this award in the spirit of a curator of some precious heirloom which holds in trust for its true owners—all those to whom beauty of genuine brotherhood and peace is more precious than diamonds, silver or gold." [31]

After Dr. King's acceptance speech the orchestra of the Norwegian Broadcasting System played excerpts from George Gershwin's "Porgy and Bess." He was then congratulated by King Olva V, Crown Prince Harald, and government officials.

The next night Dr. King followed the tradition of other Nobel Peace Prize winners and spoke to the students at Oslo University. He was greeted outside of the University Aula (Hall) by hundreds of students carrying burning fakkels, or Viking torches. Inside, he followed his family and associates

172

to the rostrum through waves of thunderous applauses. Many persons stood throughout his address.

Dr. King urged that "nonviolence become immediately a subject for study for serious experimentation in every field of human conflict, by no means excluding the relations between nations. At this point the audience interrputed with applause.

"The freedom movement is spreading in the wildest liberation in history. In its vanguard, is the spirit of nonviolence. It was used in a magnificent way by Ghandi to challenge the might of the British Empire, and in the last ten years by unarmed, gallant men and women of the United States fighting for civil rights," he declared.

Rev. King continued, "We will not build a peaceful world by following a negative path. It is not enough to say we must not wage war. It is necessary to love peace and sacrifice for it." Dr. King's address was rich in imagery, as he praised the thousands of "faceless, anonymous, relentless young people, black and white, who temporarily left their ivory towers of learning to storm the barricades of bias."

"That man must learn to live together because we can never again live without each other." In a slow and deliberate manner King spoke for more than an hour to a rapt audience.[32] At the end he received a standing ovation.

The following day Dr. King and his party visited Stockholm and stopped in Copenhagen and Paris. While in Norway, he received favorable coverage by the newspapers. At every press conference and in each of his numerous appearances on European radio and television, Dr. King emphasized his refusal to accept the Nobel Peace Prize as "an honor to him personally." He insisted he was only a trustee, accepting the prize in behalf of the million men, women and children who work for freedom in the United States, and to who all that I may be today." The Norwegian press emphasized Martin Luther King, Jr.'s faith in the United States and played down his graphic description of racial injustice.

While King was in Norway, the nineteen white men who had been arrested in the case of the three civil rights workers slaying in Mississippi were released. This action prompted

Dr. King to say that he would protest directly to President Johnson against their release. He also renewed his call for an economic boycott of Mississippi products. He declared, "action must be taken by the offices of goodwill" to impel the state to change its policies. He was of the opinion that the dismissal of charges against these men revealed again the absence of justice in the State of Mississippi as far as Negroes are concerned.

He stated further, "This miscarriage of justice will revolt the American people and will alienate people of goodwill throughout the world. Unless the Federal Government or the State of Mississippi can find methods of maintaining justice for all men in that state, I will have no alternative but to call upon the forces of goodwill of the nation to effect a complete boycott of Mississippi products."

A number of observers thought that Dr. King had gone too far in planning a national boycott of Mississippi products. One said it was not fair to penalize an entire state for the misdeeds of a few. Others, merely laughed at Dr. King's plan and called it ridiculous. Some Mississippians said, a few products may be boycotted, but most of the other would not.

Chapter Twenty

KING RETURNS HOME

The Supreme Court unanimously upheld the public accommodation section of the Civil Rights Act of 1964. This was the controversial section, known as Title II, prohibits the refusal of service or segregation in hotels, motels, restaurants, places of amusement and gasoline stations, if their operations affect interstate commerce or if the discrimination or segregation is supported by state action.

Civil rights leaders said the decision vindicated the efforts of thousands of young Negroes and whites who carried the public accommodation struggle through the South.

While Reverend King was in Paris, he praised the Supreme Court as a "refreshing contrast to the abuse of law and cynical approach in Meridian, Mississippi." He said the decision should make all Americans "proud of the Supreme Court in its constant vigilance to assure equal protection of the law." Dr. King also expressed enthusiasm over the unanimous decision upholding the constitutionality of the rights law.

King's plan for national boycott on the products of Mississippi received great support when Harold J. Gibbons, Vice President of the International Brotherhood of Teamsters," telegraphed Dr. King in Paris and told him that no goods, materials, or services from the state of Mississippi would be used in the construction of the Teamsters' $20 million Council Plaza project in St. Louis, Missouri. The Council Plaza is a housing project that has 600 units for senior citizens.

I

The NAACP urged 50 New York City financial houses to decline to participate in bidding the same week on three Mississippi bond issues totaling $32,650,000.

Roy Wilkins, of the NAACP, noted that the Civil Rights Act of 1964 required the Federal Government to withhold financial aid to states that use it unfairly. "We believe that private financial community can do no less," said Mr. Wilkins.

A spokesman for CORE said the civil rights group had urged the attorney generals of the states of New York, New Jersey, California and Massachusetts to ban the sale of bonds that would be used to intensify segregation in the South. "It's our contention that since the Supreme Court has ruled that segregation is illegal, it's improper to sell bonds for an illegal purpose," the spokesman said.

Later during the week a Mississippi water supply company found no acceptable bids for a $24.65 million bond that the NAACP had urged investment bankers to boycott. None of the underwriters that had withdrawn said that their action was based on the NAACP appeal. There is little doubt that the racial issue did play a significant role in their decision.

Mississippi was beginning to feel the economic pinch as the result of racial violence in the state, during the latter part of the year. State tax revenue fell below anticipated collections and the state had to operate on a hand-to-mouth basis.

State officials said much of the financial problems were due to an increase in the state budget. That was not entirely true. Business was down because of racial strife. Tourist business on the Gulf Coast dropped 50 per cent after the murder of the three civil rights workers. A factory in the southern part of the State moved a few miles across the border into Louisiana so that it would not have a Mississippi mailing address.

For many years the Sugar Bowl football teams trained in Biloxi during December, however, that year Syracuse University trained in Pensacola, Florida. Syracuse was afraid for the safety of the Negro players on the team if it went to Mississippi.

There was deep concern in Mississippi over the national boycott against Mississippi products planned by the civil rights organizations. In fact, former Governor Hugh L. White suggested that the state buy prime time on national television to get "the true image of Mississippi" across the nation.

Looking at the boycott on Mississippi products in retrospect, it had a far greater effect than anticipated. Therefore, one could conclude that Dr. King and the other civil rights organizations' project was a success.

II

Dr. King and his party left Paris and returned to the United States. The first city that they visited was New York. Dr. King was welcomed to the city by Mayor Robert Wagner, city, state and national officials, including Vice President Hubert Humphery and Governor Nelson A. Rockefeller.

"This city has officially welcomed many world-renowned figures," said Mayor Wagner, "I can think of no one who has won a more lasting place in the moral epic of America. New York is proud of you, Dr. King."

Mayor Wagner then gave the Medallion of Honor of the City of New York to Reverend Martin Luther King, Jr. This award is the highest for a visitor, except for the Medal of Honor, which only heads of state can receive.

The ceremony was held in the City Council Chamber and many stood in the corridors to see and hear Dr. King.

King said in a deep voice:

> I am returning with a deeper conviction that nonviolence is the answer to the crucial political and moral questions of our time—the need for men to end the oppression and violence of racial persecution, destructive poverty and war without resorting to violence and oppression.
>
> Yes, our souls have been tied in the cold and bitter Valley Forges of the Deep South, and the black and white together, we have met the test.
>
> We shall overcome.

At this point the audience, which included King's mother and father, rose and cheered. Martin Luther King, Jr. had earlier said he would give all the prize money to the civil rights movement, and at this time he specified how he would disburse it.

The Unity Council, which includes CORE, NAACP, SNCC, The National Council of Negro Women, Urban League, and the NAACP legal Defense Fund, would receive $17,000; and SCLC $12,000. The balance of the $25,000 was put into a special fund for the furtherance of education in nonviolence.

That afternoon a press conference was held at which time Dr. King said that he had been "greatly humbled" by his trip to Oslo, Norway. "The response to our cause in London, Stockholm and Paris, as well as in Oslo, was far beyond imagination, he said. "These great world capitals look upon racism in this nation with horror and revulsion, but also with a certain amount of hope that Americans can solve this problem and point the way to the rest of the world."

Later that evening the civil rights leader was a guest of honor at a cocktail party sponsored by the city at the Waldorf-Astoria Hotel. About 400 persons were present as guests of the City of New York.

A crowd of 10,000 later met at the 369th Artillery Armory, Fifth Avenue and 142nd Street to pay tribute to him. Governor Rockefeller and many leaders of the civil rights movement were on hand.

The next day Dr. King and his wife and parents attended an informal luncheon with Governor Rockefeller. George Fowler, Chairman of the New York Human Rights Commission; Jackie Robinson and Rodman Rockefeller, son of the Governor also attended the luncheon.

III

Later during the day King flew to Washington to have a conference with President Johnson. Dr. King discussed with the President the role of the Negro in the anti-poverty program. He told Mr. Johnson that Negroes wanted to be part of his "Great Society" and he hoped they would be given roles of leadership in the anti-poverty program.

The Nobel Peace Prize winner said he told the President that Negroes were very much concerned about the problem of judges who "use and misabuse" their power in dealing with civil rights cases. Mr. Johnson and Dr. King did not discuss his dispute with J. Edgar Hoover. As far as King was concerned that was a "dead issue" and was a matter of the past.

Dr King was asked to comment on a remark made by Assistant Attorney General Burke Marshall, who resigned and said that the civil rights movement would not be a matter of litigation in the courts. "It must be the department's overall responsibility," said Dr. King.

The meeting lasted for 45 minutes and King called it a "very fruitful and friendly"discussion. He and his wife, Coretta, who had accompanied him to Washington returned to Atlanta. When King returned home, he found that the predominantly Negro International Chemical Workers Union of Atlanta was striking against the Scripto, Inc. He, therefore, joined the union in their demands and even walked the picket lines. The union said the company was discriminating against its 700 Negro members (all unskilled) by offering higher wages to the 200 skilled members (only two of them were Negroes). The company, however, denied any discrimination and said wages was the issue. Dr. King said he would call a worldwide boycott of Scripto products which includes, pens, pencils and cigaret lighters, if some agreement between the company and union was not reached. King said, "what good does it do a man to have integrated lunch counters if he can't buy a hamburger," and added that Scripto's management "will treat the Negro rights voluntarily. You've got to demand it." An agreement was reached and King called the boycott off.

Another year came to a close in the life and times of Martin Luther King, Jr. It was an illustrious year for him. It was the year that he received the John F. Kennedy Award; met Pope Paul VI; and reached the apex of his career when he won the Nobel Peace Prize.

Chapter Twenty-One

TARGET: SELMA

Most people, including some Southerns, thought with the passage of the 1964 Civil Rights Act, segregation would ultimately face death or retirement and that Negroes would at least be permitted to register and vote. That belief, however, was only an illusion.

It was, therefore, necessary to dramatize the plight of the Negroes in the South. Selma, Alabama was the ideal city; it represented bitter-end resistance to desegregation and police brutality. Martin Luther King, Jr. was the ideal man to break the stranglehold Selma had on its Negroes; he represented nonviolence, leadership and determination.

During the last week in December 1964, Martin Luther King, Jr. conferred with Alabama civil rights leaders and announced that Selma would be the prime target of the Southern Christian Leadership Conference's voter registration drive for 1965.

Even though Selma had a population of 29,500, fewer than one per cent of the 15,100 Negro residents were registered voters. In fact, only twenty per cent of the entire state was registered.

After the Supreme Court passed the school desegregation order in 1954, Selma was the first Alabama town to organize a White Citizens Council. James Clark, Sheriff of Dallas County, kept Negroes down with the help of a special squad of deputies known locally as "squirrel shooters." In the summer of 1963, Clark and his men herded more than 100 Negroes off to jail with sticks and cattle prods, when they tried to register to vote.

Clark should have known that Bull Connor, with his police dogs, fire hoses and high-handed methods, gave the 1964 Civil Rights Act the additional backing that it needed to become the law of the land. Clark's temper and lack of judgment served as the Negroes greatest asset. And like Mr. Connor he had not learned the lesson of meeting violence with non-violence.

Dr. King and his aides arrived in Selma early in January and called for massive street demonstrations if Negroes there were not permitted to register and vote in large numbers.

King told 700 cheering Negroes in the Brown Chapel Methodist Episcopal Church that Alabama kept down Negroes' registration by limiting the amount of registration. "If they refuse to register us," he said, "we will appeal to Governor Wallace. If he doesn't listen, we will appeal to the Legislature." "If the Legislature doesn't listen, we will seek to arouse the Federal Government by marching by the thousands by the places of registration. "We must be willing to go to jail by the thousands. We are not asking, we are demanding the ballot," he said.

The books were opened for registration only two days a month. Therefore, a maximum of only 30 persons could register a day and fewer than that number were accepted.

That last week in January, Dr. King and his eleven aides went to Selma to begin the voter registration drive. The first thing they did was to register for a room at Selma Hotel Albert, built by slave labor over a hundred years ago as a copy of the ornate Doge's Palace in Venice. When King tried to register, James Robinson, a member of the National States Rights Party, struck him in the head and aimed two kicks at his groin, but missed. The city policemen had expected trouble and were standing near-by. They rushed over and pulled Robinson away from Dr. King and took him to jail. He was fined $100 and sentenced to 60 days in jail for assault. King finished registering and became the first Negro ever to stay there.

The next day more than 500 Negroes marched to the county courthouse and attempted to register. Most of them, however, were told to wait in a roped-in alleyway beside the courthouse. They waited in line all day and by closing time none were registered.

A rally was held at Brown Chapel that night and Dr. King told them: "When we get the right to vote, we will send to the

181

State House not men who will stand in the doorway of universities to keep Negroes out but men who will uphold the cause of justice. And we will send to Congress men who will sign not a manifesto for segregation but a manifesto for justice."

The next morning the Negroes tried to register. And again they were met by Sheriff Clark, who threatened to jail them if they did not move into the alleyway. At this point, Reverend Ralph Abernathy stepped forward and said: "We intend to enter by the front door. We have gone in the back doors from the alleys for too many years."

Seventy Negroes refused to move and were arrested, including Mrs. Amelia Boynton, chairman of the registration drive, who was seized bodily by Clark and pushed half a block along the street into a patrol car.

In 1964 Public Safety Director, Wilson Baker, was appointed to the special post by the newly elected Mayor Joe T. Smitherman. Mr. Smitherman realized that Clark's high-handed methods, like Bull Connor's, would no longer do. The mayor said, however, "We want to maintain the dignity of the town and peace."

On the Negroes third attempt to register, Mr. Baker provided a city police escort for them. As the Negroes approached the courthouse, Clark stood in the doorway with his billy club and cattle prod in his hand. Even though Baker objected to Clark's standing in the doorway, Clark still arrested 150 more Negroes when they refused to leave the front of the building. Now Clark had not only the Negroes as his antagonists, but Baker and Smitherman, as well.

Meanwhile, the Legal Defense Fund of the N.A.A.C.P. asked for and was granted a federal injunction against further interference by Clark. The injunction stated in part: "Persons legally entitled to register as voters should be permitted to do so in an orderly fashion." King announced that the Legal Defense Fund would soon send to Selma a panel of seven white lawyers to draw up "freedom registration forms," register the Negroes, and try to bypass Clark and Dallas County by submitting the forms for verification directly to a federal district court.

Dr. King had to leave Selma temporarily to attend a testimonial dinner in Atlanta. He did, however, promise to return to continue "Plaguing Dallas County—creatively and nonviolently."

I

Soon after the October announcement of Martin Luther King, Jr.'s selection for the Nobel Peace Prize, a number of Atlanta leaders began discussing the possibility of some event to honor him.

On December 16, a letter signed by the Most Reverend Paul J. Hallinan, Roman Catholic Archbishop of Atlanta, Rabbi Jacob Rothschild, Dr. Benjamin E. Mays and Ralph McGill was sent to more than 100 leaders in business, education, religion, politics and civic affairs, asking them to join as sponsors of a banquet at the Dinkler Plaza Hotel in Atlanta.

The letter to the prospective sponsors of the dinner read:

> This is the second Nobel award that any Southerner has received. We believe it reflects on the South, and particularly, on our state and city. It is with this pride in mind that we join in this undertaking.

At first, most of them receiving the letters were slow in replying. A few replied negatively. A substantial number of those asked, however, accepted. Their names alone would be sufficient to give the occasion a stamp of approval by what might be called the moderate-liberal element of the community.

The issue at hand was whether the city's principal business and industrial leaders would endorse the banquet. The business and industrial leaders were not originally informed of it.

There was one high-level bank executive making telephone calls to discourage anyone from participating. The president of one of the city's biggest companies, however, persuaded others to endorse the banquet.

King's part in the Scripto, Inc. dispute was cited as the obstacles for lack of some participation. The Scripto events were taking place at the same time the dinner was being planned. Some business leaders felt that Dr. King was intruding in a matter in which he should not have been involved and that the boycott threat was a forced move during a time of collective bargaining.

Opposition came from segregationist bankers as well as some of Atlanta's top merchants, who feared that their participation in the testimonial might cost them white customers. The Ku Klux Klan, as expected, inevitably threatened to picket the affair.

For a while things got so touchy Mr. McGill considered calling the banquet off. As time passed, however, a number of prominent leaders in the community began endorsing the dinner, including some white college presidents and some leading professional men.

The most active participants in the controversy was Mayor Ivan Allen and former Mayor William Hartsfield. These men moved in forcefully but quietly to prevent any incident that would become an insult to Dr. King.

A group of the most influential leaders met to discuss the dinner and active opposition to plans for the dinner were no longer evident. At the meeting a widely known corporate executive argued forcefully for support of the event and his views were opposed by some present. Most however, supported the dinner.

On January 27, some 750 whites, including most civic leaders and about the same number of Negroes, honored Martin Luther King, Jr. The dinner was held in the Dinkler Plaza Hotel ballroom. Mayor Allen told the participants at the banquet:

> Through the years, as history is wrought, some men are destined to be leaders of humanity and to shape the future course of the world. Dr. King is such a man. I take great pride in honoring this citizen of Atlanta who is willing to turn the other cheek in his quest for full citizenship for Americans. . .

Martin Luther King, Jr. received thunderous applause as he came forward. He told the audience that the tragedy of the civil rights movement has been "the appalling silence and indifference of the good people."

Moved to tears, King said, "Our generation will have to repent not only for the words and acts of the children of darkness, but also for the fears and apathy of the children of light . . . "

"The South's native sons are best suited to handle their own problems. This hour represents a great opportunity for white persons of good will, if they will only speak the truth, and suffer, if necessary, for what they know is right," continued King.

II

After two weeks of protesting, not a single Negro was added to the registration rolls, despite a federal court order against Sheriff Clark and his deputies—to stop interfering with orderly registration. The Sheriff and his men still arrested 60 applicants and civil rights workers and brought the number arrested to nearly 300.

The county officials used every legal and illegal maneuver to halt the voter registration drive. Some Negroes stood in line, approximately six hours a day, waiting to enter the courthouse to register. Only 95 persons got in during the two weeks period since only one applicant was admitted at a time. Each had to answer long series of confusing biographical questions. Next they had to provide written answers to a twenty-page test on the Constitution, federal, state and local governments. To prove literacy, each applicant had to write a passage from the Constitution read to him by the registrar. The registrar was the sole judge of whether the applicant's writing was passable, and whether he had givien the correct answers. These complicated registration procedures were so unjust that even some college professors could not "pass" the literacy test.

The voter registration drive was, however, helped considerably by the remorseful Mr. Clark. Mrs. Annie Lee Cooper, an aspiring registrant stood patiently in line waiting to register at the Dallas County courthouse. Mrs. Cooper and others in the line were complaining about police treatment of an arrested civil rights worker. A civil rights worker went limping into the arms of a police and yelled: "Don't hit me again!" Sheriff Clark heard her say: "There ain't nobody scared here." At this point he jerked her out of line, twisted her arm, and struck her on the head with his billy. Before she was brought down, she managed to land two blows against Clark's head appeared to be outpointing him, until three burly deputies came to his aid. She was taken to jail and charged with assault and battery.

The next day all the major newspapers carried front-page pictures and stories of Mrs. Cooper being held on the ground and three policemen hitting her with their billy sticks. That picture was worth more to the voter registration drive than all the thousands of words that could be written about it and Selma, Alabama.

In 1963, Selma passed a city ordinance and tried to put a halt to any protest marches, by banning "any parade or procession or public demonstration on the streets or other public ways of the city, unless a permit thereof had been secured from the city council."

During the two week period, King and his followers did not violate the ordinance. In the third week of the campaign, however, King deliberately got himself and his aides arrested. They did not apply for a parade permit.

The trap was set and the officials fell for the bait. Dr. King led 240 Negroes on the mass march to the courthouse and they all were arrested for parading without a permit. The arrests as they had anticipated, led to more arrests and jailings. About 500 Negro children left school to protest King's arrest. They were charged with juvenile delinquency. While the state circuit court was convening, 40 Negro adults were picketing the courthouse and were charged with contempt of court. The following day over 100 more adults were arrested on the same charge. In fact, some adults only wanted to see the voting registrars. The same day nearly 40 more students were arrested.

The next day over 350 Negro students locked arms on the sidewalk outside of the courthouse and sang civil rights songs. They changed some of the words to include the name of Sheriff James Clark. "I love Jim Clark in my heart," they sang, and "Ain't gonna let Jim Clark turn me round." Clark arrested all of them and marched them through the center of Selma to the armory. Many of the students spent the night sleeping on the cement floor.

King stayed in jail four days and was released on a $200 bond. While he was there he wrote for the *New York Times* a "Letter from a Selma, Alabama Jail" stating correctly that there were more Negroes in jail with him than there were on the voting rolls.[33]

Because of the pressure brought by Martin Luther King, Jr. Selma Negroes were beginning to make some visible progress in speeding the registration procedures. The county board of registration ordinarily sat for only two days a month. In January, however, it sat for twelve days. On a single day during the second week in February it processed 60 Negro applications. Later during the week, a federal judge responded to a suit brought by the U. S. Department of Justice, decreed that Alabama's onerous 20-page voting test on government and the United States Constitution, aimed at disqualifying Negroes, must be discarded and that Dallas County registrars must process at least 100 applicants each day their offices are open.

The effects of the Selma demonstration spread to other Alabama cities. In nearby Marion, where Negroes outnumbered whites 11,500 to 6,000, Negroes tested the public accommodations section of the Civil Rights Act. They entered a drugstore and were served. They ordered cokes and received them filled with salt. And were charged the ridiculous price of $5.00, for a mere hamburger. The next day 15 Negroes were arrested after protesting in front of the drugstore. Later during the day nearly 700 Negro students boycotted their classes and marched toward the jail where the other students were being held. A state policeman stopped and told them: "Sing one more song and you are under arrest." James Orange, one of King's aides, told the students: "Sing another song." They did and were arrested.

King moved his voter registration drive to Montgomery, Alabama. He called for Negroes to march to the ballot boxes by the thousands. Instead of the thousands that he called for, only about 200 Negroes turned up.

Since 1962 Montgomery had gone out of its way to register all eligible voters. That same year Federal District Judge Frank M. Johnson, Jr. ordered an end to discrimination by city registrars. Those who were not registered were done so swiftly. Apparently Montgomery had learned the lesson of meeting violence with nonviolence!

King immediately returned to Selma, where segregationists had not learned their lessons. After four weeks of protesting over 3,500 people had been arrested and more were still going to jail.

The Negroes tried to register; again and again they were refused. After they were turned away, they merely went to the end of the waiting line. After seeing what the Negroes were doing, Sheriff Clark became so furious that he cried out vehemently: "You are making a mockery of justice."

The next day he and his men arrested 160 Negro teenagers for truancy outside of the court house. Clark emerged and commanded: "You like to march, so we'll let you. Move out!" He started marching them to the Fraternal Order of Police Lodge, some six miles away. Clark said the city jail was full.

Clark's men forced the children to double time and then trot by brandishing billy sticks and electric prods. Several of the youngsters slogged along and some dropped out, vomiting, while others faltered and cried.

The children's march went on for nearly three miles, until finally, Clark and his deputies became wearied and let them "escape." Actually, the students broke ranks and ran into the yards of nearby Negro farmhouses.

The following day wire services carried front-page pictures and editorials of the forced march. The Selma white community was beginning to finally take notice of what was happening to their city. Mass arrests were bad enough for the city's image. Now, in a front-page editorial, *The Selma Time Journal* said it could find "no reasonable explanation" for the march. The "march" did more harm than good, and it only swelled attendance on the daily picket lines," the paper said.

The marches, picketing, demonstrations and criticisms from both whites and Negroes took its toll on Sheriff Clark. At the end of the week, he was suffering from chest pains and exhaustion and was taken to Vaughan Memorial Hospital, for observation and rest.

Outside of the hospital about 200 demonstrating Negroes knelt—unmolested to pray for him. Some carried signs that bore the message: "Jim Clark, get well in mind and body."

Martin Luther King, Jr. was also in bed with a cold but not in the hospital. He stayed in bed for two days, but arose to renew his voter registration drive. He led about 1,500 Negroes to the courthouse. This time he had his first parade permit. Ninety-one Negroes were permitted to apply. This was the largest number for a single day in Selma's history.

The next day, Clark also arose from his bed to halt anymore gains by Negroes. He appeared outside of the courthouse, in the rain, and read a court order forbidding demonstrations. The Reverend C. T. Vivian, a close associate of Dr. King, said to Clark, "Maybe you're not as bad as Hitler, but you are an evil man!" At this point Clark planted a solid punch to his mouth and knocked him to the ground.

Later Clark declared: "If I hit him, I don't know it. One of the first things I ever learned was not to hit a nigger with your fist because his head is too hard. Of course, the camera might make me out a liar. I think I have a broken finger."

A newsreel was present when the incident occurred. James Clark still had not learned how not to handle a racial demonstration: Don't make any mistakes that can be photographed!

Selma was not the only place where violence was occurring. Some of the worse violence during that time broke out in Marion, Alabama. About 425 Negroes started marching from Zion Methodist Church to the town jail. They were protesting the arrest of a fellow worker. Eight Marion policemen, 50 state Policemen and a number of agitators, including Sheriff James Clark, who was dressed in civilian clothes, waited for the Negroes outside the church.

When they came out, Marion Police Chief T. O. Harris told the Negroes: "This is an unlawful assembly. You are hereby ordered to disperse. Go home or go back to the church." Some Negroes kept walking. At that point the policemen launched forward. Some Negroes ran and tried to take refuge in Mac's Cafe, about a block from the church, but State troopers crashed in after them. Jimmy Lee Jaskson, a Negro, made a break for the door, and was shot in the stomach. He was taken to a hospital in critical condition and later died. About fifteen Negroes were treated for injuries, including six women. Three newsmen were also beaten by white segregationists, as they tried to take pictures.

The next day the *Montgomery Journal* called the violence in Marion "a nightmare of state police stupidity" and the "worst outrage since the church bombing in Birmingham." The newspaper also said: "Alabama is, once again worse than ever before disgraced by mindless 'police work' and blood."

The next week funeral services were held for Jimmy Lee Jackson at the Zion Methodist Church. About 1,000 Negroes attended the funeral. Reverend Ralph Abernathy attended the services and declared: "Jimmy Jackson had taken his rightful place alongside such men as Crispus Attacks, Abraham Lincoln, John Kennedy, John Brown, Medgar Evers . . . "

Reverend Martin Luther King, Jr. attended the services also and offered this consolation: "There is an amazing democracy about death." cried King: "Farewell, Jimmy, you died that all of us could vote, and we are going to vote."

After the funeral services King and Abernathy immediately returned to Selma to begin the seventh week of the voter registration campaign.

During this drive, Kenneth Crawford wrote a brilliant article in *Newsweek* on Martin Luther King, Jr., Selma, Alabama and the "RIGHT TO VOTE." [34]

The same week King led 400 Negroes, in drenching rain, to the courthouse, where Sheriff Clark was, as usual, standing resolutely in the doorway. King appealed to Clark "in the name of humanity" to let the applicants enter and get out of the pouring rain. "There isn't room. It would interfere with orderly procedures. In the name of common sense, they will have to stay out," said Clark. That statement seemed strange. After all, when have the registration procedures, in Selma, Alabama, ever, been orderly. By the end of the day, however, a record of 200 applications had been received.

Chapter Twenty-Two

FROM SELMA TO MONTGOMERY

Later the Negroes gathered again. While they were waiting to register, they were singing "We Shall Overcome." Sheriff Clark replied by pinning a button on his shirt reading "Never!"

After the shooting of Jimmy Lee Jackson, King called for a march from Selma to the state capitol at Montgomery, a distance of over 50 miles.

The same night King told a mass crowd at a rally at the Brown Chapel African Methodist Episcopal Church, "I can't promise you that it won't get you beaten. I can't promise you that it won't get your house bombed. I can't promise you that it won't get you scarred up a bit. But we must stand up for what is right."

Governor George Wallace had been silent until now and had made no plea for peace in Selma. After he heard of the planned march, he forbid it. The march, however, had gained too much momentum for him to stop it.

The march was held on the Sunday afternoon of March 7. King had orginally planned to lead it, but was persuaded at the last minute by his aides, to stay in Atlanta—for his safety's sake. Approximately seven hundred Negroes gathered at Brown Chapel Church on Sylvan Street for the march. The group was headed by S.N.C.C.'s John Lewis, and S.C.L.C.'s Hosea Williams. The Negroes filed through the back streets of Selma, turned down Broad Street, and marched toward the Edmund Pettus Bridge.

The marchers stopped when they were 25 yards from the bridge. State Police Major John Cloud told them over a bullhorn: "Turn around and go back to your church! You will not be allowed to march any further! You've got two minutes to disperse!"

Everyone was in suspense as the seconds ticked by. Would the marchers go back? Or would they continue? The Negroes stood their ground! Then Major Cloud gave the order: "Trooper-forward!" The patrolmen had formed a solid wall and pushed the Negroes back. The troopers then started swinging clubs.

The marchers retreated for a hundred yards, and the troopers still advanced on them. They then threw tear gas. By this time, possemen and deputies joined the patrolmen.

The possemen on horseback chased the marchers. One posseman's horse trampled a woman who had fallen. He told her, "O.K., nigger! You want to march—now march."

"Please! No!" begged a Negro, while a cop was beating her. "My God, we're being killed," cried another. Lewis described the plight, "We were helpless. The tear gas simply drove our folk to the heights of desperation. We screamed, hollered, prayed, ran everywhere to escape the suffocating fumes. Women vomited. Men gasped for breath and fell out exhausted." Meanwhile, now circled by the troopers, these suffering people were whipped, kicked by horses and shocked by cattle prods. One marcher cried, "God, how can they hate us so?" Still being chased by the sheriff's deputies, the Negroes finally managed to stagger across the bridge and make it to the Brown Chapel Church. About 80 Negroes were treated for injuries at a hospital.

The next day, all the major newspapers carried front-page pictures of the march. Rarely in history has public opinion reacted so spontaneously and with such sincerety.

President Johnson publicly declared that he "deplored the brutality" in Selma. He urged the city officials to cool down.

Governors usually do not interfere in other states' affairs, however, some did find it necessary, after seeing police brutality in the raw. Governor Edmund Brown of California sent a telegram to Governor Wallace declaring, "I have never seen anything more brutal." Governor Brown had just finished watching television films of Sunday's march.

Governor Richard Hughes of New Jersey urged the Federal Government to intervene. And his own legislature passed a resolution strongly condemning Alabama's actions. Governor John King of New Hampshire joined in a public prayer for Alabama.

Detroit's Mayor Jerome Cavanaugh and Michigan's Governor George Romney led a protest parade of 10,000 protesters. In New Jersey, California, New York, Connecticut, Washington, D. C., Wisconsin and Illinois demonstrators streamed into the streets and tied up traffic for hours, to express their rage.

An editorial in *The Atlanta Constitution* lashed the Selma brutalities and Alabama Governor Wallace: "It is a sad and morbid commentary that bleeding American citizens must fill hospitals, while a governor permits them to be clubbed down in the name of 'the law', when all they are asking under the law, is the simplest, most basic American right—to vote."

In her *New York World Telegram and Sun* column, Harriet Van Horne asserted, " . . . Guns, clubs, ropes and tear gas grenades" are the necessities of the "well-dressed Alabama trooper." All these items they consider "essential in holding the traditions of the Old South," she claimed. In lamenting the gassing and beating of the marchers in Selma, she wrote, "The police . . . had their masks snugly in place. The masks . . . were probably less sinister than the naked faces."

The march had been a failure! Martin Luther King, Jr. had only one course—to lead another march from Selma to Montgomery. The march was scheduled for Tuesday, March 9.

I

King said, in Atlanta, as a "matter of conscience" and in an attempt to arouse the deepest concern of the nation, he was compelled to march again.

King's plea was overwhelmingly received by whites and Negro clergymen, from city after city. From Indianapolis came A. Garnett Day, Jr., an official of the Disciples of Christ and Jewish Mission Worker, David Goldstein, Episcopal Bishop James Pike of California, Methodist Bishop John Wesley Lord, vice president of the National Council of Churches, Msgr. George L. Gingras of the Roman Catholic archdiocese of Washington, D. C., Rabbi Richard G. Hirsch of the Union of American Hebrew Congregation was there. James Wilcoxen, an instructor at the University of Chicago Divinity School came along with eight other faculty members. Several came from Yale and Harvard Universities Divinity Schools.

Mrs. Paul Douglas, wife of the Illinois Senator, Mrs. Harold Ickes, widow of Franklin D. Roosevelt's Interior Secretary, Mrs. Charles Tobey, widow of the former Republican Senator from New Hampshire also came. All that came to Selma had dropped what they were doing and headed for the nearest airport. Overnight more than 425 ministers, priests, rabbis, lay leaders, marchers and crusaders poured into Selma for the march. Many came without a toothbrush or any notion of where they would be sleeping for the night, but they came anyway.

In Washington, D. C., airline officials put on extra help to handle groups flying to Selma. In Atlanta, Delta Airlines scheduled extra flights for volunteers pouring into the area. In St. Louis, the local Conference on Race and Religion sent two chartered planes of religious leaders and kept others on standby for relief. The Reverend Ken Field of Des Moines, Iowa, explained the mass mobilization for civil rights when he asserted: "My six year-old daughter was so proud of me when I told her I was going to join Dr. Martin Luther King."

Colonel Al Lingo was in town with 500 of the state's 750 troopers. John Doar, Assistant U. S. Attorney General in charge of civil rights and LeRoy Collins, chairman of the U. S. Community Relations Service came at the request of President Johnson. F.B.I. agents also came to Selma.

At 4:30 Monday afternoon, the day before the march, four attorneys for King appeared in the Montgomery office of U. S. District Judge Frank M. Johnson, Jr. and asked him to issue an injunction to keep state and Dallas County police from interfering with the Tuesday march.

Judge Johnson told the attorneys that he would have to hear evidence on their petition, and scheduled a hearing for Thursday—the first available date. Mr. Johnson also advised them that King should call off the march.

The same night King and other civil rights leaders were under going extreme pressure from U. S. Attorney General Nicholas Katenbach and other attorneys. They wanted them to call off the march also but the leaders refused.

The next morning, the attorneys appeared before Judge Johnson and told him that King had decided to march. Mr. Johnson immediately issued an order enjoining the march until after the hearing on Thursday. This decision placed King in an even deeper dilemma. He had been criticized for not being present in the earlier march. Besides, he felt that he owed an obligation to the out-of-state people that had come to march.

The entire success of the civil rights movement had been based on upholding the laws of the land. If he marched, now, he would be defying a federal court order. Finally, King came to a decision of sorts. He would march to Montgomery, but, stop it before trouble occurred.

Despite the federal court order, most of the 1,500 people in and around the Brown Chapel Church still wanted to march and sentiment was strong.

According to Mrs. Paul Douglas, "going to Selma to stand up with the natives is consistent with all I believe in. We Americans cannot afford any community to defy the Constitution or American principles. We must act on our convictions. This is no funny business. They are not exhibitionists." She was particularly impressed by the young men and women who had showed moral superiority and staying power. "Northern youth, both Negro and white, could follow the example of young Selmans," stated Mrs. Douglas.

Mrs. Douglas also declared that "It seems if we wait two more days we are losing a great deal of public support." A Roman Catholic priest suggested "It's about time we walked that last mile."

Rabbi Israel Dresner of Springfield, New Jersey said, "There is a higher law in God's universe and that is God's law. There is a time when man must choose between man's law and God's law."

Reverend George Docherty of the Washington's New York Avenue Presbyterian Church, expressed the feeling of all the clergymen, when he said, "I'm here for three reasons. One, I think the fundamentals of the Christian church are at stake in this hour. Someone said this is the largest gathering of ministers since the Council of Trent. I'd venture to say it is

195

also just as important. We differ in the way we interpret the Scripture. But at this moment the church is being challenged." Two, "The constitution of the United States is at stake here. Three, "We are in the midst of a revolution regarding human rights. Sunday evening my wife and I watched T.V. and saw those ghastly scenes our stomachs turned."

Earlier mediator LeRoy Collins had met with Smitherman, Lingo and Clark. They were willing to let the marchers cross the bridge to the place where the Sunday's march had ended in disaster. Then the troopers would turn King and the marchers back and King would leave peaceably. King had agreed to this arrangement.

King arrived about a half-hour before the march started. He told the crowd, "I have made my choice. I have to march. I do not know what lies ahead of us. There may be beatings, jailings, tear gas. But I would rather die on the highways of Alabama than make a butchery of my conscience! There is nothing more tragic in all this world than to know right and not do it. I cannot stand in the midst of all these glaring evils and not take a stand. There is no alternative in conscience or in the name of morality."

II

The march began as scheduled. In the front line were four S.N.C.C. workers. Behind them were King, his brother, A. D. King, James Farmer, Ralph Abernathy, and others. The marchers were stopped at the foot of the bridge by a United States Marshal who read portions of Judge Johnson's court order. King replied to the order and he spoke of his painful and difficult decision. The U. S. Marshal stepped aside and the march continued.

King and the marchers crossed the bridge and at this point King stopped the procession as planned. Major John Cloud raised his bullhorn and said, "I ask you to stop this march. You will not continue—you are ordered to stop and stand where you are." King asked Mr. Cloud if it were all right to "have some of the great religious leaders of our nation lead us in prayer." Cloud granted his permission. At this point, King motioned Reverend Ralph Abernathy to lead the prayer. Hundreds in the procession knelt and Abernathy said, "We come to present our bodies as living sacrifice. We don't have much to offer, but we do have our bodies, and we lay them on the altar today." Later other ministers prayed. When they had finished, Cloud turned to his troopers and said, "Clear the road completely—move out! The troopers, then moved to the sides of the highway.

According to plans, King was supposed to turn back only because he had been told to by the authorities. But King did not fall for the trap. Instead, King walked back and told the marchers to turn back. The crowd proceeded to the church. The march was part failure and part success.

The only thing that could add up to total victory for the civil rights movement would be some foolish act by white racists. As usual, they came to the rescue of the movement.

That night three white ministers, including James Reed, dined at a Negro restaurant in Selma. As they left the restaurant, they passed the Silver Moon Cafe which was for white only. Several white men came toward them and yelled, "Hey Nigger." The white men then started hitting them unmercilessly on their heads with clubs. Several white men in the Cafe saw the fight, but did not try to stop it. The victims staggered for three blocks, before they found help.

Reverend Reed remained in a coma for two days. Twice his heart stopped and twice doctors managed to start it beating again. Mr. Reed never came out of the coma and later died.

Everyone from President Johnson, Congressmen, Mr. Katzenbach and Dr. King, were besieged by telegrams, telephone calls, and personal visits, protesting Reverend Reed's untimely death.

By Friday of that week, President Johnson was convinced that a presidential statement to the nation was in order. He was determined to make the Government's position unmistakably clear!

Meanwhile, Governor George Wallace, who had remained silent, suddenly was a visitor at the White House. President Johnson told the Governor bluntly, the Negro was obviously going to win his right to participate in his own Government.

Then he said, "You ought to be thinking of where you will stand in 1995, not 1965."

The President held a news conference, after his meeting with the Governor, and stated that he would propose to Congress a bill that would guarantee every citizen's franchise. The President said:

> It is wrong to do violence to peaceful citizens in the streets of the town. It is wrong to deny Americans the right to vote. It is wrong to deny any person full equality because of the color of his skin. The promise of America is a simple promise: Every person shares in the blessings of this land, and they shall share on the basis of their merits as a person. They shall not be judged by their color or by where they were born or the neighborhood in which they live.

> Those who do injustice are as surely the victims of their own acts as the people that they wrong. They scar their own lives and they scar the communities in which they live. If we put aside disorder and violence, if we put aside hatred and lawlessness, we can provide for all our people great opportunity almost beyond our imagination.

> I advised the Governor of my intention to press with all the vigor at my command to assure that every citizen of this country is given the right to participate in his Government at every level through the complete voting process. We are a nation that is governed by laws, and our procedure for enacting and amending and repealing these laws must prevail. I told the Governor that we believe in maintaining law and order in every county and in every precinct in this land. If state and local authorities are unable to function, the Federal Government will completely meet its responsibilities.

> I told the Governor that the brutality in Selma last Sunday just must not be repeated. I urged that the Governor publicly declare his support for universal suffrage in the state of Alabama and the United States of America.

Even as the President spoke, hearings were being held before Judge Johnson on the injunction. No decision had been reached, and things were continuously getting worse in Selma, and across the country protests had erupted everywhere. In San Francisco students waded into the Federal Building's ornamental pool. In New York City, Sisters of Charity marched with large SNCC's posters. In Boston, students from Harvard, MIT, Brandeis and Radcliffe universities protested at the Federal building. And in Philadelphia about thirty five students slept in rolled blankets around the Liberty Bell.

III

Later during the week Judge Johnson finally authorized the march from Selma to Montgomery and told the State of Alabama to provide protection. Governor Wallace tried to appeal the decision, but was turned down.

Mr. Wallace sent two telegrams to President Johnson telling him that he would not protect the marchers. He said it would cost about $400,000 and 6,171 men to police the march. Wallace demanded "federal civil authorities" to protect the marchers. President Johnson told the Governor, "responsibility for maintaining law and order in our federal system properly rests with state and local government." The President, however, sent the Alabama National Guard onto the parade route.

The civil rights leaders planned the march to military percision. Every conceivable detail was taken care of, from tents for overnight stops to portable latrines to ambulances. It would be the March on Washington, only on a smaller scale! The parade would follow the same route that was attempted two weeks ago.

Violence was continuing to flare elsewhere also. In Montgomery 600 students assembled at the Jackson Street Baptist Church to march to the capital. On the way to the Church they sang a song:

> What do you want, what do you want?
> Freedom, Freedom, Freedom!
> When do you want it, when do you want it?
> Now, Now, Now!
> How much do you want, how much do you want?
> All of it, All of it, All of it!
> What do you want . . . .

As they started down Decatur Street, they were stopped by city and state policemen. When they refused, the policemen beat them with clubs. One policeman had cornered a teenager against a porch and a priest ran down to protect him. "Please let the boy go," cried the priest. The policeman paid no attention to the priest. Instead he said, "You bastard preacher!"

The president of the United States was fully aware of the racial situation and he went before Congress to express his concern.[33] Mr. Johnson's speech was well received. At first, then like a great wave, for several minutes, the members of Congress stood pouring out thunderous applause. President Lyndon B. Johnson strode from the chambers a changed man—more hopeful and confident in American democracy.

IV

Airplane after airplane and bus after bus brought more people to Selma. There was one-legged James Leatherer, from Michigan, walking on crutches. A nun from Kansas City. Blind participant Joe Young, from Atlanta, resting on the arm of his 64-year old mother. Beatniks from New York City were there. Sam Farr of Ontario, Canada was there. Representatives from fifty states were present—all determined to march and be part of this mammoth event. Everything and everyone was ready to begin.

It started on the Sunday afternoon of March 21. There were 4,000 marchers led by Dr. Martin Luther King, Jr., and Dr. Ralph Bunche. The first day, they marched eleven miles. They were well protected by 1,000 military police sent by President Johnson, by 1,900 federalized Alabama National Guardsmen, by U.S. Marshals and F.B.I. agents. At night, before the marchers were permitted to enter the open field to bed down, soldiers would check it thoroughly for bombs, mines or booby traps.

On the second day, the procession walked eleven more miles. Meanwhile, the Alabama Legislature passed a resolution claiming that there had been "evidence of much fornication" at the marchers' camps. No one, however, came forward with the "evidence." John Lewis of SNCC stated his answer to the allegation: "All these segregationists can think of is fornication, and that is why there are so many different shades of Negroes."

On the third day, the marchers covered seventeen miles. That night they were entertained by Nipsey Russell, Odetta, Tony Bennett, Joan Baez, Nina Simone, Dick Gregory and Billy Eckstine. Actresses Ina Balin and Shelley Winters along with actors Gary Merrill, William Marshall and Purnell Roberts were there. Sammy Davis, Jr. closed his hit Broadway show "Golden Boy" and flew in from New York City, to entertain the marchers. Harry Belafonte, left his troupe on the coast and came also. Floyd Patterson, former heavyweight champion of the world, was there. Writer James Baldwin and Alexander Aldrich, cousin of Governor Rockefeller, were there. Leonard Bernstein came from New York City and performed for thousands in a muddy field near Montgomery.

Martin Luther King, Jr. left the same day to make a speech in Cleveland, Ohio. He, however, returned a few miles outside of Montgomery.

Roger Lee, 82-year old grandfather of Jimmy Lee Jackson, was perhaps, the most apologetic pilgrim of all. He walked only a few miles on the first day and had to quit with tears in his eyes. He, however, returned off and on to put in a few miles to show his interest in the march. "Just got to tramp some more," he said repeatedly. Thousands more kept tramping until the day of "freedom."

The big day came on Thursday, the final day of the march. The parade was outside the state capitol. At the entrance stood state troopers. On the steps most of the leaders gave long, and sometimes boring and tiring addresses for two hours.

Finally, Martin Luther King, Jr. arose and gave the crowd what they were waiting to hear. He was magnificent! He started in a slow deep voice:

> We have walked on meandering highways and rested our bodies on rocky byways. They told us we would not get here. And there were those who said that we would get here only over their dead bodies, but all the world today knows that we are here and that we are standing before the forces of power in the state of Alabama, saying, "We ain't goin' let nobody turn us around. . . ."
>
> I know you are asking today, How long will it take? I come to say to you this afternoon however difficult the moment, however frustrating the hours, it will not be long because truth pressed to earth will rise again. How long? Not long, because no lie can live forever. How long? Not long, because you still reap what you sow. How long? Not long, because the arm of the moral universe is long, but it bends toward injustice . . . .

He reached the climax and cried out the words of the "Battle Hymn of the Republic", with a rhythmic chant: "Glory hallelujah! Glory hallelujah! Glory hallelujah!

Glory Hallelujah!" According to *Ebony,* in the four days the march had attracted nearly 50,000 people. The march was a success! No violence had occurred up to this point.

The entire purpose of the march had been to present to Governor Wallace a petition protesting voting discrimination. Earlier the Governor had said he would see "any citizen of Alabama." Twenty Alabamaians had signed a petition and wanted to give it to him. An aide came forward and told the petitioners, "This capitol is closed today."

Later the Governor went on television and denounced the march again. He called it a "prostitution of lawful process." Mr. Wallace declared: "I see that Ralph Bunche, the United Nations man, was here. He's supposed to be defending us against Communists, but today he was consorting with known communists."

V

Later during the evening a motorcade moved along U.S. Highway 80 returning from Montgomery to Selma. A period of peace prevailed for a short time. In characteristic fashion, however, it was disturbed by white racists of Alabama. Mrs. Viola Gregg Luizzo, white and 39 years old, was shot in the temple, while returning to Selma. LeRoy Moton, a Negro, and 19 years old and a member of the S.C.L.C., was in the car with Mrs. Luizzo. He laid on the floor of the 1963 Oldsmobile, pretending to be dead, as the gunmen searched the car. After the gunmen left, Moton hitchhiked about 20 miles out of Selma for help. By the time help arrived, Mrs. Luizzo was dead.

The following morning Governor Wallace was interviewed on NBC's "Today Show." The Governor was asked to comment on the murder of Mrs. Luizzo. He said: "Of course, I regret this incident. I would like to point out, though, that people are assaulted in every state in the Union. It's still safer on Highway 80 than it is riding a subway in New York. You can't blame any one individual about things that happen in Alabama anymore than you can blame Governor Rockefeller about Malcolm X being slain in New York. And I regret this incident, but I can say with 25,000 people marching in the streets and chanting and maligning and slandering and libeling the people of this state as they did for several hours on your network and other networks, I think the people of our state were greatly restrained."

Mr. Wallace was only adding venom to the violence, by making such reckless allegations.

About sixteen hours after Mrs. Luizzo's death, the FBI had arrested four members of the KKK in connection with the slaying.

President Johnson was obviously angered at what had happened and the statements made by the Governor of Alabama. The President deemed it necessary to go before the nation on national television and express his feelings for the murder of Mrs. Luizzo. Mr. Johnson labeled the KKK as a "hooded society of bigots." The President said:

> "Mrs. Luizzo went to Alabama to serve the struggle for justice . . . She was murdered by the enemies of justice who for decades have used the rope and the gun and the tar and the feathers to terrorize their neighbors. They struck by night as they generally do, for their purpose cannot stand the light of day . . .
>
> If the Klansmen hear my voice today, let it be both an appeal— and a warning—to get out of the Ku Klux Klan now and return to a decent society— before it is too late. Justice must be done, in the largest city as well as the smallest village, on the dirt road or on the interstate highway. We will not be intimidated by the terrorists of the Klu Klux Klan anymore than we will be intimidated by the terrorists in North Viet Nam . . ."

Violence was continuing to spread to other cities in Alabama. In Camden, demonstrators took up where they had left off in Selma—only 33 miles away. In Birmingham, scene of 25 racial bombings over a ten year period, a bomb with 15 sticks of dynamite was discovered before causing more deaths.

The white racists' highhanded methods of trying to halt the civil rights movement only added impetus to it. Because of the incidents in Camden and Birmingham, Martin Luther King, Jr. threatened an economic boycott of the whole state of Alabama, as a means of ending "this reign of terror." The boycott was received unfavorably by friend and foe. Mostly because of the effect it would have on the Negroes and the innocent whites in Alabama.

President Johnson said at a news conference, "We must be very careful to see that we do not punish the innocent while we are trying to protect our people."

The same week, Dr. King attended a meeting of the Southern Christian Leadership Conference in Baltimore, Maryland. He was asked by reporters, "What would you do if President Johnson personally asked you to call off the boycott?" "I'm afraid, I would have to say no to him," said King.

Dr. King proposed a three-stage boycott, instead of a total and immediate boycott. The first stage would begin with a cutoff of all federal funds. The second stage would be to appeal to the major United States companies, such as International Paper, Dan River Mills, Hammermill Paper and about 30 others to cancel plans to build factories in Alabama. The final stage would be to use as a last resort—a nationwide boycott of all Alabama-made consumer products.

Chapter Twenty-Three

WATTS: AN AMERICAN DILEMMA

Between April and August, Martin Luther King, Jr. dropped from headlines for a while. He was traveling around the country making speeches. King visited mostly Northern states. He was not only speaking about the civil rights movement and nonviolence but also about international affairs.

King visited New York City and addressed the New York City Bar Association. He told the lawyers that the civil rights groups have a right to defy the law if only because "they had no part in making" so many laws that affect Negroes. "What the United States needs is a divine discontent," King declared. He also spoke on the test ban, religious bigotry, the madness of militarism and the self-defeating effects of physical violence. He also urged the formation of an "International Association for the Advancement of Creative Maladjustment."

King left New York City, and went to Boston, Massachusetts. He appeared before the Massachusetts Legislature and also met Governor John A. Volpe.

At a news conference King said he did not mind having fellow civil rights leaders speak out against the United States' involvement in Viet Nam. He also spoke against nuclear bomb testing. "One cannot be just concerned with civil rights. What good does it do me to integrate a lunch counter if the milk I drink there is loaded with strotium 90?" said King.

The civil rights groups were continuously taking stands on broader issues, such as the United States foreign policy. Many observers of the civil rights movement believe that the organizations should tend to their own cause. It should be noted that the leaders voiced their opinions on foreign affairs, not as leaders of their respected organizations, but as individual citizens.

Dr. King felt that the civil rights movement must become involved with issues that affect the United States whether home or abroad, and that the movement must not be afraid to address itself to the problems of war.

"It's marvelous to talk about integration, but we've got to have a world in which to be integrated. I'm not going to sit silently by the wayside and see war being escalated in our world and never rise up to say a word about it. All I know is that the war in Viet Nam must be stopped. And I also know that there must be a negotiated settlement," declared King.

Martin Luther King, Jr. and other civil rights organizations had become more and more involved in foreign affairs. The Congress of Racial Equality passed a resolution at its 21st national convention that called for the withdrawal of United States troops in Viet Nam. Roy Wilkins of the National Association for the Advancement of Colored People said, as far as his organization is concerned, "we think we have enough Viet Nam in Alabama. . . ."

On August 5, 1965, King led nearly 6,000 persons in a 15-block march to the White House in appreciation of President Johnson's endorsement of the home rule for the District of Columbia. The march climaxed a two-day visit by Dr. King during which time he looked at Negro housing, education, and employment possibilities in Washington.

The following day, President Lyndon B. Johnson signed into law the Voting Rights Act of 1965. The President went before national television and radio and spoke of the bill. He recalled that the first Negro slaves in the United States were landed at Jamestown in 1619. "They came in darkness and chains. Today we strike away the . . . major shackles of those fierce and ancient bonds," he said.

"Today is a triumph for freedom as huge as any victory won on any battlefield. Today the Negro story and the American story fuse and blend," declared President Johnson.

The President continued, "the time for waiting is gone." He concluded: ". . . Let me now say to every Negro in this country: you must register, you must vote. And you must learn, so your choice advances your interest and the interest of our beloved nation. Your future depends upon it. . . ."

The 1965 Voting Right Act would add millions of American Negroes to the nation's voting rolls if vigorously enforced.

In a matter of days after the signing of the bill, Federal Examiners were sent to parts of seven states with authority to register disenfranchised persons.

Even though federal registrars were not sent into Georgia, Negroes in Americus, scene of a militant drive for equality, had been registering in unprecedented numbers. In America, it took 100 years to get 1,000 Negroes on the segregated voting rolls. With the impetus of the new voting bill and the prodding of the S.C.L.C. and S.N.C.C., 1,003 Negroes were registered in just three days!

Even in Mississippi, many of the most intimidated delta-area Negroes flocked out to registration offices, signed their "X", then left within minutes.

The Justice Department worked over-time preparing lists of all counties that fail to meet the franchise requirement set by the bill.

The civil rights organizations had already made preparations for getting Negroes out to register. The organizations had actually enrolled several thousand Negroes before President Johnson had signed the bill.

President Johnson warned that the right to vote was not the end of the Freedom Road for the Negroes; ahead lay the long twilight struggle to erase "the wounds and the weaknesses, the outward walls and the inward scars," the Voting Rights Acts of 1965 was a milestone measuring the long way traveled by Americans, black and white, from the streets of Selma and the docks of Jamestown. "This is a victory . . . for freedom of the American nation, and every family across this entire searching land will live stronger in liberty, more splendid in expectation, and prouder to be Americans because of the Act which you have passed and I will sign today," said President Johnson.

I

Less than two weeks after President Johnson signed the 1965 Voting Rights Act, a major riot broke on the southeastern fringe of Los Angeles, the Negro ghetto of Watts.

Two white highway patrolmen arrested a Negro man, Marquette Frye, for reckless driving. According to eye-witness reports, the patrolmen had beaten and kicked Frye into the squad car. The policemen, however, denied that there was any brutality. But the word of the arrest spread and the crowd grew quickly. Soon about 2,000 Negroes started throwing rocks at stores and passing cars in a ten-square-block area.

Later during the week, stores were looted and Negroes carted off TV sets, lamps, radios, air conditioners, clothing and anything that was not nailed down.

The riot, by this time, had spread over a 150 square block area. And even police and news helicopters were fired upon.

The following night 2,000 helmeted National Guardsmen moved into the riot torn area with mounted machine guns. The Negroes had purchased guns and armed themselves also. It was policemen versus rioters and looters and Guardsmen were wounded and killed in gun battles.

President Johnson was in Texas at his ranch and branded the disorders as "tragic and shocking." The President urged every person in a position of leadership to make every effort to restore order in Los Angeles. Mr. Johnson sent LeRoy Collin and White House Assistant, Lee White to California to confer with Governor Edmund G. Brown.

Violence was erupting in other sections of the United States also—Chicago, Illinois and Springfield, Massachusetts. Those incidents probably would not have been noticed in less volatile times.

When the riots started in Los Angeles not a single Negro leader even bothered going to Watts, other than Martin Luther King, Jr. He was in Miami, Florida and could not immediately avail himself. In fact, before King came, Governor Brown discouraged him from coming. But King came anyway.

Dr. King met with local Negro leaders and told them that Negroes must join hands and work together.

Martin Luther King, Jr. was rarely received hostilely by Negroes. This time, however, his plea for peace and non-violence was received most chillily and disrespectfully.

He addressed a crowd, at the Westminister Neighborhood Association Center that really did not care to hear what he had to say. As he walked through the crowd to the platform, he could see the expressions of anger on the Negroes' faces.

Dr. King began anyway and the audience buzzed so noisily that Bayard Rustin stepped forward and demanded that they at least allow him to finish. King continued and again the buzzing started. Again King began. "What this community needs is to get together and . . ." "Burn, baby . . ." a voice yelled to finish the sentence King started.

Without blinking an eye, he continued his address. To convey his message, he evoked all the symbols of Christianity and brotherly love. His deep voice and sermon-like oratory began to sway the audience. Now the mood was changing!

He called the roll of the dead, both whites and Negroes, who had laid down their lives in defense of freedom and equality. He spoke of Reverend James Reed, Mrs. Viola Luizzo, Andrew Goodman, and Michael Schwerner. King's point was simply this: All white people should not be put in the same category, despite the injustices injected by some upon Negroes.

If any one thing reached the Negroes, it was the name of Elijah Muhammad, leader of the Black Muslims. King cried, "Even he is my brother, even though our methods are different."

The audience expressed its approval by cheering and smiling. It was obvious, by now, that he had won at least one round in his mission to change the mood of the Negroes. His mission was a success and the people present were obviously impressed by his plea!

The local Negro leaders generally agreed that Dr. King's plea had a positive effect on the community. The leaders appreciated his help and they felt that he was needed to give the ghetto dwellers new hope. They, however, felt that Reverend King should leave the real task of cleaning up the ghettos to them. After all, they knew how to combat the problem best.

King also met with Major Sam Yorty (who did his best to avoid being photographed with him) and Police Chief William Parker, who burst into a fist-pounding tirade against "black agitators," including King himself. King suggested a civilian board to review complaints against policemen. Chief Parker refused to even listen! Instead he "just blew and said he wouldn't even think about it." King met with the city officials for two hours and left in dismay. He later said, "I really don't see a willingness here to do anything."

About 35 persons died and 1,000 were injured during the riot. Property damage was estimated at $50 million, with 750 buildings damaged or destroyed by fires. Nearly 5,000 had been arrested for possession of stolen goods, disorderly conduct, disturbing the peace and possession of fire arms.

What caused the riot? Who was to blame? How did it happen? Why did it happen? There were as many explanations as there were points of views. Dr. King, perhaps, gave the most accurate explanations: "I strongly deplore the violence. It is absolutely wrong, socially detestable and self-defeating. On the other hand, I equally deplore the continuation of ghetto life that millions of Negroes have to live in. They are in hopeless despair, and they feel they have no stake in society."

Senator Robert F. Kennedy said of the riot: "All these places—Harlem, Watts, South Side—are riots waiting to happen and one of the reasons is the alienation of the ghetto from the responsible leaders. The army of resentful and desperate is larger in the North than in the South—but it is an army without generals, without captains, without sergeants." One answer, the Senator said, is that middle-class Negroes themselves will have to provide "more leadership."

News commentator Edward P. Morgan declared of the riot: "If responsible officials had paid more than passing attention to conditions in the 'Black Ghetto', as the Negro neighborhood of Watts is called, the dynamite of human frustration and fury might have been weakened somewhat. On his way back from Greece, California's Governor Edmund G. Brown was quoted as saying he couldn't understand why in the world there had been such a disturbance. It is irresistible to wonder when was the last time the governor had walked the streets or talked to the inhabitants of Watts. Civil rights workers and sociologists had been warning for a long time that trouble was brewing there. . . ."

Mr. Morgan concluded, "Legislation won't solve the problems of Watts or Harlem, or Chicago's South Side or the ugly little crisis in Springfield, Mass., for that matter. . . But the struggle must go on." What can be done? "Better education . . .

210

better housing ... better job opportunities ... Something more is needed, not only in Los Angeles but in every other bi-racial community in the land: acceptance. Acceptance of the black man by the white man as a fellow human being."

Several periodicals commented on Watts and the role Martin Luther King, Jr. played there. *Newsweek* for August 30, 1965, declared, "In all the history of the Negro revolt, no single leader has moved more men to disciplined, non-violence action in the name of God and the cause of equality than Martin Luther King, Jr. . . . "[36] *Life* magazine also published an editorial on the riot and Martin Luther King, Jr. for August 27, 1965, entitled "Some Negroes Riot But Most Go Forward." [37]

Los Angeles was the only city in the nation which refused to carry out local anti-poverty programs because Mayor Samuel Yorty did not want to appoint poor people from the impoverished, slum-ridden areas to the local economic opportunity board, according to Sargent Shiver, Director of the Office of Economic Opportunity. Mr. Shiver said the attitude of Los Angeles officials could be described as "welfarism without representation" policy. "That doesn't solve any problem, people have to feel they are participating in society. That feeling of participation never developed," Mr. Shiver added.

The riot in Watts made one thing unmistakably clear—the civil rights organizations had not reached the Negroes in the slums and ghettoes of the West and North. The leaders, especially Martin Luther King, Jr., had pleaded the ghetto Negro's cause and it went unheeded.

After the riot in Watts, King immediately announced that he would launch a full assault on the slums and ghettoes in the West and North. He was well aware that the struggle in the West and North would be tougher than the ones in the South. He began by proposing an expansion of the Jobs Corps, public-works projects, federal aid, and more participation by the middleclass Negroes.

In August the Southern Christian Leadership Conference also held its Ninth Annual Convention in Birmingham, Alabama. The conference discovered a different city from the one it left in 1963.

The delegates stayed in the Thomas Jefferson Hotel in the heart of the city. The various committees of the Conference worked out of the remodeled Sixteenth Street Baptist Church.

Reverend Fred Shuttleworth, then President of the Alabama Christian Movement for Human Rights introduced Dr. King to the audience. Mr. Shuttleworth said, "There is still loose dynamite around. . . But some changes have been made. Police smiled less than they do now. And now, there is a marked degree of friendliness."

Reverend King gave his annual report and told the delegates, "this is the community that did so much to bring freedom to the South." He warned new demonstrations were being planned for Birmingham . . . King paid tribute to the four little girls who died in a bombing there and others who had given their lives for freedom, including Jimmy Lee Jackson, Reverend James Reed and Mrs. Viola Luizzo who died in the Selma Campaign.

Reverend Andrew Young gave the keynote address. He said that the next phase of the movement must be an experiment in political power in the South. Young concluded: "There are now ten Negroes sitting in the Georgia legislature and the next election will at least triple the number . . . across the Southland."

Not a single incident occurred during the Conference. In fact, the delegates were received warmly by the city. Birmingham, apparently, had learned the lesson of meeting violence with nonviolence.

Mrs. Coretta King was also doing her part to help the civil rights movement. In August, she went on a nine day singing tour. She appeared on the nation's concert stages in a dramatic, one-woman production featuring, in narrative and song, the struggle of her husband and other militant activists from the Montgomery bus boycott to the March on Washington. The song tour, which grossed an estimated $20,000 for the civil rights movement, took her to San Diego, Los Angeles, and San Francisco, California; Seattle, Washington and Portland, Oregon.

On stage Mrs. King captivated each audience with her natural charm and elegance. She moved them to tears with her moving narratives about beatings and the bombings, the love and the anger, the setbacks and the victories connected with Dr. King's struggle.

More such engagements, called Freedom concerts, were planned by Coretta. "My husband feels it is important that one parent remain at home to give the children security. But I would like to make a more complete witness by marching, and if necessary, going to jail," said Mrs. Martin Luther King, Jr.

II

In November, three months after the racial riot in Watts, Martin Luther King, Jr. wrote an article "Beyond the Los Angeles Riot" for the *Saturday Review* stating the meaning of the riot and how others can be averted.[38] He said: "The flames of Watts illuminated more than the Western sky; they cast light on the imperfections in the civil rights movement and the tragic shallowness of white racial policy in the explosive ghettos." He contended that Los Angeles could have expected the holocaust when its officials tied federal aid in political manipulation; when the rate of Negro unemployment soared above the depression level of the Thirties and when the population density of Watts became the worst in the nation.

Yet, even these tormenting visible conditions are less than the complete story. In 1964 California repealed its law forbidding racial discrimination. This revocation left many Negroes disillusioned. California, by its own shortsighted acts, was actually endorsing ghettos!

The question in focus is whether the civil rights movement, both North and South, would be nonviolent. King, more than anyone, believed that nonviolence would prevail. Not because Northern Negroes would settle for no-win tranquillity and calm; but because they could be convinced that there was a more effective method and a more moral one in nonviolent action.

King concluded: "The rushing history of change has been late to reach the North but it is now on a fixed northerly course.

The urban slums need not be destroyed by flames: earnest people of good will can decree their end nonviolently—as atrocious relics of a persisting unjust past." [39]

In November, Dr. and Mrs. King went to Paris, France, on their tour of European cities. While in Paris, King received several hundred dollars, from some of the city's top jazz musicians, for the Southern Christian Leadership Conference. The musicians staged an all-Sunday afternoon, standing room only jazz festival at the American Student Center, to raise money for the civil rights struggle "back home." The benefit was organized by Crawford Johnson.

The entertainers included: pianists Hazel Scott, Joe Turner and Michael Sardaby; horn men Dexter Gordon, Jacques Bulter, Bill Coleman and Nathan Davis; singers, Herbie Colman, Mae Mercer, Bobbie Parker and Marge McGlory; drummers, Charles Bellonzi, Sam Kali and Roland Hayenes; organist Lou Bennett and actresses Marpressa Dawn and Nancy Holloway. Mrs. King also appeared on the program. She recited Langston Hughes' poem, "Crystal Stairs."

Martin Luther King, Jr.'s last major tour of the United States was in December. He closed out the year, 1965, by sweeping across Alabama's "Black Belt" urging Negroes to continue voter registration drives, prodding them into increasing political action, and warning his people not to be lulled to sleep because an all-white jury convicted three Klu Klux Klansmen on federal conspiracy charges in the death of Mrs. Viola Luizzo.

Reverend King journeyed to Eutaw, Jackson and Selma, Alabama. The dominant theme throughout the tour was his warning that federal officials were backing off on promises of legislation to insure equal justice for Negroes in Southern courts.

In Selma, King called for a job training plan for Negroes, similar to the GI Bill for World War II veterans. He insisted that Negroes are unable to get good jobs because they lack the training and America must atone for this sin by going out of its way to provide job training for them similarly to the GI Bill which helped World War II servicemen. "If this is not done, America will suffer the consequences," King concluded.

Another year comes to an end in the life and times of Martin Luther King, Jr. It was another violent year and one of massive demonstrations and riots. It was the year that 50,000 people marched from Selma to Montgomery, Alabama, to petition their government. Martin Luther King, Jr. led the mammoth march and again was acclaimed as the unchallenged voice of the Negro American people.

The year 1965 gave the Negro the Voting Rights Act and Watts—an American dilemma. Yet, even in Watts, Martin Luther King, Jr., gave new hope to disillusioned Negroes.

After 1965, with the help of Martin Luther King, Jr., Negroes will never again be where they were or what they were!

Chapter Twenty-Four

KING MOVES NORTH

In early January 1966, Martin Luther King, Jr. announced that one of the major drives of the Southern Christian Leadership Conference for the year would be a "full-scale assault" against slum conditions in Chicago. This was the first campaign against a major Northern city by the SCLC. Chicago was selected because it was typical of those cities creating urban race problems throughout the North. Another reason was that King and his organization were invited by the Coordinating Council of Community Organizations (CCCO). This organization represented more than 40 local groups. King, therefore, had the support of all the major civil rights and civic groups in Chicago. King reasoned that if Chicago made progress, it would set the example for other cities, both Northern and Southern, in the United States.

More than 22 Southern Christian Leadership Conference members and staff had come to Chicago in August of 1965 and laid the groundwork for the massive campaign. Dr. King went to Chicago in early January to confer with Al Raby and other members of CCCO concerning the anti-slum drive for the coming year. He left Chicago in mid-January. However, King returned in late January and rented a $90.00 apartment in a faded brick building in the Lawndale ghetto. The apartment was in an all-Negro section and a short drive from the SCLC's office on the West Side. King rented the apartment so that he could personally experience slum conditions and to dramatize the SCLC's "end to slums" campaign. The civil rights leader stayed in Chicago two and sometimes three days a week; commuting back and forth from Atlanta.

One of the first things that Rev. King did was to inform Police Superintendent O. W. Wilson, of his group activities. He met with Mr. Wilson and told him that the same conditions that caused riots in Watts and other cities were present in

Chicago. He further stated that his staff's Southern experience had made Negroes regard the policemen as enemies and not friends.

After meeting with the Police Superintendent, King addressed a group at the Church of the Brethren on the West Side. He said: "There is no threat—the same problems are here and if something isn't done in a hurry we can see a darker night of social disruption." The church was crowded, and the slum residents told him of their problems. Some told him that there were overcrowded schools that had classrooms "like closets," gymnasiums "like dungeons," with no showers but a $2.00 shower towel fee. Others stated that there were history courses that ignored Negro history, and hospitals that refused Negroes entrance and housing without door locks. Of all the people that spoke of their despairs, Mrs. Millie Thompson, expressed the views of a large number present when she stated: "I get down and scrub all day. I'm tired of being mistreated. I thank God you came here Rev. King. My house, just now the kitchen is falling in. I'm not going to pay no rent where there are rats and nobody going to throw me out." King told the audience that a change was going to come and gave them hope of a brighter day.

King was fully aware that this campaign would have to be conducted differently than the ones in the South because there were no Bull Conners or Jim Clarke. He also realized that politics in the North was generally, if not always, run by Northern style political machinery. In the South, King knew his enemies from the outset. In the North, however, his opponents would try and remain neutral and play both sides against the middle by offering token accommodations to each side. In fact even Mayor Richard J. Daley of Chicago, "Welcomed" King and his staff to the windy city.

His drive to end slums got a boost from Charles H. Percy, who was the Republican candidate for the U. S. Senate from Illinois. Percy stated that "clocked in hypocrisy, discrimination in the North is just as real as discrimination anywhere." He also said that "Martin Luther King had made no mistake in coming to Chicago to mount an assault against our wretched slums."

Not all people, however, were glad to see King come to Chicago. In fact several threats were made on his life. On several occasions uniformed policemen had to accompany him when he spoke at mass rallies because of these threats. During the same time that threats were being made the House Un-American Activities Committee was hearing testimony that a plot to assassinate King had been planned in June of 1965, when he spoke at Antioch College at Yellow Springs, Ohio.

William Dawson, a Negro Congressman from the Illinois first district, unlike Percy, did not welcome King, either out of leadership jealousy or political fear. Dawson announced at a mass rally: "There are some who have come to Chicago to lead you astray. If those boys would get things straight where they live, we'll take care of things here." Even though Rep. Dawson was careful not to call any names, all present knew that he was referring to Martin Luther King, Jr.

The Nobel Peace Prize winner realized that if the campaign in Chicago were to be successful, he would need the assistance of other groups. He, therefore, used the forces of the churches, neighborhood unions, student movements, mass meetings, neighborhood rallies, workshops, and demonstrations against slums.

King even joined forces with Elijah Muhammad and both agreed to form a "common front" to eradicate slums in Chicago. Rev. King declared that he obviously had religious differences with Muhammad, but there were some areas, slums and areas other than slums, in which both could work together. The conference between the two was a historical one because it was the first meeting between these great leaders. King told Muhammad that he might not always agree with the Black Muslims in their philosophy or method. After the meeting, some observers were of the opinion that Dr. King had changed his nonviolence position. He had not. In fact, King also told Mr. Muhammad that his movement would continue to be nonviolent.

The movement in Chicago had some immediate effects on the slum conditions. Mayor Daley declared that every Chicagoan would be living in a building that would meet minimal code standards by 1967. He also remarked that the "full power of the resources of the city would be used in an unlimited way to erase the slum blights." Some landlords, also, saw the handwriting on the wall and made some much needed repairs to their buildings. The anti-slum campaign in Chicago also had profound effects on other cities across the nation.

In New York, slum occupants in some areas who did not have heat in their apartments were housed at the Astor Hotel at reduced rates. In Los Angeles, plans were announced to lease 1,000 vacant apartments from private owners and sublease them to low income families. Plans were made in other cities also to help slum dwellers in Newark and Trenton, New Jersey; in Nassau, Suffold and Queens counties in New York.

To help finance the massive anti-slum drive, the CCCO and SCLC sponsored a Freedom Festival, in March, in Chicago's International Amphitheater. More than 14,000 people paid an estimated $100,000 to see and hear Harry Belafonte, Sidney Poiter, Mahalia Jackson, Liz Lands, Dick Gregory, and Martin Luther King, Jr.

King was the principal speaker at the rally. He realized that he did not have the support of all Chicagoans and he took this opportunity to assure the gathering that the Chicago Freedom Movement would continue to encourage sit-ins, stand-ins, rent strikes, boycotts, picket lines, and every kind of protest, including civil disobedience and demonstrations, as long as they were nonviolent.

He continued to say that Southerners coming to Chicago "found themselves interwoven within a decaying infested slum community on the south and west sides of the city which has the largest concentration of colored citizens in an urban ghetto of any major city in the United States." In his closing remarks he said that he agreed that the colored citizens should lift themselves by their bootstraps. "But you can't do it, if you have no boots," he concluded.

In late March King left Chicago and went to Stockholm to help raise funds for his organization. On the way there he stopped in Paris for a rally. About 5,000 persons turned out to hear him. Harry Belafonte, Yves Montand and Hughes Affray, two French singers, and Dr. Jacques Monod, winner of the Nobel Prize for medicine, were also on the program. Dr. King spoke about the achievements American Negroes had made in recent years. He said, however, the gains were "almost miraclous" and that the Negroes existence was threatened by their economic conditions. Rev. King, Mrs. King, and Harry Belafonte, left Paris for Stockholm. While they were there, they had a half-hour audience with King Gustan VI Adolf. After the audience, they attended the Royal Opera House that night. Profits from the performance went to the Southern Christian Leadership Conference. Later that week they returned to the United States. King went to Atlanta and then to Chicago.

Three months had passed and King and his staff had not adopted a program that would eliminate the slum problem. Many Chicagoans were becoming skeptical of the organization's ability to succeed. King understood the problems of the slum residents, but he did not know the best method of attacking them. He knew that landlords collected rent but could not make needed repairs. King was aware that businessmen, in the slums, made large profits but would not invest any of the money back in these areas. He was not unmindful that most of the people that had interests in the slums did not live there. Rev. James Bevel, program director for the West Side Christian Parish, said what they had to do was to find a way to reverse all this, so that money will be coming in as well as going out. He further contended: "That when that happens people won't have to leave the slums to find a better life. They can stay right there and the slums will disappear."

In the latter part of May all the major civil rights organizations were invited to participate in the White House Civil Rights Conference. The Student Nonviolent Coordinating Committee, however, refused the invitation. King spoke out against their refusal and gave his views on Black Nationalism. He declared: "We see integration as an insidious subterfuge for white supremacy in this country. The goal of integration is irrelevant. Political and economic power is what black people have to have."

Martin Luther King, Jr. left Chicago in early June to join Floyd McKissick, national director of CORE, and Stokley Carmichael, chairman of SNCC, in Mississippi, to continue the 220-mile walk from Memphis to Jackson planned by James H. Meredith. Meredith's walk was cut short after 28 miles when a white man shot him in the back.

As the marchers and about 15 supporters were walking, the state troopers of Mississippi told them that they would have to march single or double file and off the pavement. At that point King said, "We marched on the pavement from Selma to Montgomery," one trooper replied, "I don't care if you march to China as long as you march on the side of the road." Another trooper began pushing King and said, "Let's get them off the pavement now." King asked, "Can't you stop pushing as he fell."

Mr. Meredith was marching to dramatize voter registration and to help Negroes conquer their fear of white Mississippians. Rev. King said that he hoped the march would help pass the Administration's pending civil rights bill. The bill provided for stiffer handling of persons who injured civil rights workers and give the Justice Department power to step in and prosecute.

The shooting of Meredith brought angry reactions from people all across the country and especially from Washington. Among those deploring the shooting and predicting it would stir Congress to act on the civil rights bill was Rep. Emanuel Cellar of the House Judiciary Committee and one of the sponsors of the bill. He declared: "There are times when the civil rights movement has no greater friend than its enemy. It is the enemy of civil rights who again and again produces the evidence to convince this nation that we cannot afford to stand still."

The next day King, along with Floyd McKissick, Stokley Carmichael, Charles Evers and Arthur Thomas, signed a manifesto which stated in part:

> This march will be a massive public indictment and protest of the failure of American society, the Government of the United States and the state of Mississippi to fulfill these rights. . . .

221

Mississippi is symbolic of every evil that American Negroes have long endured. Most important of all the President of the United States, who is charged with the duty of enforcing the laws of the United States, must enforce those laws justly and impartially for all men. . . .

King left Mississippi and went back to Chicago to resume his anti-slum campaign. He stayed there for a few days and returned to Mississippi because he was concerned over the criticism that the march had been receiving. Charles Evers said he was worried that many of the marchers were in the state for publicity and fund-raising purposes and that they "leave with the cameramen," instead of staying to help with voter registration. King said that they were not there to engage in publicity stunts, but they were there because things were not right in that state. He also thought the march would stimulate interest in registration by dispelling Negro fear.

Although he left Mississippi again and went to Atlanta and then to Chicago, King returned for the final few miles of the march. James H. Meredith, who started the walk also returned and took over the leadership. One of the many goals of the marchers was to persuade the Justice Department to send Federal registrars into over 500 Southern counties. They did not, however, succeed in accomplishing that goal. They did succeed in registering about 2,500 to 3,500 Negroes and encouraging more than 10,000 to join in the march at one time or another.

The next day the marchers brought the walk to an end at the State Capitol, where hundreds of National Guard troops, state highway patrolmen, and other state agents looked on with tear gas and riot guns in their hands.

As James H. Meredith began to speak, he was interrupted again and again by loud applause. He said:

> From what you've seen on television and what you have read in the newspapers, you might assume that I had been shot by a Negro, since all you've been hearing is about Negroes being divided. But from this day on, our focus is going to be on the issue freedom.

222

Later Martin Luther King, Jr. began to speak, and his voice was drowned out at times by the cheers of the more than 15,000 marchers. His speech was a variation of his now famous "I Have A Dream" he delivered for the equally famous March On Washington in 1963. He said that his dream had turned into a nightmare. He continued to remark that he had seen too much injustice in the administration of laws toward Negroes. But he still had a dream that even there in Mississippi justice would come to all of God's children. Dr. King also declared that the march and rally would go down in history as the greatest demonstration for freedom ever held in the state of Mississippi.

Stokely Carmichael was cheered when he declared "that Negroes must build a power base in this country so strong that we will bring them (whites) to their knees every time they mess with us."

Dr. Alvin Poussaint of the Medical Committee for the Human Rights was likewise cheered when he asserted: "The civil rights movement was doing more for the mental health of Negroes in this country than anything else."

Whitney M. Young, Jr. attended the rally and told the crowd that more Federal job training programs were on the way for Mississippi. He also said, "I assume you were not marching for your feet's sake but for jobs and education."

Although there were a few tense moments, the march and rally were a success and were without serious incidents. After the march King returned to Atlanta and then to Chicago where he continued his anti-slum campaign.

In mid-July King held a huge civil rights rally at Soldier's Field in Chicago where more than 50,000 attended. At the rally, he called for "open and just city and an end to the cement reservation of the city's Negroes." He further stated: "This day we must declare our own emancipation proclamation. This day we must commit ourselves to make any sacrifice necessary to change Chicago. We must decide to fill up the jails of Chicago, if necessary in order to end slums."

After the rally King led more than 40,000 in a massive march to the city's Loop and affixed 14 demands on the door of City Hall. They covered jobs, education, welfare, and housing. The mayor ignored the demands. Later that day violence broke out when policemen cut off a fire hydrant at Roosevelt Road and Throop St. Negro teenagers had turned it on to apparently get relief from the near 100 degree temperature and the police turned it off again. Residents pointed out that when fire hydrants in the Italian community, about four blocks away, were turned on, the police looked the other way. The policemen there told them "that was not their precinct." A crowd was now beginning to mount and the police began to disperse it. Someone threw a stone and for nearly five hours, hundreds of teenagers rioted and many were arrested. More than a hundred windows were smashed by the teenagers and some threw Molotov cocktails. Many stores near the area boarded up their windows and nearly 200 helmeted policemen rushed to the area. Dr. King called a meeting that night at the Shiloh Missionary Baptist Church and urged the youths to be nonviolent in their actions. He was booed and about a fourth of the 600 youths walked out. He explained to the crowd that he had discussed with Mayor Daley the very things that took place and all suggestions fell on deaf ears.

The next day Mayor Daley tried to appease the residents by setting up one portable swimming pool and ten hydrant sprinklers. He apparently thought that with those token concessions things would cool down. He was mistaken. The mood of the Negro had changed more than he had expected. In the meantime, King had found his catalyst-housing. Therefore, immediately after the riot he and his group began marching into white middle-class communities that boxed Negroes into ghettoes. One of the first sections the marchers visited was the Cage Park area of Chicago. It had approximately 100,000 residents and all but seven or eight were white. Violence broke out when the demonstrators turned off the residential streets and marched through a small business area. This is where whites tore up an effigy of Martin Luther King, Jr. The whites also smashed windows of cars driven by Negroes.

About 700 policemen protected King and about 800 marchers from stones, firecrackers, and bottles thrown by whites. King was hit above the right ear by a stone. He fell to his knees, but got up and continued to march for another hour.

In order to control the whites, who at one point numbered near 5,000, the police shot over the rioters' heads and arrested hundreds over a period of five hours.

King personally witnessed a number of abuses and insults. Along with various epithets were such phrases as —"We want Martin Luther Coon-Kill those niggers-loving cops. Elect George Wallace for President. King would look good with a knife in his back. Go home, Communist, go home Red, race mixers, queers, junkies, winoes, muggers, rapists . . . you are all persona non grata here."

King later remarked: "I've never seen anything like it in my life. I think the people from Mississippi ought to come to Chicago to learn how to hate." One veteran marcher also said: "It's worse than Mississippi or Selma. Down there, white people had the guts enough to wade in and physically assault you. Up here, they hide behind buildings and hurl rocks."

Dr. Alvin F. Poussaint, a psychiatrist, explained some reasons why the whites behaved the way they did: "It showed that these people were suffering from a deep, psychological disturbance. They saw Negroes as more of a threat. . . It's simply a projection of all the bad parts of themselves. They will tell you that Negroes are violent, lack culture, are obsessed with sex, when really they are the ones who are projecting these traits. The men have real doubts about their masculinity and the women are taking what we call in the profession, a reaction formation, that is the opposite stand from what they really feel and want."

After the incident in the white community, King commented on the police protection: "It was clear the police were either unwilling or unable to disperse the rioters mob that so brutally attacked Negroes and whites who had come to the community to seek open housing in compliance with the law. . . It was clear that this bigoted mob destroyed more property on the Southwest Side than did the West Side rioters." It was pointed out by the observers that some of the policemen were even seen joking with the white rioters. After the criticism by King, the police made special efforts to protect him and the other marchers. In all fairness to the Chicago Police Department, it should be mentioned that Dr. King later praised them for their protection.

Early the Governor of the State, Otto Kerner, issued an executive open housing order. The civil rights workers tested the fair housing law compliance. White civil rights workers were sent to realty offices in select areas, requested houses for sale or rent, and obtained a listing of such houses. When the white workers obtained the list of houses that were available, Negroes would then go to the same realty offices and apply for the same houses. When they were refused or were told that there was nothing available, a prima facie case of discrimination was established. The Governor's executive order was not effective because it was not enforced by real estate brokers and others who owned apartments and houses.

King left Chicago in mid-August to attend the SCLC's annual convention. It was held in Jackson, Mississippi with nearly 1,000 delegates attending. These delegates approved a resolution to put white members on the conference's executive board. Previously the executive was composed of all Negroes.

Martin Luther King, Jr. became ill at the convention. His father, substituted for him and told the group "that the next time we meet, some men with white faces will be introduced as members of this board and that is as it ought to be." The SCLC added 10 new members to the then 29-man executive body—five white and five blacks.

Martin Luther King, Jr. recovered sufficiently from the cold to give his annual report and made some proposals for the remainder of the year. After the convention, King immediately returned to Chicago to continue his anti-slum movement.

Along with several other civil rights leaders King met for ten hours with city officials, real estate brokers, and religious leaders to discuss open housing. No agreements were reached: it was the concensus, however, that the meeting was "very fruitful."

After the meeting the civil rights groups continued marching in white communities protesting for open housing, until Cook County Circuit Judge Corneluis Harrington ordered an injunction against King and other civil rights leaders. King thought that the injunction was "unjust, illegal and unconstitutional." He did, however, obey the injunction and later appealed it. The injunction limited King and the demonstrators to 500. King and the other marchers got around the court order by marching in several small suburban communities.

Mayor Daley went on city-wide television a few hours after the injunction was issued and stated that the past months of demonstrations had put a severe strain on Chicago's police force. King was of the opinion that if the city of Chicago could not protect nonviolent marchers with their police force, then the national guard should have been called in. He declared: "We are not the culprits, the people of Chicago should be good enough not to be throwing bottles and causing disturbances."

King and the leaders of CCCO met again with Mayor Daley and other city officials, but no agreement was reached. King accused Mayor Daley of being more concerned with stopping the marchers than about justice.

The only way to bring the issue of open housing out in the open was to continue demonstrating. Believing this, King and the other leaders, prepared to conduct a demonstration in Cicero, an all-white suburb that was the scene of racial violence in the early 1950's A few days before the planned march, King, Al Raby, Edwin Berry and other officials of the Freedom Movement met again with civic and political officials in an effort to resolve the open house crisis. The meeting was successful. Martin Luther King, Jr. also, emerged as the chief negotiator and with improved prestige.

In the settlement between the two groups, open housing was proclaimed as a city-wide policy. Many labor unions and other groups actually located Negro families in previous all-white sections of the city. King was well aware that integrated housing in Chicago would present some problems. He, however, rightly pointed out that "integrated eating in the South also presented problems but that "it is a way of life accepted by almost everyone." King was confident that the problem of open housing would be accepted in Chicago.

The following Sunday after the agreement for open housing was reached, King appeared on "Meet the Press." He said that anti-Negro hatred that has existed for a long time was at the base of the trouble in Chicago. He attributed it to unfounded fears that Negroes create slums and constitute a threat to jobs held by others. King denied that civil rights demonstrations create this hatred, rather they merely "arouse" latent hostility. The demonstrations are needed, he remarked, to call attention to the underlying social ills.

In the latter part of October, King met with Sargent Shriver, then director of the Office of Economic Opportunity, concerning his decision to withhold Federal funds from the Child Development Group in Mississippi until the project made major changes in personnel and policies.

Opponents of the program stated that its staff had been too closely connected with certain civil rights organizations.

Shriver said that laws governing the war on poverty would not permit him to fund the development group as it was constituted. The director contended that as a matter of record some of the group's federally financed equipment had been used for civil rights activities. Rev. King pointed out to Mr. Shriver that the program had been providing Negro Mississippians with one of the nation's outstanding war on poverty programs until it was discontinued by the Office of Economic Opportunity.

He also told Mr. Shriver that if he did not continue funding the program that it would lead to many questions about the war on poverty itself and who is actually controlling it. Dr. King praised the project and said one value of the development was that it had been controlled from the beginning by impoverished Negroes in Mississippi. He, however, failed to persuade Shriver to change his position. Both men implied that the meeting was rewarding.

After going through the Chicago movement and speaking and traveling around the country, Martin Luther King, Jr. decided to take a two-month leave to rest and write another book. One of the reasons King was writing the book was that there was an uneasy feeling in the civil rights movement that the leaders may have lost their sense of direction and that the forces of goodwill were in disarray. He also felt a need to reassure the course of the movement and to suggest new ideas and programs.

In mid-December King's vacation was interrupted so that he could appear before a Senate Subcommittee of Executive Reorganization. At the hearing he declared that the Federal Government had a system of national priorities that made the war in Vietnam a national obsession while reducing the war on poverty to a skirmish. He warned that without a "rebalancing of priorities-without a huge "commitment" by White Americans to the problem of The Urban Negro—there would be renewed violence in the slums." His own experience in the slums of Chicago had convinced him that it would be necessary to form on a national scale some type of union of slum dwellers.

King told the Subcommittee that the Johnson Administration had failed to provide an "efficient timetable for achieving the Great Society and it was merely a phase so long as no date was set for the achievement of its promises. Senator Abraham A. Ribicoff, chairman of the Subcommittee, said that the problems of urban America are as important as Vietnam. He however, declared: "We would always have foreign problems." King saw the Vietnam war as being incompatible with any sustained effort to relieve the deplorable conditions in ghettoes in America. He put it more clearly when he declared: "The security we profess to seek in foreign adventures, we will lose in our decaying cities. The bombs in Vietnam explode at home, thereby destroying the hopes and possibilities for a decent America."

Another year comes to an end in the life and times of Martin Luther King, Jr. The year 1966 was a critical one for him. He, however, emerged once again as the most prolific apostle of nonviolence and the number one champion for the cause of the black people in America.

Chapter Twenty-Five

KING AND THE PEACE MOVEMENT

In early 1967 King went to Chicago to seek political leverage with an intensive and massive campaign to register Negroes to vote before the February elections for Aldermen and Mayor. He sent for Hosea L. Williams from the SCLC's headquarters in Atlanta to come to Chicago and organize voter registration drives there. Williams arrived within a few days with 12 other staff members who had worked with them in previous registration drives in the South.

Williams and the other workers made little headway in getting Negroes to register during the first few weeks. Williams later declared: "I have never seen such hopelessness. The Negroes of Chicago have a greater feeling of powerless than any I ever saw. They don't participate in the governmental process because they're beaten down psychologically." Other civil rights workers expressed the same point of view.

Williams was of the opinion that a lack of interest in the civil rights movement could be attributed partly to dissention among the leaders of CCCO. Al Raby, one of the leaders of that organization said that there was a sharp split in the civil rights leadership on how to gain political strength in Chicago. King left Williams in charge of the Chicago campaign and returned to Atlanta. He, however, said that he would return.

In late February, King attended an anti-Vietnam conference in California. The conference was entitled "National Priority No. 1: Redirecting American Power." About 1,555 persons attended this conference, including four United States Senators—Eugene J. McCarthy of Minnesota, George S. McGovern of South Dakota, Ernest Gruening of Alaska, and Marck O. Hatfield of Oregon.

Martin Luther King, Jr. was the principal speaker at the meeting. The main issue of his speech was that the United

States activities in Vietnam amounted to supporting a new form of colonialism covered up by certain niceties of complexity.[40]

The Senators present also spoke out against Vietnam. Senator McCarthy contended: "We should not hesitate to waste our strength—economic, military and moral—in so highly questionable a course. We must not do the wrong things for the right reason."

Senator Hatfield made this suggestion: "We must reorder our priorities. We must rationally decide if our goal of preserving is better served through huge expenditures to beat Russians, or through developing methods to feed a hungry world."

Senator McGovern also surmised: "We have neither the mission nor the capacity to play God in Asia by unilateral United States police operation."

King returned to Chicago in late March as he had avowed he would. This time, however, he came to address an anti-Vietnam rally. King and the SCLC were now pressing their new emphasis on seeking an end to the war in Vietnam. He had stated earlier that the war situation was not helping the antipoverty program and was becoming a major obstacle to the civil rights movement. Over 5,000 peace demonstrators heard him declare:

> The Vietnam was a blasphemy against all that America stood for. Our nation which initiated so much of the revolutionary spirit of the modern world was now cast in the mold of being an arch anti-revolutionary. . .
> Certainly this stream of events was not contributing to freedom and democracy abroad. It leaves us in the weakest posture of world stature since our birth as a nation. . .
> We are committing atrocities equal to any perpetrated by the Vietcong. We are left standing before the world glutted by our own barbarity. We engaged in a war that seeks to turn the clock of history back and perpetuate white colonialism. . .
> We often arrogantly feel that we have some divine messianic mission to police the whole world; we are arrogant in not allowing young nations to go through the same growing pains, turbulence and revolution that characterized our history. Our arrogance can be our doom.

The peace rally included many Negroes and whites, from all walks of life and organizations, including Dr. Benjamin Spock, co-chairman of the National Committee for a Sane Nuclear Policy. This committee, also, was one of the sponsors of the rally. The rally was peaceful and only a few minor incidents occurred. An incident occurred, however, when a few members of the American Nazi Party shouted "Treason" and seized one of the anti-war signs. The police were able to stop the brief skirmish.

On March 30, 1967, while Martin Luther King, Jr. was attending a conference, of the board of directors of the Southern Christian Leadership Conference, in Louisville, Kentucky, he expressed his views on the war in Vietnam in a recorded interview with John Herbers of the *New York Times*. King listed three reasons why he spoke out against the war: "First, the war is playing havoc with our domestic destinies. As long as the war in Vietnam goes on, the more difficult it would be to implement the program that would deal with the economic and social problems of the Negro people and poor people in our country. Secondly, the constant escalation of the war in Vietnam can lead to a grand war with China and to a kind of full world war that could mean the annihilation of the human race. Thirdly, I have preached nonviolence in the movement in our country, and I think it is very consistent for me to follow a nonviolent approach in international affairs."

After leaving the conference in Louisville, Kentucky, King went to Atlanta for a few days and then carried his anti-war drive to New York. He was invited by the Clergy and Laymen Concerned About Vietnam. He spoke to more than 3,000 at Riverside Church at 122nd Street and Riverside Drive.

It was here that King made his strongest appeal by calling on Negroes and all white people of goodwill to boycott the Vietnam war by becoming conscientious objectors to military service.

King offered a five-point plan to end the war in Vietnam: (1) The end of all bombing in North and South Vietnam. (2) The declaration of a unilateral cease-fire in the hope that such action would create an atmosphere of negotiation. (3) The taking of immediate steps to prevent other wars from developing in Southeast Asia by curtailing in Thailand and interference in Laos. (4) The recognition that the National Liberation Front has substantial support in Vietnam and must therefore play a role in any meaningful negotiations and in any future Vietnam Government. (5) The establishment of a date on which the United States will remove foreign troops from Vietnam in accordance with the Geneva Agreement of 1954.

In suggesting his program King said that in order to atone our sins and errors in Vietnam, we should take the initiative in bringing a halt to this tragic war. He concluded his speech by saying that "a nation that continues year after year to spend more money on military defense than on programs of social uplift is approaching spiritual death."

Among the people that shared the platform with King was historian Henry Steele Commager who said the Vietnam war was a product of a body of political and historical miscalculation and of moral and psychological obsessions. Professor Commager continued: "It is the product of an obsession with Communism—we call it a conspiracy just as the Communists used to talk about capitalist conspiracies. Something that is, therefore, not nearly a rival political or economic system, but an irradicable moral evil."

There were no major incidents. About 40 or 50 pickets, however, marched and chanted protest against King's position. After his speech, King was criticized by powerful forces in the United States, including newspaper editors, senators, private citizens and other civil rights leaders. He probably had never been so bitterly attacked in his life.

The *New York Times* in an editorial for April 7, 1967, questioned King's linking of the Vietnam war with the cause of Negro equality in the United States. The editorial stated in part:

. . . As an individual, Dr. King has the right and even the moral obligation to explore the ethical implication of the war in Vietnam, but as one of the most respected leaders of the civil rights movement he has an equally weighty obligation to direct that movement's efforts in the most constructive and relevant way. . .

There are no simple or easy answers to the war in Vietnam or the racial injustice in this country. Linking these hard, complex problems will lead not to solutions but to deeper confusion."

The *New York Amsterdam News* editorial of April 15, 1967 declared:

" . . . While upholding his rights to make any observation and proposal as an individual, we do not think that he should equate civil rights and the war at the same time. But this is what Dr. King did. . .

There is justification in what Dr. King says and he has a perfect right to his stand, but we do not share his views at this time. . . "

Life magazine was likewise critical of Martin Luther King, Jr. Its April 21 editorial read—

" . . . Dr. King has claimed that bugetary demands of the war in Vietnam are the key hindrance to progress in civil rights. Not so. If the drive for equal rights falters now, in the difficult times when life must be given to laws already on the books, Dr. King and his tactics must share the blame. . . "

Senator Jacob K. Javits of New York said he disapproved very strongly of Dr. King's attitude in identifying the Negro's struggle for civil rights with the opposition to the war in Vietnam. He called it unfair to Negroes because it by no means necessarily characterized the view of the overwhelming machine of them. . .

Former Senator Barry Goldwater said of King's speech: "This could border a bit on treason." Vice President Hubert H. Humphrey declared: "I think he is in error. I think it will hurt the civil rights movement."

The 60-member board of the N.A.A.C.P. at its quarterly meeting in mid-April called King's plan "a serious tactical mistake" to link the civil rights drive with the war in Vietnam. The N.A.A.C.P. also adopted a resolution that said "Civil Rights battles will have to be fought and won on their own merits, irrespective of the state of war or peace in the world."

Dr. Ralph J. Bunche, a longtime friend of King, asserted that he should not try to lead both a civil rights campaign and a crusade against American involvement in Vietnam. Dr. Bunche thought that King should positively and publicly give up one role or the other, because the two efforts have too little in common.

Martin Luther King, Jr. later replied to his critics: "No one can pretend that the existence of the war is not profoundly affecting the destiny of civil rights progress." He also stated that he would remain as president of the Southern Christian Leadership Conference and do all he could in that role. He, however, declared that he deemed it his responsibility to speak out positively and forthrightly on the war in Vietnam.

Although King was bitterly criticized for linking Vietnam with the civil rights movement, he received some laudable support. Rabbi Israel Margolies of New York City, declared: "To suggest as some do, that the recipient of that coveted award has no right to oppose our deepening involvement in a bloody and brutal war against people of color, is to deny Dr. King that which is not only his right as an American citizen, but his duty as a man of God." King also received support from Stokely Carmichael, Floyd McKissick, Bayard Rustin, Benjamin Spock, and the SCLC.

On April 15, 1967, over 125,000 to 150,000 people attended a rally at the United Nations protesting the war in Vietnam. It was no doubt the largest peace demonstration ever staged in New York since the Vietnam war began. The march was led by Martin Luther King, Jr., Dr. Benjamin Spock, Floyd McKissick, Stokely Carmichael, James Bevel, and Harry Belafonte.

Before the march King and several leaders presented a formal letter to Ralph Bunche, Undersecretary for Special Political Affairs at the United Nations. The note read:

"We rally at the United Nations in order to affirm support of the principles of peace, universality, equal rights and self-determination of people embodied in the Charter and acclaimed by mankind, but violated by the United States."

After the leaders left Dr. Bunche's office, the rally officially began. In his speech at the United Nations rally Rev. King called on the United States to honor its word and stop the bombing of North Vietnam. He urged students from colleges and universities all over the country to use this summer and the coming summers educating and organizing communities across the nation against the Vietnam war. He concluded his speech by saying:

235

" . . . This is just the beginning of a massive outpouring of concern. . . I would like to see the fervor of the civil rights movement infused in the peace movement. . .

. . . Let us save our national honor—stop the bombing. Let us save American lives and Vietnamese lives—stop the bombing. Let us take a single instantaneous step to the peace table—stop the bombing. Let our voices ring out across the land to say the American people are not vain-glorious conquerors—stop the bombing. . . "

Floyd McKissick, Stokely Carmichael, and James Bevel also spoke at the meeting. McKissick called for the immediate withdrawal of American troops from Vietnam and predicted that the turnout of marchers would bring some positive action from Washington. Carmichael described the United States presence in Vietnam as "brutal and racist," and declared that he was against drafting young men, particularly young black Americans." Rev. Bevel declared that he would give President Johnson "one month to stop murdering those folks in Vietnam. Just one month."

There were no major incidents during or following the peace rally. After this mass rally there was no doubt in anyone's mind that Martin Luther King, Jr. was not fully and unequivocally committed to the peace movement. Needless to say his opposition to the Vietnam war cost him some financial support. However, King said it was offset by contributions linked with the peace movement.

Although King continued to travel throughout the United States speaking out on the Vietnam war, he still visited some cities and helped launch civil rights campaigns. Cleveland was one such city. He went to Cleveland in the middle of May to work with local Negro leaders.

In June Martin Luther King, Jr. attended a luncheon given for him by his publishers at Sardi's in New York, to mark the publication of his book, *Where Do We Go From Here: Chaos or Community?* At the luncheon, he made the following observations: "Everyone is worrying about the long hot summer with its threat of riots. We had a long cold winter when little was done about the conditions that create riots." King continued "There has to be a long-range commitment by the nation. Economic deprivation, the slums, the terribly inadequate schools—these are the problems that must be dealt with. Riots will not be stopped by sermons by Martin Luther King, Jr. nor by programs got up as we see summer approaching."

In June and July violence erupted in several major cities. Some people were killed, thousands were arrested, and damages to property totaled many millions of dollars. Almost everyone in public and private life protested the violence in the streets. Roy Wilkins, Whitney M. Young, A Philip Randolph and Martin Luther King, Jr., issued a joint protest.

> Developments in Newark, Detroit and other strife-torn cities make it crystal clear that the primary victims of the riots are the Negro citizens. That they have grave grievances of long standing cannot be denied or minimized. That the riots have not contributed in any substantial measures to the eradication of these just complaints is by now obvious to all. . .
>
> We are confident that the overwhelming majority of the Negro community join us in opposition to violence in the street. . .
>
> Killing, arson, looting, are criminal acts and should be dealt with as such. Equally guilty are those who incite, provoke, and call specifically for such action. . .
>
> No one benefits under mob law. Let's end it now!

Because of the violence and discord in the United States, President Johnson deemed it necessary to appoint a special eleven-man commission to investigate the disorders. The members were Illinois Governor Otto Kerner, commission chairman; New York Mayor John V. Lindsey, co-chairman; Sen. Edward Brooks of Mass.; Atlanta, Ga., Police Chief Herbert Jenkins; Kentucky Commerce Commissioner Katherine Peden; Sen. Fred Harris of Okla.; I. W. Abel, United Steel-Workers President; Roy Wilkins, executive director, NAACP; Charles Thornton, President of Litton Industries; Rep. William McCulloch of Ohio; and Rep. James Corman of Calif. The commission included two Negroes—Roy Wilkins and Sen. Edward Brooks. Many people questioned President Johnson's selection of the commission members and especially the selection of Wilkins and not Martin Luther King, Jr. Some observers were of the opinion that King would give the commission greater prestige. After all most public opinion polls still considered him the number one spokesman for the Negro people in America. Mr. Johnson obviously had his reasons for the selection of the commission members and the exclusion of the Nobel Peace Prize winner.

In mid-August, Martin Luther King, Jr. was feeling so strongly about the Vietnam war that he thought the entire country should express its opposition to it. He thought one way to do that was by a popular vote. Therefore, he proposed a nationwide referendum on the war in Vietnam. He was of the opinion that Congress and President Johnson had been unresponsive or indifferent to deepening grass-roots opinion about our policy in Vietnam. The local initiative, therefore, was a unique and dramatic way for the people to deliver their mandate against the war. In 1966 a referendum was held in Dearborn, Michigan, calling for "an immediate cease-fire and withdrawal of American troops from Vietnam" and received 40 per cent of the votes.

On August 15, the Southern Christian Leadership Conference held its annual convention in Atlanta. The delegates were welcomed to the city by its Mayor, Ivan Allen. This was the first time in the history of the SCLC that its delegates were welcomed to a city by a mayor. Martin Luther King, Jr. gave his annual report. He was also one of the main speakers. He told the delegates of the SCLC's plans for the coming year, namely, to dislocate Northern cities with massive but nonviolent disobedience before Congress adjourned its current session. The President of the Southern Christian Leadership Conference remarked:

> To dislocate the functioning of a city without destroying it can be more effective than a riot because it can be longer-lasting, costly to the society but now wantonly destructive. Moreover, it is more difficult for Government to quell it by superior force. . .
> Our real problem is that there is no disposition by the Administration nor Congress to seek fundamental remedies beyond police measures. The tragic truth is that Congress, more than the American people, is now running wild with racism. . .
> It is purposeless to tell Negroes they should not be enraged when they should be. Indeed, they will be mentally healthier if they do not suppress rage but vent it constructively to cripple the operations of an oppressive society. Civil disobedience can utilize the militance waste in riots to seize clothes or groceries many do not even want. . .

238

King also spoke out against escalating the war in Vietnam, President Johnson's Commission on Civil Disobedience, Congress cutting back several poverty programs and voting down a rat control bill. He declared that Congress had shown itself to be more "anti-Negro than anti-rat."

The Southern Christian Leadership Conference stated also that it would oppose President Johnson, if he decided to seek re-election in 1968, unless he changed his stand on the war in Vietnam. It would, however, support a "peace candidate." The SCLC also passed a resolution that called for a series of "identity workshops" and "Afro-American unity conferences." It should be mentioned that about 300 whites attended several sessions of the convention.

Immediately after King's SCLC speech, his critics began to try and show that he was contradicting his past position and that there was no such thing as "nonviolent confrontation." Others stated that the civil rights leader's quest was unrealistic because his organization did not have the necessary funds needed or staff for such a massive attack upon the Northern cities. *The New York Times* stated that . . . its mere announcement will give added strength to the powerful Congressional elements already convinced that the answer to urban unrest lies in repression rather than in expanded programs for eradicating slum problems." King did not let the critics deter him. Between August and October he continued to speak out on Vietnam and the Negroes' quest for full equality.

On October 10, the U. S. Supreme Court refused to review the convictions of Martin Luther King, Jr., and several ministers that stemmed from the 1963 demonstrations in Birmingham, Ala. The civil rights leaders were found guilty of violating a court injunction that prohibited demonstrations. The sentence was five days in jail and a $50.00 fine. Several ministers served their jail sentences in mid-October. However, Martin Luther King, Jr., Wyatt Tee Walker, Ralph D. Abernathy, and A. D. King did not begin their sentences until October 30. The four men surrendered to the sheriff's deputies in Birmingham. They flew there from Atlanta. At the airport King held a news conference and made the following statement:

"The 1963 demonstrations led to the enactment of the Civil Rights Act of 1964, and the sentence was "a small price to pay for that and other accomplishments. . .

But I am sad that the Supreme Court of our land in a 5 to 4 decision could not uphold the rights of individual citizens in the courts of the State of Alabama as a means of oppression. . .

Perhaps these five days will afford all of us an opportunity for a more intense and serious evaluation of our situation, for all the signs of our times indicate that this is a darker hour in the life of America."

When King went to jail he was dressed in his "jail attire" —denim shirt,, blue jeans, and brown sweater. He carried three books with him: A *Bible, The New Industrial State,* and *The Confessions of Nat Turner.*

While King was in jail, he was confined to bed with a virus infection. His condition, however, was not serious. The civil rights leaders spent most of their days worshipping and reading. About 500 Negroes marched in front of the jail protesting their heroes' arrest. There were no incidents.

King was transferred from the jail in Bessemer, about 18 miles from Birmingham, to a jail in Birmingham. His aides requested the transferral because they were afraid that harm would come to him and his companions since Bessemer was alleged KKK territory. Sheriff Mel Bailey, however, disagreed. He stated that there were better medical facilities in Birmingham than Bessemer. This reasoning seemed strange to the aides because Mr. Bailey had not worried about other prisons' health before.

After serving four days, King and the other three ministers were released from jail on November 3. The same day that he was released from jail, King continued his plea for national civil disobedience and said more demonstrations were planned on Washington and other cities.

In early December Martin Luther King, Jr. announced that Washington, D. C. had been chosen as the target for massive disobedience for 1968. One of the purposes of the protest was to force Congress and the Administration to provide jobs or income for all.

King and his top aides selected Washington as the city during a meeting at Frogmore, S. C. He explained why the massive rally was necessary:

"It is impossible to underestimate the crisis we face in America. The stability of a civilization, the potential of free government, and the simple honors of men are at stake. . .

A clear majority in America are asking for the very things which we will demand in Washington. The Government does not move to correct the problem involving race until it is confronted directly and dramatically. . ."

Martin Luther King, Jr. and his aides were well aware that the rally in Washington could have dangerous repercussions. However, they were apparently willing to take the chance. He said not to act represented moral irresponsibility. Other civil rights organizations were asked to participate, including the militant SNCC. All participants, however, must pledge to be nonviolent.

Another year comes to a close in the life and times of the late Dr. Martin Luther King, Jr. It was a critical year for him. It was the year that he was bitterly criticized for views on Vietnam. It was the year that he led the largest peace march since the Vietnam war had begun. He also spent four days in jail. It was not one of his better years! Yet he still emerged as the number 1 champion for the cause of black people in America.

Chapter Twenty-Six

UP ON THE MOUNTAIN

When Martin Luther King, Jr. announced in late December, 1967 that his organization would "dislocate" Washington, D. C. many observers wanted to know how King would keep it nonviolent. In January he gave them the answer. A corps of 3,000 from six Southern states and nine Northern cities would be trained in the discipline of nonviolence, and what the massive mobilization was all about. After the 3,000 had set the nonviolent tone, the campaign would then include thousands and thousands of people. The demonstrations would not violate the life of a person or his property. However, demonstrators would insist upon confronting the offending party (even Congress) and demanding justice by refusing to cooperate economically, by withdrawing their labor, their political support or by using any means that would disrupt in order to bring about justice.

King and the Negro people waited a year for some action by Congress on their behalf and nothing happened. Therefore he reached the conclusion that something needed to be done to shock the United States to her senses. The poor people's march on Washington would be the catalyst.

President Johnson had remained silent about King's planned invasion of Washington. But at his February 2 news conference he was asked:

> Mr. President, some people interested in civil rights, including Martin Luther King, are planning a massive march on Washington this spring. There is some talk that they would like to stop the wheels of Government. Are you planning to try to talk them out of this? Would you assess that for us?

To this question he answered:

> I don't know what their plans are. I am not sure that they have developed them yet.

242

Of course, I would be hopeful that our energies, our talents and our concerns could be directed in a more productive and a more effective manner.

I would hope that some of these people who are leaders of the causes could recognize that the Congress is having hearings every day on subjects of vital important to their cause.

By coming here and following constitutional methods, presenting their evidence to the Congress and persuading the Congress, it would be more helpful than just trying to stop the functioning of the Government who is also trying very much to help their cause to eliminate discrimination, get more jobs and improve housing. Whatever time and attention the Government had to give to these things that they could be doing to help them.

So we will do all we can to work with all groups in this country to see that their views are heard, considered and acted upon with promptness and understanding.

A few days after Mr. Johnson held his news conference, King called a news conference and rejected Mr. Johnson's appeal. He told newsmen that he deemed it necessary to have the march to dramatize the plight of the underprivileged.

While King was planning for the massive march on Washington, he still continued to participate in anti-war demonstrations. In fact in February, on the lawns of Arlington National Cemetery, he led nearly 3,000 members of the Clergy and Laymen concerned about Vietnam in silent prayers for the military that died in Vietnam.

After the services at the grave sides the worshipers boarded buses and went to the New York Avenue Presbyterian Church where Rev. King declared that "The war in Vietnam was 'playing havoc' with the nation's affairs. Somewhere along the way we have allowed means by which we live to outdistance the ends for which we live."

King was well aware that Negro Americans alone could not move Congress to take the action it must take. He believed that white Americans would not see the cities go up in flames because that was where they made their money, even though they lived in the suburbs. The civil rights leader declared that the "self-interest" of the whites, would therefore convince Congress that it must adopt a $10 billion-a-year program providing jobs or income for the urban poor. King wanted a cross-section of the American people to be represented at the mammoth march on Washington, including Indians, Mexican-Americans, Puerto Ricans, and poor whites.

King realized that the massive "invasion" on Washington would be no easy task. He remembered the problems he and his staff encountered when they organized the 1963 March on Washington. Besides they did not have the service of Baynard Rustin, who helped organize the first March on Washington. The second major problem, besides, finance was the participants themselves. This march would be more difficult because thousands of poor people were involved. The people wanted to know how they would get to Washington? Where would they stay. How long would they be there? In January and February, Martin Luther King, Jr. traveled across the country recruiting poor people for his march. It was during this time that he answered all their questions, concerning transportation, living conditions, and food.

From the time Dr. King announced his nonviolent poor people's march on Washington, people all over the country wanted to know the exact date and plans for it. On March 4, King set Monday April 22, as the starting date. On April 22, he and other leaders would go to Washington and call formally on administration and congressional leaders. This would begin the "educational phase" of the march. On the same day, a caravan of some 3,000 Negroes in wagons drawn by mules and horses, would start out to Washington from Mississippi. On the way from Mississippi, the marchers would move in buses and by foot picking up others as they moved through Alabama, Georgia, South Carolina, North Carolina, Virginia, and finally into Washington.

Ten days after King announced the opening day of the poor people's rally in Washington, he met in Atlanta with 78 leaders of 53 non-Negro minority organizations, from 17 states and representing American Indians, Mexican-Americans, Puerto Ricans, Applachian whites and migrant workers, to discuss plans for the march. All the leaders agreed in theory with the march and King was confident that they would join.

On March 14, the internationally known civil rights leaders announced that he would begin a nationwide tour of 19 communities between Mississippi and Boston, to get a first hand view of "poverty-stricken slum areas" and to hold hearings to learn grievances.

A few days later Dr. King went to Mississippi and opened his planned three weeks recruiting drive for marchers to go to Washington. He traveled by car and chartered plane across Mississippi, including Marks, which is among the poorest in the United States. After seeing half-starved and poorly dressed children, he stated that he had been deeply moved and was more determined than ever to continue his plans for the poor people's rally in Washington, D. C.

King and his aides went to the Eudora African Methodist Episcopal Zion Church and heard Negroes tell of their despairs. King listened for nearly 30 minutes, then responded: "Even though Quitman County is the poorest in the United States, it's criminal for people to have to live in these conditions. I am very deeply touched. God does not want you to live like you are living."

With his party King left the church and continued the tour of the states. Surprisingly, they met no white resistance. In fact, one white man in Marks handed King a new $100 bill to help finance the rally in Washington. King took the money and thanked him. It was gestures like this that made him have faith and realize that there were still some good and honest white citizens that wanted to help the cause of the Negro—even in Mississippi.

King and the civil rights workers left Mississippi and went to Georgia to enlist supporters. He told the poor people there that the housing in Washington would be temporary and would last only until a shanty town—a town within a town—could be built. One of the purposes of the shanty town was to let the world know how America was treating its poor. Dr. King said that activities would include regular physical check-ups at Walter Reed Hospital, organized classes on Negro history and entertainment by national known entertainers.

From Georgia King went to New York City as part of his nation-wide campaign to develop support for his poor people's rally in Washington. While in New York, he spoke in Harlem. He declared: "We need an alternative to riots and to timid supplication. Nonviolence is our most potent weapon."

He also spoke out against the war in Vietnam, Congress, and the Presidential race. King was also scheduled to visit other areas in New York but he cancelled them because he was overly tired.

After he rested a day, he left New York and continued his drive for supporters of the poor people's march by visiting several cities in New Jersey—Patterson, Orange, Jersey City and Newark. He was greeted in every city with prolonged applause, cheers, and whistles. It was at the predominantly Negro South Side High School in Newark, that he received his greatest reception. He told an overflowing crowd of 1,400 that black people must develop and maintain a continuing sense of somebodyness. He further inserted: "Stand up for dignity and self-respect. Too long black people have been ashamed of themselves. Now I'm black, but I'm black and beautiful."

While in Newark, King also held a news conference. It was here he said that the crucial nature of election issues at home and abroad might force him to abandon his customary nonpartisan stand and declare publicly for a Presidential candidate.

On March 28, King interrupted his campaign for support for the poor people's march on Washington, and went to Memphis, Tennessee, to help the striking sanitation workers to settle their disagreements. More than 1,400 of the city's sanitation workers had been on strike since February 12, asking for higher wages, union recognition and a union dues check-off. Most of the garbage colllectors were Negroes.

The local leaders planned to march to City Hall and confront Mayor Henry Loeb, once again, with their grievances. King and the other leaders led the procession from the Clayborn Temple African Church. However, before they reached City Hall violence broke out and the march was halted. There were conflicting reports as to whether the youths blamed for the disorder were part of the march or whether they were merely running along the sidewalks beside the marchers.

The shooting of Larry Payne, a 16-year old Negro, triggered the riot. Police officials said Payne was shot when caught looting. According to police authorities, the teenager attacked a policeman with a butcher knife. When word of the shooting reached the Negroes, a number of teenagers broke out windows and looted a few stores. Policemen quickly merged on the youths with clubs and pounded many into submission. Some of the Negroes fought back, hurling bricks and bottles. A number of policemen received minor injuries. As the day ended one person was dead, about 75 persons injured and at least 150 persons were arrested, and damages were estimated at $400,000.

King was discouraged by the disorders that broke out around the march. Rev. Bernard Lee, later said he was confident that if the protest had been organized by the SCLC the violence could have been avoided.

The next day King held a news conference and told the newsmen his plans for Memphis. He said he would plan another protest there soon to show that demonstrations could be conducted without violence. After the news conference he consulted with local leaders. He later returned to Atlanta and consulted with his staff to determine how many people would be available to go to Memphis and plan another mass demonstration, without delaying plans for the poor people's march on Washington.

Martin Luther King, Jr. returned to Memphis a week later to organize the sanitation workers. The day before, he came to Memphis, however, he was delayed in Atlanta because threats were made on his life and his plane had to be searched. He arrived in Memphis that Wednesday and addressed a mass rally that night. He told them of the threats, but said it really did not matter because God "has allowed me to go up to the mountain. And I've looked over, and I've seen the promised land. . ."[41]

The next day, Thursday April 4, 1968, Martin Luther King, Jr.'s prophecy came true. He was assassinated that night, by an alleged white man, while he leaned over a second-floor railing outside his room at the Lorraine Motel. King was immediately taken to St. Joseph's Hospital where he was given emergency surgery for the gunshot wound on the right side of the neck. He died at 8:30 P.M.

Mrs. King was informed that her husband had been wounded and she was rushed to the Atlanta Airport by Mayor Ivan Allen, Jr. While she waited in a private room with her two children, Yolanda Denise and Martin Luther King, III, Mayor Allen broke the news of her husband's death. Then he returned her to her residence. She occasionally broke into tears, but otherwise she was composed.

Rev. Jesse Jackson, an aide to Dr. King, later described the incidents surrounding the assassination: "Dr. King had been in his room most of the day. Later that day, about 6:00 P.M., he came out of his room wearing a black suit, tie and white shirt. His driver, Solomon Jones, Jr. had been waiting to take him by car to the home of the Rev. Samuel Kyles, of Memphis, for dinner. Mr. Jones told King to put on his topcoat because it was cold outside. King replied: "O.K. I will." King then leaned over a green iron railing to talk to him (Rev. Jackson), standing just below him in a courtyard parking lot. Do you know Ben? Mr. Jackson asked, introducing Ben Branch of Chicago, a musician, who was to play at the rally that night. "Yes, that is my man!" King remarked. "I want you to play "Precious Lord, Take My Hand," at the rally." Branch said that he would. Rev. Abernathy was just about to come out of the motel room when suddenly a loud noise burst out. King fell to the concrete second-floor walkway. . .

Needless to say the whole world was shocked over Martin Luther King, Jr.'s death. As expected, violence broke out all across the country. The same night President Johnson [42] and Vice President Humphrey, [43] went on nation-wide television, and issued a statement on the slaying of the civil rights leader. The United States Senate passed a resolution expressing "profound sorrow" over Rev. King's death.[44] It was adopted by a voice vote after numerous eulogies on the floor.

President Johnson also announced that he would address a joint session of Congress and urge them to promptly pass open housing legislation and also urge immediate passage and financing of measures he recommended previously to relieve big city crisis in housing, jobs, and education. The President, however, postponed his scheduled speech to Congress to avoid any conflict with the funeral of Rev. Dr. Martin Luther King, Jr.

The day before the funeral, Mrs. Coretta King along with Ralph Abernathy, Walter P. Reuther, Dr. Benjamin Spock, Rabbi Joachim Prinz, Mario Procaccino, Eugene Nickerson, Harry Belafonte and Ossie Davis, led a silent march in Memphis in support of the striking garbage workers. Nearly 50,000 people from all over the nation came to Memphis to participate in this mammoth event. The march was successful and no disorders were reported.

Dr. King's death had a profound effect upon every segment of American life. Television programs were cancelled; banks, schools, colleges, stores, and other institutions were closed; sporting events were re-scheduled—all in honor of Martin Luther King, Jr. The Nobel Peace Prize winner's death even pushed the Wall Street Stock Market down. The Exchange also observed a minute of silent tribute to him. This was the first time that the Stock market paid tribute to a private citizen.

Between King's death and his funeral riots broke out in most of the major cities in America, including the nation's capitol. More than 150 cities were effected. Over 50 persons died and at least 3,000 were injured. At least 25,000 persons were arrested, and property damages were roughly estimated at nearly $50 million.

Tuesday April 9, Rev. Dr. Martin Luther King, Jr. was buried in Atlanta. Funeral services were held in the church of which he was co-pastor, along with his father—Ebenezer Baptist Church. The principal mourners, including his immediate family, could not get into the church because there were about 40,000 people jammed outside. Not until Dr. King's brother, A. D. King, emerged and pleaded with the crowd to be orderly, did the mourners finally enter the church.

Inside the church the audience heard the Rev. Ralph Abernathy, Dr. King's closest friend, begin the eulogy by calling Dr. King's murder "one of the darkest hours of mankind." Prayers were given by Rev. Ronald English, [45] assistant pastor of the Ebenezer Baptist Church and Dr. L. Harold DeWolfe, [46] one of King's former teachers.

A taped excerpt from the last sermon Dr. King preached at the church, on February 4, was played also at the services. The request was made by Rev. King's wife, Mrs. Coretta King. Some of the mourners had tears in their eyes as they heard the voice of Dr. King say:

" . . . If any of you are around when I have to meet my day, I don't want a long funeral. And if you get somebody to deliver the eulogy, tell him not to talk too long. . . Tell him not to mention that I have a Nobel Peace Prize—that isn't important. . .

Tell him not to mention where I went to school. I'd like somebody to mention that day that Martin Luther King, Jr. tried to give his life serving others. . .

I'd like for somebody to say that day that Martin Luther King, Jr. tried to love somebody. . .

I want you to be able to say that day that I did try in my life to clothe the naked. I want you to say on that day I did try in my life to visit those who were in prison. And I tried to love and save humanity."

Because the church seated about 1,300, only the congregation and "invited" guests attended the private services. After the services, the coffin was carried through the streets of the city by a farm wagon pulled by two mules. Thousands of mourners walked silently before and behind the coffin as it journeyed on its way to Morehouse College, where an open-air general service was held.

At Morehouse College Rev. Abernathy was joined by Dr. Benjamin E. Mays, [47] retired president of Morehouse and Mahalia Jackson who moved the crowd to tears, as she sang "Precious Lord, Take My Hand."

The body of Dr. King was later placed in a temporary marble tomb in South View Cemetery in Atlanta. The family would later decide on a permanent resting place.

Nearly 150,000 people from all walks of life made up the vast procession in Atlanta. There were bishops, African envoys, labor representatives, famous names, both white and black, in the theater and the sport's world. There were 50 or more members of the House of Representatives and 30 or more Senators, including Wayne Morse, Robert F. Kennedy, Jacob K. Javits, Eugene J, McCarthy, Edward F. Kennedy and Edward Brooks. Vice President Humphrey was there representing the White House. President Johnson had planned earlier to come to Atlanta for the funeral, but the Police Department there advised against it for security reasons. Mrs. Jackie Kennedy was also there. Many mayors, some coming from riot torn cities, were there. It was a gathering of "Who's Who in America."

In addition to the many participants about 130 million people in the United States watched some part of the funeral services on television. The television networks carried the funeral for 7½ hours. The services were also beamed by Early Bird communication satellite to Europe, where they were transmitted by Eurovision.

Millions of Americans, both white and black, marched side by side in memorial parades and prayed together in public places, the same time that the services were being held. Few, if anyone in America, passed the day without some thought of Martin Luther King, Jr. This was one day that the words of Emile Zola could be truly applicable: "He was a moment in the conscience of man."

The day after King's funeral, the House of Representatives passed a civil rights bill that opened 80 per cent of the nation's houses and apartments. The following day, April 11, 1968 President Johnson signed the Civil Rights Act of 1968. Needless to say the assassination of Martin Luther King, Jr. prompted the passage and signing of the Act. The following week the sanitation workers in Memphis, also, settled their labor dispute. Thus, Dr. King's efforts in Memphis were not in vain. He died for a cause that was fulfilled.

The author would like to conclude this book with an Epitaph for Martin Luther King, Jr. and a challenge for the world.

EPITAPH AND CHALLENGE

Just a few months ago one of the most shocking tragedies, since the assassination of President John F. Kennedy, occurred in our great nation. Men, women and children were horrified at the stupefacient assassination of Martin Luther King, Jr. Because of a close identity with that great leader, a peace loving world, still refuses to believe that he is no longer among the living.

As unreal as it may seem, we must face the fact that Martin Luther King, Jr. is dead. Although he may be dead physically, spiritually and morally he will always be among us.

The epitaph of Martin Luther King, Jr. reveals that he was an apostle of nonviolence and a disciple of Gandhi. Yet like Gandhi, he met a violent death. He died at a time when the United States and the world needed him the most. He had the courage of his convictions and the vision of a prophet. Dr. King was a friend to the rich and the poor, black and white, the high and the low, the faithful and the unfaithful. He was a friend to ALL mankind. This was a leader among men!

So Martin Luther King, Jr. has something important to say to each of us in his death. He has something to say to every racist who has convinced his constituent to believe that one man is superior to another. He has something to say to the man who remains silent and knows in his heart that he should speak out. He has something to say to a nation that preaches love and brotherhood and practices hatred and bigotry. Rev. King has something to say to the white and the black, not only in the United States but the whole world. He, himself, gave the answer to the problem of the world, when he declared: "Nonviolence, the answer to the Negroes' need, may become the answer to the most desperate need of all humanity."

Thus the epitaph of Martin Luther King, Jr.'s life shows us the way to solve our problem and destroy the chains of racial segregation and discrimination and live like brothers in this great world of ours.

NOTES

Footnotes 1, 2, 3, 4, 5, 6, 7, 8, 9, 14, 18, were taken from L. D. Reddick, *Crusader Without Violence*, Reprinted by permission.

10. Martin Luther King, Jr., *Stride Toward Freedom*, p. 13 Reprinted by permission.

11. *Ibid.*, p. 58.

12. *Ibid.*, p. 63.

13. *Ibid.*, p. 67

15. See *Christian Century*, April 10, 1957.

16. See *Chicago Defender*, May 22, 1957.

17. See *New York Amsterdam News*, June 1, 1957.

19. See *New York Times*, Tuesday, March 29, 1960.

20. Arthur M. Schlesinger, Jr. *A Thousand Days*, p. 73.

21. See Appendix I

22. See Appendix II

23. See Appendix III

24. Martin Luther King, Jr. *Why We Can't Wait*, pp. 15-26.

25. *Ibid.* p. 152.

26. See Appendix IV

27. See Appendix V

28. See Appendix VI

29. See Appendix VII

30. See Appendix VIII

31. See Appendix IX

32. See Appendix X

33. See Appendix XI

34. See Appendix XII

35. See Appendix XIII

36. See Appendix XIV

37. See Appendix XV

38. See *Saturday Review*, November 13, 1965. Reprinted by permission.

39. *Ibid.*

40. See Appendix XVI

41. See Appendix XVII

42. See Appendix XVIII

43. See Appendix XIX

44. See Appendix XX

45. See Appendix XXI

46. See Appendix XXII

47. See Appendix XXIII

Appendix I

MY DEAR FELLOW CLERGYMEN:

We have waited for more than 340 years for our constitutional and God-given rights. The nations of Asia and Africa are moving with jetlike speed toward the goal of political independence, and we still creep at horse-and-buggy pace toward the gaining of a cup of coffee at a lunch counter. I guess it is easy for those who have never felt the stinging darts of segregation to say "wait."

But when you have seen vicious mobs lynch your mothers and fathers at will and drown your sisters and brothers at whim; when you have seen hate-filled policemen curse, kick, brutalize and even kill your black brothers and sisters; when you suddenly find your tongue twisted and your speech stammering as you seek to explain to your six-year-old daughter why she can't go to the public amusement park that has just been advertised on television, and see tears welling up in her little eyes when she is told that "Funtown" is closed to colored children, and see the depressing clouds of inferiority begin to form in her little personality by unconsciously developing a bitterness toward white people; when you are humiliated day in and day out by nagging signs reading "white" and "colored," when your first name becomes "nigger" and your middle name becomes "boy" (however old you are) and your last name becomes "John," and when your wife and mother are never given the respected title "Mrs.," when you are harried by day and haunted by night by the fact that you are a Negro, living constantly at tiptoe stance, never quite knowing what to expect next, and plagued with inner fears and other resentments; when you are forever fighting a degenerating sense of "nobodyness"—then you will understand why we find it difficult to wait. . .

In your statement you asserted that our actions, even though peaceful, must be condemned because they precipitate violence. Isn't this like condemning the robbed man because his possession of money precipitated the evil act of robbery? Isn't this like condemning Socrates because his unswerving commitment to truth and his philosophical drivings precipitated the misguided popular mind to make him drink the hemlock? Isn't this like condemning Jesus because his unique God-consciousness and never-ceasing devotion to God's will precipitated the evil act of the Crucifixion?

The question is not whether we will be extremist but what kind of extremist will we be. Will we be extremists for hate or will we be extremists for love? Will we be extremists for the preservation of injustice or will we be extremists for the cause of justice? In that dramatic scene on Calvary's hill, three men were crucified for the same crime—the crime of extremism. Two were extremists for immorality, and thus fell below their environment. The other, Jesus Christ, was an extremist for love, truth and goodness, and thereby rose above his environment. So, after all, maybe the South, the nation and the world are in dire need of creative extremists. . .

Before the Pilgrims landed at Plymouth, we were here. Before the pen of Jefferson etched across the pages of history the majestic words of the Declaration of Independence, we were here. For more than two centuries, our foreparents labored in this country without wages; they made cotton "king", and they built the homes of their masters in the midst of brutal injustice and shameful humiliation— and yet out of a bottomless vitality, they continued to thrive and develop. If the inexpressible cruelties of slavery could not stop us, the opposition we now face will surely fail. We will win our freedom because the sacred heritage of our nation and the eternal will of God are embodied in our echoing demands. . .

Appendix II

I HEREBY PLEDGE MYSELF—MY PERSON AND BODY—TO THE NONVIOLENT MOVEMENT. THEREFORE I WILL KEEP THE FOLLOWING TEN COMMANDMENTS:

1. MEDITATE daily on the teaching and life of Jesus.

2. REMEMBER always that the nonviolent movement in Birmingham seeks justice and reconciliation—not victory.

3. WALK and TALK in the manner of love, for God is love.

4. PRAY daily to be used by God in order that all men might be free.

5. SACRIFICE personal wishes in order that all men might be free.

6. OBSERVE with both friend and foe the ordinary rules of courtesy.

7. SEEK to perform regular service for others and for the world.

8. REFRAIN from violence of fist, tongue, heart.

9. STRIVE to be in good spiritual and bodily health.

10. FOLLOW the directions of the movement and of the captain of a demonstration.

I sign this pledge, having seriously considered what I do and with the determination and will to persevere.

Name _____

Address _____

Phone _____

Nearest Relative _____

Address _____

Besides demonstrations, I could also help the movement by (circle the proper items): Run errands, drive my car, fix food for volunteers, clerical work, make phone calls, answer phones, mimeograph, type, print signs, distribute leaflets.

ALABAMA CHRISTIAN MOVEMENT FOR HUMAN RIGHTS
BIRMINGHAM AFFILITATE OF S. C. L. C.
505½ North 17th Street
F. S. Shuttlesworth, President

Appendix III

The City of Birmingham has reached an accord with its conscience. The acceptance of responsibility by local white and Negro leadership offers an example of a free people uniting to meet and solve their problems. Birmingham may well offer for Twentieth Century America an example of progressive racial relations; and for all mankind a dawn of a new day, a promise for all men, a day of opportunity and a new sense of freedom for all America. Thusly, Birmingham may again become a Magic City.

Responsible leaders of both Negro and white communities of Birmingham, begin desirous of promoting conditions which will ensure interest of all citizens of Birmingham, after mutual consideration and discussion of the issues relating to the recent demonstrations in the city, have agreed to the following:

1. The desegregation of lunch counters, restrooms, fitting rooms and drinking fountains in planned stages within 90 days. Cooperative, prayerful planning is necessary to insure smooth transition.

2. The upgrading and hiring of Negroes on a nondiscriminatory basis throughout the industrial community of Birmingham. This will include the hiring of clerks and salesmen within the next 60 days, and the immediate appointment of a committee of business, industrial and professional leaders for the implementation of an area-wide program for acceleration of upgrading and the employment of Negroes in job categories previously denied to Negroes.

3. Our movement has made release of all persons on bonds or their personal recognizance. Our legal department is working with further solutions in this problem.

4. Through the Senior Citizens Committee, or the Chamber of Commerce, communications between the Negro and white will be publicly re-established within the next two weeks. We would hope that this channel of communication between the white and Negro communities will prevent the necessity of further protest demonstrations as have been conducted.

MARTIN LUTHER KING, JR.'S STATEMENT:

I am very happy to be able to annnounce that we have come today to the climax of a long struggle for justice, freedom and human dignity in the city of Birmingham. I see the climax, and not the end, for though we have come a long way, there is still a strenuous task before us and some of it is yet uncharted.

257

Nevertheless, it can now be said that this great struggle . . . this day is clearly the moment of a great victory. The greatness of the triumph is measured by this one fact: it is a victory that cannot possibly be confined to the limited area of one race.

Indeed, the agreements which have been reached over the last few days are signal accomplishments which rebound to the credit of all Birmingham's citizens. As a matter of fact, I believe sincerely that this victory cannot even be confined within the limits of this sprawling metropolis, for Birmingham now stands on the threshold of becoming a great enlightened symbol shedding the radiance of its example throughout this entire nation.

Credit for what has been done must go to many persons. Without question, of course, the name of the Reverend Fred Shuttlesworth stands as clear as the magic name in this Magic City. He has walked a long and often lonesome road to reach this day—and even now his health is impaired, but he has just reason to be thankful and glad for all of his great sacrifice.

Moreover, the many men and women who worked with him, by his side and behind.

The scenes in the Alabama Christian Movement for Human Rights must also be praised. And without a doubt the thousands of children and adults who gave up their own physical safety and freedom of all men.

I must say this too: In these recent days, I have been deeply impressed by the quality of the white persons of the community who worked diligently for just solutions to our mutual problem. They must also be given real credit. They are men of goodwill. However, when all is seen in perspective of eternity, ultimate credit and glory and honor must be given to Almighty God, for He has clearly been at work among us. And it is He alone who has finally gained the victory for all His children.

Under His guidance, we now enter into a new day for Birmingham's people, a day when men will no longer fear to speak the truth, when citizens will no longer cringe before the threats of misguided men. We look forward now to continued progress toward the establishment of a city in which equal job opportunities, equal access to public facilities, and equal rights and responsibilities for all its people will be the order of the day.

However, even these needful things are not our final goal. The deepest hope that surges up within our hearts is this: that Birmingham is on its way to the creation of a new kind of community not simply a new image, but a new reality . . . violence must not come from any of us . . . we must be loving enough to turn any enemy into a friend . . . we must now move from protest to reconciliation. . . Then and only then, will all the citizens of this community be able to say in joyful response "Thank You! It's great to be in Birmingham—a city of honor, respect and brotherly love."

Appendix IV

CIVIL RIGHTS MESSAGE

Good evening, my fellow citizens.

This afternoon, following a series of threats and defiant statements, the presence of Alabama National Guardsmen was required on the University of Alabama to carry out the final and unequivocal order of the United States District Court of the Northern District of Alabama. That order called for the admission of two clearly qualified young Alabama residents who happened to have been born Negro.

That they were admitted peacefully on the campus is due in good measure to the conduct of the students of the University of Alabama, who met their responsibilities in a constructive way.

I hope that every American, regardless of where he lives, will stop and examine his conscience about this and other related incidents. This Nation was founded by men of many nations and backgrounds. It was founded on the principle that all men are created equal, and that the rights of every man are diminished when the rights of one man are threatened.

Today we are committed to a world-wide struggle to promote and protect all of those who wish to be free and when Americans are sent to Viet-Nam or West Berlin, we do not ask for whites only. It ought to be possible for American students of any color to attend any public institution they select without having to be backed up by troops. It ought to be possible for American consumers of any color to receive equal services in places of public accommodations, such as hotels and restaurants and theaters and retail stores, without being forced to resort to demonstrations in the street, and it ought to be possible for American citizens of any color to register and vote in a free election without interference or fear of reprisal.

It ought to be possible, in short, for every American to enjoy the privilege of being American without regard to his race or color. In short, every American ought to have the right to be treated as he would wish to be treated, as one could wish his children to be treated.

The Negro baby in America today, regardless of the section of the Nation in which he is born, has about one half as much chance of completing high school as a white baby born in the same place on the same day, one third as much chance of completing college, one third as much chance of becoming a professional man, twice as much chance of becoming unemployed, about one seventh as much chance of earning $10,000 a year, a life expectancy which is seven years shorter, and the prospects of earning only half as much.

This is not a sectional issue. Difficulties and discrimination exist in every city, every state of the Union, producing in many cities a rising tide of discontent that threatens the public safety. Nor is this

259

a partisan issue in a time of domestic crisis. Men of good will and generosity should be able to unite regardless of party or politics. This is not even a legal or legislative issue alone. It is better to settle these matters in the courts than on the streets, and new laws are needed at every level, but law alone cannot make men see right.

We are confronted primarily with a moral issue. It is as old as the Scriptures and is clear as the American Constitution. The heart of the question is whether all Americans are to be afforded equal rights and equal opportunities, whether we are going to treat our fellow Americans as we want to be treated.

If an American, because his skin is dark, cannot eat lunch in a restaurant open to the public, if he cannot send his children to the best public school available, if he cannot enjoy the full officials who represent him, if, in short, he cannot enjoy the full and free life which all people want, then who among us would be content to have the color of his skin changed and stand in his place? Who among us would then be content with the counsels of patience and delay?

One hundred years of delay have passed since President Lincoln freed the slaves, yet their heirs, their grandsons, are not fully free. They are not yet freed from the bonds of injustice. They are not yet freed from social and economic oppression, and this Nation, for all its hopes and all its boasts, will not be fully free until all its citizens are free.

We preach freedom around the world, and we mean it, and we cherish our freedom here at home. But are we to say to the world, and much more importantly, to each other that this is a land of the free except for the Negroes; that we have no second class citizens except Negroes, that we have no class or caste system, no ghettos, no master race except with respect to Negroes?

Appendix V

I HAVE A DREAM

I am happy to join with you today in what will go down in history as the greatest demonstration for freedom in the history of our nation.

Five score years ago a great American in whose symbolic shadow we stand today signed the Emancipation Proclamation. This momentous decree is a great beacon light of hope to millions of Negro slaves who had been seared in the flames of withering injustice. It came as a joyous daybreak to end the long night of their captivity. But 100 years later, the Negro still is not free. One hundred years later the life of the Negro is still badly crippled by the manacles of segregation and the chains of discrimination. One hundred years later the Negro lives on a lonely island of poverty in the midst of a vast ocean of material prosperity. One hundred years later the Negro still lanquished in the corners of American society and finds himself in exile in his own land. So we've come here today to dramatize a shameful condition.

In a sense we've come to our nation's capital to cash a check. When the architects of our Republic wrote the magnificent words of the Constitution and the Declaration of Independence, they were signing a promissory note to which every American was to fall heir. This note was a promise that all men—yes, black men as well as white men—would be guaranteed the unalienable rights of life, liberty and the pursuit of happiness. It is obvious today that America has defaulted on this promissory note insofar as her citizens of color are concerned. Instead of honoring this sacred obligation, America has given the Negro people a bad check, a check which has come back marked "insufficient funds."

But we refuse to believe that the bank of justice is bankrupt. We refuse to believe that there are insufficient funds in the great vaults of opportunity of this nation. So we've come to cash this check, a check that will give us upon demand the riches of freedom and the security of justice.

We have also come to this hallowed spot to remind America of the fierce urgency of now. This is no time to engage in the luxury of cooling off or to take the tranquilizing drug of gradualism. Now is the time to make real the promises of democracy. Now is the time to rise from the dark and desolate valley of segregation the sunlit path of racial justice. Now is the time to lift our nation from the quicksands of racial injustice to the solid rock of brotherhood.

Now is the time to make justice a reality for all of God's children. It would be fatal for the nation to overlook the urgency of the moment. This sweltering summer of the Negro's legitimate discontent will not pass until there is an invigorating autumn of freedom and equality—1963 is not an end but a beginning. Those who hope that the Negro needed to blow off steam and will now be content will have a rude awakening if the nation returns to business as usual.

There will be neither rest nor tranquility in America until the Negro is granted his citizenship rights. The whirlwinds of revolt will continue to shake the foundations of our nation until the bright days of justice emerges. And that is something that I must say to my people who stand on the worn threshold which leads into the place of justice. In the process of gaining our rightful place we must not be guilty of wrongful deeds. Let us not seek to satisfy our thirst for freedom by drinking from the cup of bitterness and hatred.

We must forever conduct our struggle on the high plane of dignity and discipline. We must not allow our creative protests to degenerate into physical violence. Again and again we must rise to the majestic heights of meeting physical force with soul force. The marvelous new militancy which has engulfed the Negro community must not lead us to distrust all white people, for many of our white brothers, as evidenced by their presence here today, have come to realize that their destiny is tied up with our destiny.

They have come to realize that their freedom is inextricably bound to our freedom. We cannot walk alone. And as we walk we must make the pledge that we shall always march ahead. We cannot turn back. There are those who are asking the devotees of civil rights, "When will you be satisfied?" We can never be satisfied as long as the Negro is the victim of the unspeakable horrors of police brutality.

We can never be satisfied as long as our bodies, heavy with the fatigue of travel, cannot gain lodging in the motels of the highways and the hotels of the cities.

We cannot be satisfied as long as the Negro's basic mobility is from a smaller ghetto to a larger one. We can never be satisfied as long as our children are stripped of their adulthood and robbed of their dignity by signs stating "For Whites Only."

We cannot be satisfied as long as the Negro in Mississippi cannot vote and the Negro in New York believes he has nothing for which to vote.

No, no, we are not satisfied, and we will not be satisfied until justice rolls down like waters and righteousness like a mighty stream.

I am not unmindful that some of you have come here out of great trials and tribulation. Some of you have come fresh from narrow jail cells. Some of you have come from areas where your quest for freedom left you battered by the storms of persecution and staggered by the winds of police brutality. You have been the veterans of creative suffering.

262

Continue to work with the faith that unearned suffering is re-demptive. Go back to Mississippi, go back to Alabama, go back to South Carolina, go back to Georgia, go back to Louisiana, go back to the slums and ghettos of our Northern cities, knowing that somehow this situation can and will be changed. Let us not wallow in the valley of despair.

I say to you today, my friends, though, even though we face the difficulties of today and tomorrow, I still have a dream. It is a dream deeply rooted in the American dream. I have a dream that one day this nation will rise up, live out the true meaning of its creed: "We hold these truths to be self-evident, that all men are created equal."

I have a dream that one day on the red hills of Georgia sons of former slaves and the sons of former slave-owners will be able to sit down together at the table of brotherhood. I have a dream that one day even the state of Mississippi, a state sweltering with the heat of injustice, sweltering with the heat of oppression, will be trans-formed into an oasis of freedom and justice.

I have a dream that my four little children will one day live in a nation where they will not be judged by the color of their skin but by the content of their character. I have a dream . . . I have a dream that one day in Alabama, with its vicious racists, with its governor having his lips dripping with the words of interposition and nullification, one day right there in Alabama little black boys and black girls will be able to join hands with little white boys and white girls as sisters and brothers.

I have a dream today . . . I have a dream that one day every valley shall be exalted, every hill and mountain shall be made low. The rough places will be made plain, and the crooked places will be made straight. And the glory of the Lord shall be revealed, and all flesh shall see it together. This is our hope. This is the faith that I go back to the South with. With this faith we will be able to hew out of the mountain of despair a stone of hope. With this faith we will be able to transform the jangling discords of our nation into a beautiful symphony of brotherhood. With this faith we will be able to work together, to stand up for freedom together, knowing that we will be free one day.

This will be the day when all of God's children will be able to sing with new meaning, "My country, 'tis of thee, sweet land of liberty, of thee I sing. Land where my fathers died, land of the pilgrim's pride, from every mountain side, let freedom ring." And if America is to be a great nation, this must become true. So let freedom ring from the prodigious hilltops of New Hampshire. Let freedom ring from the mighty mountains of New York. Let freedom ring from the heightening Alleghenies of Pennsylvania. Let freedom ring from the

263

snow-capped Rockies of Colorado. Let freedom ring from the curvaceous slopes of California.

But not only that. Let freedom ring from Stone Mountain of Georgia. Let freedom ring from Lookout Mountain of Tennessee. Let freedom ring from every hill and molehill of Mississippi, from every mountain side. Let freedom ring. . .

When we allow freedom to ring—when we let it ring from every city and every hamlet, from every state and every city, we will be able to speed up that day when all God's children, black men and white men, Jews and Gentiles, Protestants and Catholics, will be able to join hands and sing in the words of the old Negro spiritual, "Free at last, Free at last, Great God a-mighty, We are free at last."

Appendix VI

EPITAPH AND CHALLENGE

We stand just a few days removed from one of the most shocking and horrible tragedies that has ever befallen our nation. Men everywhere were stunned into sober confusion at an incredible assassination of John F. Kennedy. It is still difficult to believe that one so saturated with vim, vitality and vigor is no longer in our midst.

As unreal as it seems to our senses, we must face the fact that John Fitzgerald Kennedy is dead. Dead, physically, but the posture of his life has written an epitaph that lives beyond the boundaries of death.

The epitaph of John Kennedy reveals that he was a leader unafraid of change. He came to the presidency in one of the most turbulent and catoclysmic periods of human history. A time when the problems of the world were gigantic in intent and chaotic in detail. On the international scene there was the ominous threat of mankind being plunged into the abyss of nuclear annihilation. On the domestic scene the nation was reaping the harvest of its terrible injustice toward the Negro. John Kennedy met these problems with a depth of concern, a breadth of intelligence, and a keen sense of history. He had the courage to be a friend of civil rights and a stalwart advocate of peace. The unmistakable cause of sincere grief expressed by so many millions was more than simple emotion. It revealed that President Kennedy had become a symbol of peoples' yearnings for justice, economic well being and peace.

Our nation should do a great deal of soul-searching as a result of President Kennedy's assassination. The shot that came from the fifth story building cannot be easily dismissed as the isolated act of a madman. Honesty impels us to look beyond the demented mind that executed this dastardly act. While the question "who killed President Kennedy?" is important, the question "what killed him" is more important. Our late President was assassinated by a morally inclement climate. It is a climate filled with heavy torrents of false accusation, jostling winds of hatred and raging storms of violence.

It is a climate where men cannot disagree without being disagreeable, and where they express dissent through violence and murder. It is the same climate that murdered Medgar Evers in Mississippi and six innocent Negro children in Birmingham, Alabama. So in a sense we are all participants in that horrible act that tarnished the image of our nation. By our silence, by our willingness to compromise principle; by our constant attempt to cure the cancer of racial injustice with the vaseline of graduation; our readiness to allow arms to be

265

purchased at will and fired at whim; by allowing our movie and television screens to teach our children that the hero is one who masters the art of shooting and the technique of killing; by allowing all of these developments we have created an atmosphere in which violence and hatred have become popular pastimes.

So President Kennedy has something important to say to each of us in his death. He has something to say to every politician who has fed his constituents the stale bread of racism and the spoiled meat of hatred. He has something to say to every clergyman who had observed racial evils and remained silent behind the safe security of stained glass windows. He has something to say to the devotees of the extreme right who pour out venomous words against the supreme court and the United Nations, and branded everyone a communist with whom they disagree. He has something to say to a misguided philosophy of communism that would teach man that the end justifies means, and that violence and the denial of basic freedom are justifiable methods to achieve the goal of a classic society. He says to all of us that this virus of hate that has seeped into the veins of our nation, if unchecked, will lead inevitably to our moral and spiritual doom.

Thus the epitaph of John Kennedy's life illuminates profound truths that challenge us to set aside our grief of a session and move forward with more determination to rid our nation of the vestiges of racial segregation and discrimination.

Appendix VII

EVANGEL OF NONVIOLENCE

In April of last year the Reverend Dr. Martin Luther King, Jr. sat in a Birmingham jail cell. There he filled page after page of note paper with a scrawled reply to eight fellow clergymen who had protested his participation in civil rights demonstrations as "unwise and untimely."

That letter has become a classic statement of his conviction that "injustice anywhere is injustice everywhere"—a conviction to which he has given nonviolent expression on scores of testing grounds, North and South, and one which has found a substantial measure of legal fulfillment in the passage of the most comprehensive civil rights law in the nation's history.

Dr. King's insistence on accomplishing the Negro's march toward full equality through peaceful means has now brought him the 1964 Nobel Peace Prize—an award that exalts the prize as much as it does this brave crusader for human understanding and brotherhood. Characteristically, he accepts the prize as a tribute to the discipline restraint and courage of millions of Negroes and whites who followed the doctrines of nonviolence in seeking to establish "a reign of justice and a rule of love across this nation of ours."

As Dr. King fully recognizes, demonstrations alone will not provide answers to the hard problems now facing the Negro—better schools, better housing, better jobs. The watchword for these times may lie in this earlier admonition of his "Human progress never rolls in on wheels of inevitability; it comes through the tireless efforts of men willing to be co-workers with God, and without this hard work time itself becomes an ally of the forces of social stagnation."

Such leaders as Dr. King, working with men of such dedication in the community, represent the best insurance that progress will be both peaceful and prompt.

Appendix VIII

I was appalled and surprised at your reported statement maligning my integrity. What motivated such an irresponsible accusation is a mystery to me. I have sincerely questioned the effectiveness of the FBI in racial incidents, particularly where bombing and brutalities against Negroes are at issue, but I have never attributed this merely to the presence of Southerners in the FBI. This is a part of the broad question of federal involvement in the protection of Negroes in the South and the seeming inability to gain convictions in even the most heinous crimes perpetrated against civil rights workers.

It remains a fact that not a single arrest was made in Albany, Georgia, during the many brutalities against Negroes. Neither has a single arrest been made in connection with the tragic murder of the four children in Birmingham, nor the three civil rights workers in Mississippi. Moreover, all FBI agents inevitably work with local law enforcement officers in car thefts, bank robberies and other interstate violations. This makes it difficult for them to function effectively in cases where the rights and safety of Negro citizens are being threatened by these same law enforcement officers.

I will be happy to discuss this question with you at length in the near future. Although your statement said that you have attempted to meet me, I have sought in vain for any record of such a request. I have always made myself available to all FBI agents of the Atlanta office, and encouraged our staff and affiliates to cooperate with them in spite of the fact that many of our people have suspicions and distrust of the FBI as a result of the slow pace of justice in the South.

Appendix IX

EXCERPTS OF DR. KING'S SPEECH IN NORWAY

Your Majesty, your Royal Highness, Mr. President, excellencies, ladies and gentlemen:

I accept the Nobel prize for peace at a moment when 22 million Negroes of the United States of America are engaged in a creative battle to end the long night of racial injustice. I accept this award in behalf of the civil rights movement which is moving with determination and a majestic scorn for risk and danger to establish a reign of freedom and a rule of justice.

I am mindful that only yesterday in Birmingham, Ala. our children, crying out for brotherhood, were answered with fire hoses, snarling dogs and even death. I am mindful that only yesterday in Philadelphia, Miss., young people seeking to secure the rights to vote were brutalized and murdered.

I am mindful that debilitating and grinding poverty afflicts my people and chains them to the lowest rung of the economic ladder.

Therefore, I must ask why this prize is awarded to a movement which is beleagured and committed to unrelenting struggle: to a movement which has not won the very peace and brotherhood which is the essence of the Nobel prize.

After contemplation, I conclude that this award which I receive on behalf of the movement is profound recognition that nonviolence is the answer to the crucial political and moral question of our time—the need for man to overcome oppression and violence without resorting to violence and oppression.

Civilization and violence are antithetical concepts. Negroes of the United States, following the people of India, have demonstrated that nonviolence is not sterile passivity but a powerful moral force which makes for social transformation. Sooner or later all the people of the world will have to discover a way to live together in peace and thereby transform this pending cosmic elegy into a creative psalm of brotherhood.

If this is to be achieved, a man must evolve for all human conflict a method which rejects revenge, aggression and retaliation. The foundation of such a method is love.

The tortuous road which has led from Montgomery, Ala., to Oslo bears witness to this truth. This is a road which millions of Negroes are traveling to find a new sense of dignity. This same road has opened for all Americans a new era of progress and hope. It has led to a new civil rights bill, and it will, I am convinced, be widened and lengthened into a superhighway of justice as Negro and white men in increasing numbers create alliances to overcome their common problems. . .

I accept this award today with an abiding faith in America and audacious faith in the future of mankind. I refuse to accept the idea that the "isness" of man's present nature makes him morally incapable of reaching up for the eternal "oughtness" that forever confronts him.

I refuse to accept the idea that man is mere flotsam and jetsam in the river of life which surrounds him. I refuse to accept the view that mankind is so tragically bound to the starless midnight of racism and war that the bright daybreak of peace and brotherhood can never become a reality.

I refuse to accept the cynical notion that nation after nation must spiral down a militaristic stairway into the hell of a thermonuclear destruction. I believe that unarmed truth and unconditional love will have the final word in reality. This is why right temporarily defeated is stronger than evil triumphant.

I believe that even amid today's mortar bursts and whining bullets, there is still hope for a brighter tomorrow. I believe that wounded justice, lying prostrate on the blood-flowing streets of our nation, can be lifted from this dust of shame to reign supreme among the children of men.

I have the audacity to believe that peoples everywhere can have three meals a day for their bodies, education and culture for their minds, and dignity, equality and freedom for their spirits. I believe that what self-centered men have torn down men other-centered can build up. I still believe that one day mankind will bow before the altars of God and be crowned triumphant over war and bloodshed, and nonviolent redemptive goodwill proclaim the rule of the land. "And the lion and the lamb shall lie down together and every man shall sit under his own vine and fig tree and none shall be afraid." I believe that we shall overcome. . .

This faith can give us courage to face the uncertainities of the future. It will give our tired feet new strength as we continue our forward stride toward the city of freedom. When our days become dreary with low-hovering clouds and our nights become darker than a thousand midnights, we will know that we are living in the creative turmoil of a genuine civilization struggling to be born.

Today I came to Oslo as a trustee, inspired and with renewed dedication to humanity. I accept this prize on behalf of all men who love peace and brotherhood. I say I come as a trustee, for in the depths of my heart I am aware that this prize is much more than an honor to me personally.

Every time I take a flight I am always mindful of the many people who make a successful journey possible, the known pilots and the unknown ground crew.

So you honor the dedicated pilots of our struggle who have sat at the controls as the freedom movement soared into orbit. You honor once again, Chief (Albert) Lithuli of South Africa, whose struggle with and for his people are still met with the most brutal expression of man's inhumanity to man.

You honor the ground crew without whose labor and sacrifices the jetflights to freedom could never have left the earth.

Most of these people will never make headlines and their names will not appear in Who's Who. Yet the years have rolled past and when the blazing light of truth is focused on this marvelous age in which we live—men and women will know and children will be taught that we have a finer land, a better people, a more noble civilization—because these humble children of God were willing to suffer for righteousness' sake. . .

I think Alfred Nobel would know what I mean when I say that I accept this award in the spirit of a curator of some precious heirloom which he holds in trust for its true owners—all those to whom beauty is truth and truth beauty—and in whose eyes the beauty of genuine brotherhood and peace is more precious than diamonds or silver or gold.

Appendix X

EXCERPTS OF DR. KING'S ADDRESS TO OSLO STUDENTS IN NORWAY

I experience this high and joyous moment not for myself alone but for those devotees of nonviolence who have moved so courageously against the ramparts of racial injustice and who in the process have acquired a new estimate of their own human worth. Many of them are young and cultured. Others are middle age and middle class. The majority are poor and untutored. But they all are united in the quiet conviction that it is better to suffer in dignity than to accept segregation in humiliation. These are the real heroes of the freedom struggle: They are noble people for whom I accept the Nobel Peace Prize.

This evening I would like to use this lofty and historic platform to discuss what appears to me to be the most pressing problem confronting mankind today. Modern man has brought this whole world to an awe-inspiring threshold of the future. He has reached new and astonishing peaks of scientific success.

Yet, in spite of these spectacular strides in science and technology, and still unlimited ones to come, something basic is missing. There is a sort of poverty of the spirit which stands in glaring contrast to our scientific and technological abundance. . .

Every man lives in two realms, the internal is that realm of spiritual ends expressed in arts, literature, morals and religion. The external is that complex of devices, techniques, mechanisms and instrumentalities by means of which we live. Our problem today is that we have allowed the internal to become lost in the external. We have allowed the means by which we live to outdistance the ends for which we live.

This problem of spiritual and moral lag, which constitutes modern man's chief dilemma, expresses itself in three larger problems which grow out of man's ethical infantilism. Each of these problems, while appearing to be separate and isolated, is inextricably bound to the other. I refer to racial injustice, poverty, and war.

The struggle to eliminate the evil of racial injustice constitutes one of the major struggles of our time. The present upsurge of the Negro people of the United States grows out of a deep and passionate determination to make freedom and equality a reality "here" and "now". In one sense the civil rights movement in the United States is a special American phenomenon which must be understood in the light of American history and dealt with in terms of the American situation. But another and more important level what is happening in the United States today is a relatively small part of a world development.

The deep rumbling of discontent that we hear today is the thunder of disinherited masses rising from dungeons of oppression to the bright hills of freedom, in one majestic chorus the rising masses singing, in the words of our freedom song, "Ain't Gonna Let Nobody Turn Us Around." All over the world, like a fever, the freedom movement is spreading in the widest liberation in history.

Something within has reminded the Negro of his birthright of freedom, and something without had reminded him that it can be gained. Consciously or unconsciously, he has been caught up by the Zeitgeist, and with his black brothers of Africa and his brown and yellow brothers in Asia, South America and the Caribbean, the United States Negro is moving with a sense of great urgency toward the promised land of racial justice. . .

Fortunately, some significant strides have been made in the struggle to end the long night of racial injustice. We have seen the magnificent drama of independence unfold in Asia and Africa. In the United States we have witnessed the gradual demise of the system of racial segregating in the public schools gave a legal and constitutional deathblow to the whole doctrine of separate but equal. . .

Then came that glowing day a few months ago when a strong civil rights bill became law of our land. . .

The word that symbolizes the spirit and the outward form of our encounter is nonviolence, and it is doubtless that factor which made it seem appropriate to award a Peace Prize to one identified with the struggle. Broadly speaking, nonviolence in the civil rights struggle has meant not relying on arms and weapons of struggle. It has meant non-cooperation with customs and laws which are the institutional aspects of a regime of discrimination and enslavement. It has meant direct participation of masses in protest, rather than reliance on indirect methods which frequently do not involve masses in action at all.

Nonviolence has also meant that my people in the agonizing struggles of recent years have taken suffering upon themselves instead of inflicting others. The movement does not seek to liberate Negroes at the expense of the humiliation and enslavement of whites. It seeks no victory over anyone. It seeks to liberate American society and to share the self-liberation of all the people.

Violence as a way of achieving racial justice is both impractical and immoral. It solves no social problem. It merely creates new and more complicated ones. Violence is impractical because it is a descending spiral ending in destruction for all. It is immoral because it seeks to humiliate the opponent rather than win his understanding. It seeks

273

to annihilate rather than convert. Violence is immoral because it thrives on hatred rather than love.

In a real sense nonviolence seeks to redeem the spiritual and moral lag that I spoke of earlier as the chief dilemma of modern man. It seeks to secure moral ends through moral means. Nonviolence is a powerful weapon. Indeed, it is a weapon unique in history, which cuts without wounding and ennobles the man who wields it.

I believe in this method because I think it is the only way to re-establish a broken community.

Appendix XI

A Letter From

MARTIN LUTHER KING

From A

Selma, Alabama Jail

February 1, 1965

Dear Friends:

When the King of Norway participated in awarding the Nobel Peace Prize to me, he surely did not think that in less than sixty days I would be in jail. He, and almost all the world opinion will be shocked because they are little aware of the unfinished business in the South.

By jailing hundreds of Negroes, the city of Selma, Alabama, has revealed the persisting ugliness of segregation to the nation and the world. When the Civil Rights Act of 1964 was passed many decent Americans were lulled into complacency because they thought the day of difficult struggle was over.

Why are we in jail? Have you ever been required to answer 100 questions on government, some obsturse even to a political science specialist, merely to vote? Have you ever stood in line with over a hundred others and after waiting an entire day seen less then ten given the qualifying test?

THIS IS SELMA, ALABAMA, THERE ARE MORE NEGROES IN JAIL WITH ME THAN THERE ARE ON THE VOTING ROLLS.

But apart from voting rights, merely to be a person in Selma is not easy. When reporters asked Sheriff Clark if a woman defendant was married, he replied, "She's a nigger woman and she hasn't got a Miss or Mrs. in front of her name.

This is the U.S.A. in 1965. We are in jail simply because we cannot tolerate these conditions for ourselves or our nation.

We need the help of all decent Americans. Our organization, SCLC, is not only working in Selma, Alabama, but in dozens of other Southern communities. Our self-help projects operate in South Carolina, Georgia, Louisiana, Mississippi and other states. Our people are eager to work, to sacrifice, to be jailed—but their income normally meager, is cut off in these crises. Your help can make the difference. Your help can be a message unity which the thickest jail walls cannot muffle. With warmest good wishes from all of us.

Sincerely,
Martin Luther King, Jr.

Appendix XII

Dr. Martin Luther King has a talent that won't win him another Nobel Peace Prize but that almost certainly will get him something he wants much more. He has a way of picking the right opponents. With the kind of enemies he makes he scarcely needs friends. Bull Connor, the former police chief of Birmingham, Ala., is, of course the prime example. Connor, with his police dogs, fire hoses, and harsh talk, gave last year's civil-rights bill the initial impetus that ultimately carried it through Congress. Now Sheriff Jim Clark of Selma, Ala., is performing the same services for the voting-rights bill still in process of drafting but soon to be introduced under Lyndon. Johnson's imprimatur. . .

Clark, with his quick temper and lack of restraining judgement, has been almost the ideal patsy for King's demonstrators in Selma. At various times he has been goaded into using his club and his fists but never his head. He has been so grossly kept that some Northern sympathizers with the cause of Negro voting rights have wondered whether he shouldn't be more pitied than blamed. The Negro youngsters he marched out of town at double time were rewarded with the last laugh when they lined up before the court-house to pray, after he had been hospitalized, for his recovery "in mind and body." Their prayers apparently were in part answered. At least, Clark made a more rapid recovery than James Bevel, the Negro leader who was chained to a hospital bed when he fell ill after Clark arrested him. . .

The Selma demonstrations, for all their burlesque aspects, have served the purpose of dramatizing a conspicious failure in the whole civil-rights effort. Nothing so far done has assured qualified Negroes that they may vote, now, or that they have any very good prospect of voting in the near future, in many Southern communities . . . Literacy tests applied to Negroes are often so difficult that college professors can't pass them. The tests applied to whites are so simple that any fool can qualify. . .

Appendix XIII

I speak tonight for the dignity of man and the destiny of democracy. At times history and fate meet at a single time in a single place to shape turning point in man's unending search for freedom. So it was last week in Selma, Alabama.

Rarely in any time does an issue lay bare the secret heart of America itself. Equal rights for American Negroes is such an issue. And should we defeat every enemy, and should we double our wealth and conquer the stars, and still be unequal to this issue, then we will have failed as a people and as a nation.

He then quoted Matthew: "For, with a country as with a person, what is a man profited if he shall gain the whole world, and lose his own soul?" No section of the United States should "look with prideful righteousness on the troubles in another section, "for there is no Negro problem. There is no Southern problem. There is only an American problem."

The founding fathers, he recalled, believed that the "most basic right of all was the right to choose your own leaders." The harsh fact is that in many places in this country men and women are kept from voting simply because they are Negroes. Every device of which human ingenuity is capable has been used to deny this right. The Negro citizen may go to register only to be told that the day is wrong, or the hour is late. And even a college degree cannot be used to prove that he can read and write. For the fact is that the only way to pass these barriers is to show a white skin."

I will send to Congress a law designed to eliminate illegal barriers to the right to vote, "which" will provide for citizens to be registered by officials of the United States Government" when it proves necessary.

It took "eight long months" to pass the 1964 civil rights bill, this time there must be no delay, or no hesitation, or no compromise with our purpose!

Rising to a climax, he cried, "Even if we pass this bill the battle will not be over. What happened in Selma is part of a far larger movement . . . the effort of American Negroes to secure for themselves that full blessing of American life." With touching earnestness, he pleaded: "Their cause must be our cause too. Because it's not just Negroes, but really it's all of us who must overcome the crippling legacy of bigotry and injustice." He then added, emphatically: "And-we-shall-over-come!"

Appendix XIV

"In all the history of the Negro revolt, no single leader has moved more men to disciplined, non-violence action in the name of God and the cause of equality than Martin Luther King, Jr. Yet he had barely set foot into riot-shattered Watts last week when he learned, with face-slapping forces, the depth of the chasm that divides him less than white Americans from the angry black ghetto. . . He came as the marshal of the Negro's victories in the South, but, as he drove into Watts under heavy guard, a Negro teenager said dourly: "Aw, they're just sending another nigger down here to tell us what we need. . . " He came to offer hope to the ghetto, but his welcome was a mocking jeer from an onlooker: "I have a dream, I have a dream, hell, we don't need no damn dreams, we want jobs."

Appendix XV

When Martin Luther King, with the powerful force of nonviolence at his disposal, marched from Selma to demand votes for Alabama Negroes, he gave such an impetus to the Federal voting rights law that the President of the United States linked Selma with Lexington and Concord in the history of freedom. Mr. J. L. Jackson, Mrs. Luizzo and the Reverend Reed—one Negro and two whites—are accounted martyrs of Selma because they lost their lives for a cause they believed in. With and without martyrs, the Negro rights movement has had many triumphs these last 10 years, including Thurgood Marshall's court fights and the breathtakingly peaceful march on Washington two years ago. It appealed to the conscience and the creed of the nation. . .

How different the battles of Los Angeles! It cost the lives of 29 Negroes and five whites whose names few knew and fewer will remember. It will not rank in the history books with Lexington and Concord or BROWN vs. BOARD OF EDUCATION. It goes instead into the sad slag heap of anonymous, purposeless, patterless, and leaderless mob frenzies of which we have already had too much. . .

. . . One name emerged from Los Angeles: Marquetts Frye, the drunken driver whose arrest triggered the catastrophe. Will any historian, black or white, rank him with Crispus Attucks of the Boston Massacre or Nat Turner of the real slave rebellion? The Negroes of Watts, God pity them, have died to history for lack of a clear purpose or cause.

The Los Angeles riot was not the most lethal of these mindlessly violent blanks in our history nor will it be the last. Months ago the Federal Community Relations Service assigned conciliators to nine cities where such an outbreak could be expected and where a chance match is all the stacked tinder needs. In the Los Angeles tinder an important ingredient was the Negroes, resentment of Police Chief Parker and what they considered his double standard toward Negroes and whites. . .

The payoff of violence is brief exhilaration, then suffering; nothing more. Violence did not assuage the hate that burned Watts; it burns still. The four days of terror were followed by insidious fear. This fear spread from black to white Los Angeles and many white people felt it with shame. . .

As hate was not exercised, neither was injustice corrected by the violence. Negroes, their lives and property, were the chief victims of Negro rage. Most Negroes so yearn for law and order that many in Watts seem ready now to put up with the police chief they hate. He is the man who announced at the end of the riot with the phrase, "We are on the top and they are on the bottom," and that is the way it will evidently remain for a while. . .

While Los Angeles searches for its answers, the rest of urban America had better search too. . . At the federal level, the Negro has indeed achieved about all the equality that the law can give. But the enforcement of the laws is still far from equal in many cities. Anyway the promise of American democracy has always aroused expectations that take more than laws to fulfill.

To many the Los Angeles violence seems strangely timed, so soon after the great Negro achievement of the voting bill. But it is the nature of revolutions (and Negro equality is a revolution) to discover new demands after the first ones are achieved. The remaining grievances of the Negroes are social and personal and will be satisfied only by personal conquest, in black and white individuals and neighborhoods, of suspicion, fear and hate. White people do not bridge this gap by treating Negroes as an undifferentiated and underprivileged mass, nor yet by indulging them like children out of the misplaced sense of inherited guilt. . .

The Negro revolution aims at full equality within and under the law, the kind other Americans have always enjoyed. This equality must include the right of both whites and Negroes to treat each other as responsible individuals and to criticize each other when the occasion demands. It is no service to the Negro revolution either to begrudge Negro rights or to exaggerate them, nor to mistake its pathologies for its goal.

Appendix XVI

The United States involvement in Vietnam had violated the United Nations Charter and the principle of self-determination; had crippled the antipoverty program; and had impaired the right of dissent.

The United States activities in Vietnam amounted to supporting a new form of colonialism covered up by certain niceties of complexity. For nine years we supported the French in their abortive effort to recolonize Vietnam. The United States Government officials began to brainwash the American public. We supported Ngo Dinh Diem in his betrayal of the Geneva accord, leaving his country in an untenable position morally and politically.

The promises of the Great Society have been shot down on the battlefield of Vietnam. The pursuit of this widened war has narrowed domestic welfare programs, making the poor, white and Negro, bear the heaviest burdens both at the front and at home. The recently revealed $10 billion mis-estimate of the war budget alone is more than five times the amount committed to antipoverty programs. The security we profess to seek in foreign adventures we will lose in our decaying cities.

We are willing to make the Negro 100 per cent a citizen in warfare, but reduce him to 50 per cent of a citizen on American soil. Half of all Negroes live in sub-standard housing and he has half the income of whites. There is twice as much unemployment and infant mortality among Negroes. There were twice as many Negroes in combat in Vietnam at the beginning of 1967, and twice as many died in action—20.6 per cent—in proportion to their numbers in the population as whites.

We are presently moving down a dead-end road that can lead to national disaster. It is time for all people of conscience to call upon America to return to her true home of brotherhood and peaceful pursuits as effectively as the war hawks.

There is an element of urgency in our redirecting of American power. We still have a choice: nonviolent co-existence or violent co-annihilation. It is still not too late to make a choice.

Appendix XVII

If a man has not found something he will die for he is not fit to live . . . . I do not know what will happen to me now, and it really does not matter . . . .

I am not old. Like any man I would like a long life but am not concerned about that now. I just want to do God's will . . . . And He has allowed me to go up to the mountain top . . . . And I have looked over and I have seen the Promised Land . . . . I may not be able to lead you all the way, but mine eyes have seen the glory of the coming of the Lord . . . .

Appendix XVIII

PRESIDENT JOHNSON

America is shocked and saddened by the brutal slaying tonight of Dr. Martin Luther King, Jr. I ask every citizen to reject the blind violence that has struck Dr. King, who lived by nonviolence.

I pray that his family can find comfort in the memory of all he tried to do for the land he loved so well. I have just conveyed the sympathy of Mrs. Johnson and myself to his widow, Mrs. King.

I know that every American of goodwill joins me in mourning the death of this outstanding leader and in praying for peace and understanding throughout the land.

We can achieve nothing by lawlessness among the American people. It's only by joining together, and only by working together, can we continue to move toward equality and fulfillment for all of our people.

I hope that all Americans tonight will search their hearts as they ponder this most tragic incident.

I have cancelled my plans for the evening. I am postponing my trip to Hawaii until tomorrow. Thank you.

Appendix XIX

VICE PRESIDENT HUMPHREY

Martin Luther King, Jr. stands with our other American martyrs in the cause of freedom and justice. His death is a terrible tragedy and a sorrow to his family, to our nation, to our conscience. The criminal act that took his life brings shame to our country.

The apostle of nonviolence has been the victim of violence. The cause for which he marched and worked I am sure will find a new strength.

The plight of discrimination, poverty and neglect must be erased from America, and an America of full freedom, full and equal opportunity, is a living memorial he deserves, and it should be his living memorial.

Appendix XX

TEXT OF RESOLUTION

Resolved, that the United States Senate of the United States has heard with profound sorrow the tragic death of the Rev. Martin Luther King, Jr., a dedicated and courageous leader in the interest of individual rights and the equality of man.

Resolved further, that the Senate condemns this vicious and senseless act which ended his life and records its respect and appreciation for the immense service and sacrifice of this dedicated American, whose timeless memorial will be the tradition on nonviolence in the struggle for social progress and human dignity.

Resolved further, that the Senate extends to his wife and members of his family its deepest sympathy in their hour of personal grief.

Resolved further, that the secretary communicate these resolutions to the family of the deceased.

Appendix XXI

Rev. English said, in part:

" . . . We have witnessed the life of the crucified Christ and we have seen the slaying of Martin Luther King, Jr. So like a wild carniverous beast that turns upon and devours them history has turned upon once more its own because it could not hear the truth that he spoke or the judgment that he brought.

And so, like Jesus, not only did Martin Luther King, Jr. challenge the status quo, but he challenged our mode of existence. Therefore, like Jesus, he had to die as a martyr for a cause that challenged the world's assumed posture of security. . .

Tune our hearts, oh God, to hear and respond to the echoes of this undying voice of love and reconciliation in the present, a voice of hope and confidence in the future.

Grant that in response to his sacrificial death we will work toward that day when the long and tragic day of man's inhumanity to man will resolve into a chorus of peace and brotherhood. Then love will tread out the baleful sign of anger and in its ashes plant a tree of peace."

Appendix XXII

Dr. L. DeWolfe paid tribute to Martin Luther King, Jr. by declaring, in part:

" . . . Martin Luther King, Jr. spoke with the tongues of men and angels. Now those eloquent lips are stilled. His knowledge ranged widely and his prophetic wisdom penetrated deeply into human affairs. Now that knowledge and that wisdom have been transcended as he shares in the divine wisdom of eternity. . .

He sought to relieve the slavery of the oppressors as well as that of the oppressed. . .

It is now for us, all the millions of the living who care, to take up his torch of love. It is for us to finish his work, to end the awful destruction in Vietnam, to root our every trace of races prejudice from our lives, to bring the massive powers of this nation to aid the oppressed and to heal the hate scared world.

God rest your soul, dear Martin. You have fought the good fight. You have finished your course. You have kept the faith. Yours is now the triumphant crown of righteousness. Your dream is now ours. May God make us worthy and able to carry your torch of love and march on to brotherhood. Amen.

Appendix XXIII

" . . . Coupled with moral courage was Martin Luther King, Jr.'s capacity to love people. Though deeply committed to a program of freedom for Negroes, he had a love and a deep concern for all kinds of people. He drew no distinction between the rich and the poor, to the high or low. He believed especially that he was sent to champion the cause of the man farthest down. He would probably have said: "If death had to come I am sure there was no greater cause to die for than fighting to get a just wage for garbage collectors. . .

This man was suprarace, supranation, supradenomination, supraclass, and supracultive. He belonged to the world and to mankind. Now he belongs to posterity. . .

Abraham staying with his country in obedience to God's call, Moses leading a rebellious people to the Promised Land, Jesus dying on a cross, Galio on his recanting knees recanting at 70, Lincoln dying of an assassin's bullet, Woodrow Wilson crusading for a League of Nations, Martin Luther King, Jr. fighting for justice for garbage collectors, none of these men were ahead of their time. With them the time is always right to do that which needs to be done. . .

I close by saying to you what Martin Luther King, Jr. believed: "If physical death was the price he had to pay to rid America of prejudice and injustice nothing could be more redemptive." John Fitzgerald Kennedy, permit me to say that Martin Luther King, Jr.'s unfinished work on earth must truly be our own."

BIBLIOGRAPHY

BOOKS

Ahmann, Mathew, ed., *The New Negro*. Notre Dame: Fides, 1962
——————, *Race: Challenge to Religion*. Chicago: Regnery, 1963.

Barndt, Joseph R., *Why Black Power?* New York,: Friendship Press, 1968.

Belfrage, Sally., *Freedom Summer*. New York: Viking, 1965.

Bennett, Lerone,. *What Manner of Man*. Chicago: Johnson, 1965; revised 1968.

Clark, Kenneth, ed., *The Negro Protest*. Boston: Beacon, 1963.

Cook, James Graham, *The Segregationists*. New York: Appleton, 1962.

Dabbs, James McBride,. *Who Speaks for the South?* New York: Funk & Wagnalls, 1964.

David, Jay., ed., *Growing Up Black*. New York: Morrow, 1968

Davis, Sammy, Jr., & Boyer, Jane and Burt., *Yes I Can*. Farrar, Straus and Giroux Co., 1965.

Douglass, James W., *The Nonviolent Cross: A Theology of Revolution and Peace*. New York: Macmilliam, 1968.

Fager, Charles, E., *White Reflections on Black Power*. Grand Rapids: Eerdmans, 1967.

Farmer, James., *Freedom—When?* New York: Random House, 1965.

Fischer, Louis, *Gandhi: His Life and Message for the World*. New York: New American Library, 1968.

Franklin, John Hope, and Isidore Starr, eds., *The Negro in Twentieth-Century America*. New York: Vintage, 1966.

Gandhi, Mohandas K., *Non-Violent Resistance*. New York: Schocken, 1962.

Gregg, Richard B., *The Power of Nonviolence*. New York: Schocken, 1965.

Grier, William H., and M. Cobbs, *Black Rage*. New York: Basic Books, 1968.

Grimes, Alan P., *Equality in America*. New York: Oxford, 1964.

Hamilton, Michael P., ed., *The Vietnam War*. Grand Rapids: Eerdmans, 1967.

Harcourt, Melville, *Thirteen For Christ*. New York: Sheed & Ward, 1963.

Hentoff, Nat., *The New Equality*. New York: Viking, 1964.

King, Martin Luther, Jr., *Stride Toward Freedom: The Montgomery Story*. New York: Harper & Row, 1959.

——————, *The Measure of a Man*. Philadelphia: United Church Press, 1959.

——————, *Strength to Love*. New York: Harper & Row, 1963.

——————, *Why We Can't Wait*. New York: Harper & Row, 1964.

——————, *Where Do We Go From Here: Chaos or Community?* New York: Harper & Row, 1967.

——————, *The Trumpet of Conscious*. New York: Harper & Row, 1968

Lincoln, Eric, *The Black Muslims in America*. Boston: Beacon Press, 1961.

Lomax, Louis E., *The Negro Revolt*. New York: Harper & Row, 1962.

Lynd, Staughton, *Nonviolence in America: A Documentary History*. Indianapolis: Bobbs-Merrill, 1966.

McGill, Ralph, *The South and the Southern*. Boston; Little, Brown, 1963.

Miller, William Robert, *Nonviolence: A Christian Interpretation*. New York: Schocken, 1966.

——————, *Martin Luther King, Jr.: His Life, Martyrdom and Meaning for the World*. New York: Weybright & Talley, 1968.

Preston, Edward, *Martin Luther King, Jr.: Fighter For Freedom*. New York: Doubleday, 1969.

Reddick, L. D., *Crusader Without Violence*. New York: Harper & Brothers. 1959.

Saunders, Doris, Ed., *The Day They Marched*. Chicago: Johnson, 1963.

Schelesinger, Arthur M., *A Thousand Days*. Boston: Houghton Mifflin Co., 1965.

Silverman, Charles, *Crisis in Black and White*. New York: Randon House, 1964.

Silver, James W., *Mississippi: The Closed Society*. New York: Harcourt, Brace and World, 1964.

Spear, Allan H., *Black Chicago: The Making of a Negro Ghetto 1890-1920*. Chicago: University of Chicago Press. 1967.

Stanfield, Edwin J., *In Memphis: More Than A Garbage Strike* Atlanta: Southern Regional Council, March 22, 1968.

Stringfellow, William, *My People is the Enemy*. New York: Holt, Rinehart & Winston Co., 1964.

Thompson, Daniel C., *The Negro Leadership Class*. Englewood Cliffs: Prentice Hall, 1963.

Warren, Robert Penn., *Who Speaks for the Negro?* New York: Randon House, 1964.

Westin, Alan F., ed., *Freedom Now!* New York: Basic Books, 1964.

White Theodore H., *The Making of the President, 1960*. New York: Atheneun Publishers, 1961.

—————, *The Making of the President, 1964*. New York: New American Library, 1965.

Wilson, James Q., *Negro Politics*. New York: Free Press, 1960.

Wright, Nathan, Jr., *Black Power and Urban Unrest*. New York: Hawthorn, 1967.

Young, Whitney M., Jr., *To Be Equal*. New York: McGraw-Hill, 1964.

COLLEGE BULLETINS AND YEARBOOKS

Antioch College, Yellow Springs, Ohio. (1948-1952).

Boston University, Boston, Massachusetts. (1952-1954).

Crozer Theological Seminary, Chester, Pennsylvania. (1948-1951).

Howard University, Washington, D. C. (1952-1958).

Morehouse College, Atlanta, Georgia. (1944-1948).

MAGAZINES

Ebony, Johnson Publishing Co. Inc., Chicago, Ill. (Selected issues, 1957-1968).

Jet, Johnson Publishing Co., Inc. Chicago, Ill. (Selected issues, 1957-1968).

Life, Time, Inc. Chicago, Ill. (Selected issues, 1957-1968).

Negro Digest, Johnson Publishing Co. Inc. Chicago, Ill. (Selected issues, 1966-1968).

Newsweek, Newsweek, Inc. New York, N. Y. (Selected issues, 1957-1968).

Redbook, McCall Corp. New York, N. Y. (Selected issues, 1957-1968).

Saturday Review, Saturday Review, Inc. New York, N. Y. (Selected issues, 1960-1968).

Time, Time, Inc. Chicago, Ill. (Selected issues, 1957-1968).

United States News and World Report, United States News & World Report, Inc. Washington, D. C. (Selected issues, 1960-1968).

NEWSLETTERS

Montgomery Improvement Association Newsletter, Montgomery, Ala. Selected issues. 1956-1958).

Southern Christian Leadership Conference Newsletter, Atlanta, Ga. (Selected issues, 1960-1966).

NEWSPAPERS

Atlanta Constitution, Atlanta, Ga. (Selected issues, 1957-1968).

Atlanta Daily World, Atlanta, Ga. (Selected issues, 1955-1968).

Atlanta Journal, Atlanta, Ga. (Selected issues, 1957-1968).

Birmingham Advertiser, Birmingham, Ala. (Selected issues, 1959-1967).

Birmingham News, Birmingham, Ala. (Selected issues, 1959-1967).

Chicago Defender, Chicago, Ill. (Selected issues, 1957-1968).

Christian Century, Chicago, Ill. (Selected issues, 1960-1966).

Montgomery Advertiser, Montgomery, Ala. (Selected issues, 1957-1966).

Montgomery Journal, Montgomery, Ala. (Selected issues, 1957-1966).

National Observer, Silver Springs, Md. (Selected issues, 1958-1966).

Neshoba County Democrat, Philadelphia, Miss. (Selected issues, 1958-1968).

New York Amsterdam News, New York, N. Y. (Selected issues, 1957-1968).

New York Herald Tribune, New York, N. Y. (Selected issues, 1960-1965).

New York Times, New York, N. Y. (Selected issues, 1957-1968).

New York World Telegram and Sun, New York, N. Y. (Selected issues, 1960-1966).

Washington Post, Washington, D. C. (Selected issues, 1957-1968).

Washington Star, Washington, D. C. (Selected issues, 1957-1965).

Index

Communist Party, 10, 202
Congress of Racial Equality (CORE), 95, 101, 130, 133, 177, 206, 221
Connor, Eugene T. ("Bull"), 128-129, 158-159, 180, 182, 217
Cooper, Anne Lee, 185-186
Coordinating Council of Community Organizations (CCCO), 216, 219, 227, 230
CORE See Congress of Racial Equality,
Corman, James, 237
Cornell University, 96
Cotton, Dorthy, 169
Council of Trent, 195
"Cradle of the Confederacy", 52, 90
Crenshaw, Jack, 44-45
Crozer, John Price, 28
Crozer Theologial Seminary, 23-28
Curry, Izola Ware, 84-86
Cushing, Richard, 158-159

Daley, Richard, 217-218, 224,227
Dallas County (Ala.), 180-191
Dallas, Texas, 139
Dansbury, Claude B., 20
Danville, Va., 113, 130
Darin, Bobby, 135
David T. Howard Sch., 14, 17
Davis, George W., 24
Davis, L. O., 145-146
Davis, Marpressa
Davis, Nathan, 214
Davis, Ossie, 249
Davis, Sammy Jr., 68, 125, 136, 200
Dawson, William, 218
Day, A. Garnett, 193
Daytona Beach, Fla. 85
Dearborn, Mich., 238
Dee, Ruby, 68
De Kalb County (Ga.), 100-103
Delaney, Hubert T., 98
Democratic Party, 5, 69, 104-106, 113, 124, 150
De Soto Hotel, 157

Des Moines, Iowa, 194
Detroit, Mich. 237
De Wolf, L. Harold, 30, 249
Dexter Avenue Baptist Church, 33-35, 62
Dexter Avenue Methodist Church, 51, 83
Dibelius, Otto, 154
Diggs, Charles, 69
Dinkler Plaza Hotel, 183-184
Dixon, Richard Jr., 169
Doar, John, 194
Docherty, George, 195
Douglas, Mrs. Paul, 194-195
Dreser, Israel, 195
Drew, John, 128
Dunbar, Leslie W., 163
Dungee, Eva A., 51
Durden, A. N., 114
Durham, N. C.,
Dylan, Bobby, 136

Eaton, Mrs. Cyrus, 114
Ebenezer Baptist Church, 12-13, 16, 27, 91, 249
Ebony, 202
Ecumenuial Council, 156
Edmund Pettus Bridge, 191
Eisenhower, Dwight D. 64-66, 71-73, 76-81, 101, 105
Elizabeth, N. J., 152
Ellington, Duke, 61
Elliot, J. Robert, 116, 119-120
English, Ronald, 249
Enslin, Morton Scott, 24
Eskstine, Billy, 200
Eurdora A.M.E.Z. Church, 245
Evers, Charles, 165, 221-222
Evers, Medger, 131, 190

Fairbanks, Mary, 36
Farmer, James, 136, 153, 163, 165, 168, 196
Farr, Sam, 200
FBI See Federal Bureau of Investigation

296

297

King, Martin Luther, Sr., 9, 12-16, 21-22, 27, 32, 33, 60, 85, 91, 105, 169, 177
King, Mrs. Martin Luther, Sr. 10, 13, 22, 60, 169, 177
King, Martin Luther III, 248
King, Olva V., 171-172
King, Slater, 122
King, Willie Christine, 10, 13-15, 17, 22, 60, 85, 169
King, Yolanda Denise, 37, 248
Ku Klux Klan (KKK), 10, 71, 108, 123, 162, 166-167, 184, 214, 240
Kyles, Samuel, 248
Kynes, James, W., 149

Laboratory Hi Sch., 14-15, 17
Lancaster, Burt, 136
Lands, Liz, 219
Langford, Charles, 50
Lautier, Louis, 72
Lawrence, George, 120-121
Lawyer Constitutional Defense Committee on Civil Rights, 163
Leatherer, James, 200
Lee, Bernard, 169, 247
Lee, Roger, 201
Leesbury, Ga. 165
Lenud, Philip, 29
"Letter From A Selma Alabama Jail," 187
Lewis, John, 137, 153, 191, 200
Liberator, 58
Lichtenberger, Arthur, 158
Life, 211, 234
Lincoln, Abraham, 129, 137
Lincoln Memorial, 67, 69, 135-136
Lindsey, John, 237
Lingo, Al, 194, 196
Little Rock, Ark., 119
Lloyds of London, 53
Loeb, Henry, 246
Logan, Mrs. Martin, 169
London, England, 112, 156, 169-170, 178
Lord, John Wesley, 193
Lorraine Motel, 247

Los Angeles, Calif., 67, 207-211, 212, 213, 219
Los Angeles Tribune, 58
Louisville, Ky., 232
Luizzo, Viola Gregg, 202-203, 209, 212, 214

Malcolm X, 169, 202
Manager Hotel, 156
Mangum, Robert, 84
"Man of the Year," 140
Manley, Norman, 62
Mann, Floyd, 108
Mansen, William, 118
March on Washington, 132-140, 152, 199, 213
Margolres, Israel, 235
Marion, Ala., 31-32, 60, 187, 189-190
Marks, Miss., 245
Martin, E. M., 12
Marshall, Burke, 130, 163, 178
Marshall, William, 200
Mathis, Johnny, 134
Mathrew, James K., 164
Maynard, Aubrey, 85-86
Mays, Benjamin, Elizah, 19-21, 183, 250
"Meet the Press," 96, 119, 227
Memphis, Tenn., 221, 246-247, 249, 251
Mercer, Mae, 214
Meredith, James H., 125, 220, 222
Meridian, Miss
Merrill, Gary, 200
Metropolitan Baptist Church, 66
MIA See Montgomery Improvement Association
Miles College, 134
Miller, Nina, 169
Ming, William R., 97-98
Mitchell, James P., 71-72
Mitchell, Nellie, 145
Mitchell, Oscar, 101-103, 107
Mohammed, Bermebarek, 126
Mohammed, Khemisti, 126
Mohammed, Sahnoun, 126

300

Nickerson, Eugene, 249
Nieburh, Reignhold, 24
Nixon, E. D., 36, 38-40, 44, 55
Nixon, Richard, 63-65, 71-73, 86, 104-105
Nkrumah, Kwame, 62-63
Nobel, Alfred, 154, 157-161, 170-173, 183, 218, 238, 249-250
Norwegian Broadcasting System, 172
Norweigan Nobel Committee, 172
Norwegian Parliament, 172

Odd Fellows, 12
Odetta, 136, 200
Office of Economic Opportunity (OEO), 211, 228
Orange, James, 187
Orange, N. J. 246
Oslo, Norway, 168-173
Oslo University, 172-173
Oswald, Lee Harvey, 161

Packinghouse Workers of America, 89
Park, Frank A. 44
Parker, Bobbie, 214
Parker, William,
Paris, (France), 136, 138, 173, 178, 214, 219-220
Parks, Frank, 93
Parks, Rosa, 38-40, 44
Paterson, N. J. 152, 246
Patterson, Floyd, 201
Patterson, John, 93-94
Pauschonbusch, Walter, 24
Payne, Ethel, 70
Payne, Larry, 246
Peabody, Mrs. Malcolm, 145
Pemberton, John, 164
Peden, Katherine, 237
Pensacola, Fla., 176
Peral Plafkner Award, 28
Percy, Charles, 217
Perez, Leander, Sr. 158-159
Peter-Paul-Mary, 136
Pettiford, Walter, 84

Phelps, Rosale, 145
Philadelphia, Miss., 167
Philadelphia, Pa., 61, 198
Pike, James, 193
Plato, 22
Poitier, Sidney, 68, 136, 219
Pope Paul VI, 155-156
"Poor People March," 313-316
Portland, Ore., 212
Poussaint, Alvin F., 223-225
Powell, Adam Clayton, 62, 69, 152
Powell, Mary, 30
"Prayer Pilgrimage For Freedom," 66-70
Perminger, Otto, 111
Presbysterian Outlook, 158
Princhett, Laurie, 116-117
Prinz, Joachim, 133, 137, 249
Procaccino, Mario, 249

Raby, Al, 216, 227, 230
Randolph, Asa Philip, 62, 66-69,, 77-80, 84, 100, 132-133, 137, 139, 153, 163, 231
Raleigh, N. C. 94
Rao, Vincent, 85
Reconstruction, 130, 151
Reddick, Lawrence D., 169
Reed, Georgia Ann, 145
Reed, James, 197, 209, 212
Reidsville, Ga., 101, 103-104
Republican Party, 5, 69, 78, 104-105, 113, 154, 214
Reuther, Walter, 133, 139, 249
Ribicoff, Abraham A., 229
Richmond, Va., 91
Rives, Richard T., 53
Robert, Purnell, 200
Robertson, Allen, 56
Robinson, Jackie, 10, 123, 178
Robinson, James, 181
Robinson, Jo Ann, 36, 43
Robinson, Lillian, 145
Rochester, N. Y., 152
Rockefeller, Nelson A., 111, 115, 177-178, 202
Rockefeller, Rodman, 178

301

Rogers, William, P., 80, 101
Romney, George, 193
Roosevelt, Mrs. Eleanor, 65
Roosevelt Hotel, 132
Rothschild, Jacob, 183
Russel, Nipsey, 200
Rustin, Bayard, 67, 132, 169, 209, 235, 244
Ryan, L. B., 157

San Francisco, Calif., 59, 198, 212
Sanders, Carl, 124
Sardaby, Michael, 214
Sasser, Ga., 123
Saturday, Review, 213
Savannah, Ga., 156-157
SCLC See Southern Christian Leadership Conference
Schewerne, Michael, 209
Scott, Bernice McMurry, 31
Scott, Coretta, 30-32
Scott, Edyth, 31
Scott, Michael, 63
Scott, Obrie, 31
Scott, Obrie Leonard, 31
Seattle, Wash., 2-12
Seigenthaler, John, 108
Selma, Ala., 151, 180-191, 207, 212, 214-218, 221, 225
Selma Time-Journal, 188
Sellers Clyde, 41, 44, 48, 82-84
Shaw University, 94
Sherman, William T., 10
Sherrod, Charles, 118
Shilon Baptist Church, 116
Shriver, Sargent, 211, 228
Shores, **Arthur, 50**
Shuttlesworth, Fred, 128, 130, 212
Siciliano, Rocco, 77, 87
Simone, Nina, 200
Simpson, Bryan, 148, 150
Sixteenth Street Baptist Church, 212
Smith College, 143
Smith, Kenneth Lee, 24
Smith, Ledger, 135
Smitherman, Joe T., 182

SNCC See Student Nonviolent Coordinating Committee
SNICK See SNCC
Southern Christian Leadership Conference (SCLC), 74, 76-77, 90, 94-95, 99-100, 112-113, 124-125, 132, 156-157, 162, 177, 180, 191, 204, 207, 211, 214, 216, 219, 220, 226, 231-232, 239
Southern Negro Leadership Conference, 65
Southern Leadership Conference on Transportation and Nonviolent Integration, 64
Southern Regional Council, 163-164
Spellman College, 19, 21
Spingar, Arthur B., 84, 132
Spock, Benjamin, 232, 235, 249
Springfield College, 149
Springfield, Mass., 208, 210
Springfield, N. J., 195
St. Augustine, Fla., 141-151
St. Joseph's Infirmary, 157
St. Joseph's Hospital, 247
St. Louis, Mo., 175, 194
Stewart, Robert, 97-98
Stoner, J. B., 189
Stride Toward Freedom, 38, 84, 88-89
Stuart, Virgil, 158-159
Student Nonviolent Coordinating Committee (SNCC), 94, 132, 207, 220-221, 241
Sullivan, L. B., 93
Syracuse University, 176

Tallahasse, Fla., 150
Tannehill, Jack, 164
Tanpsley, Jeptha C., 91
Thetford, William F., 50, 97
Thomas, Arthur, 221
Thomas Jefferson Hotel, 212
Thompson, Claude H., 59-60
Thompson, Millie, 217
Thracher, Thomas P., 44
Thronton, Charles, 237

303